PEARSON CUSTOM
Education

Legal and Social Perspectives

of Disability in Education

PEARSON

Custom
Publishing

Sponsoring Editor: Natalie Danner
Development Editor: Abbey Briggs
Editorial Assistant: Jill Johnson
Marketing Manager: Amy Dyer
Operations Manager: Eric M. Kenney
Production Manager: Jennifer M. Berry
Rights Editor: Francesca Marcantonio
Art Director: Renée Sartell
Cover Designers: Kristen Kiley

Please visit our websites at *www.pearsoncustom.com* and *www.customliterature.com*.
Attention bookstores: For permission to return any unsold stock, contact
us at *pe-uscustomreturns@pearsoncustom.com*.

ISBN-13: 9780536797056
ISBN-10: 0536797056

Package ISBN-13: N/A
Package ISBN-10: N/A

PEARSON CUSTOM PUBLISHING
501 Boylston Street, Suite 900, Boston, MA 02116
A Pearson Education Company

Contents

1

Students with Intellectual and Developmental Disabilities

From *Special Education, Contemporary Perspectives for School Professionals*, Second Edition.
Marilyn Friend. Copyright © 2008 by Pearson Education, Inc. Published by Allyn & Bacon.
All rights reserved.

Students with Intellectual and Developmental Disabilities

learning objectives

- Outline the development of the field of intellectual disabilities.

- Define terminology related to intellectual disabilities, including *mental retardation* and *developmental disabilities,* and explain the prevalence and causes of intellectual disabilities.

- Describe characteristics of individuals with intellectual disabilities.

- Explain how intellectual disabilities are identified.

- Outline how learners with intellectual disabilities receive their education.

- Describe recommended educational practices for students with intellectual disabilities.

- Explain the perspectives and concerns that parents and families of students with intellectual disabilities may have.

- Identify trends and issues influencing the field of intellectual disabilities.

Hope

Hope is in the fifth grade. If you observed her for only a few minutes in the classroom with her peers, you would say she seems like an average fifth-grader. She chats with classmates whenever the opportunity arises. She is at that in-between age: not quite a child and not quite an adolescent. However, if you observed Hope over time, you would understand why she is identified as having an *intellectual disability*, also called *mild mental retardation*. Academically, she is doing quite well, reading at a second-grade level, but she simply does not learn at the rate of her classmates. Mr. Rosen, Hope's resource teacher, works closely with fifth-grade teacher Ms. Moretti to identify the most important concepts for Hope to learn from the curriculum. Hope receives reading instruction in the resource room four times per week, which she attends with two other students reading at approximately her level. Hope's special needs are especially apparent at this age in her social skills and interactions with classmates. The other girls are beginning to worry about their hair, think about boys, and read fashion magazines; Hope still has a favorite doll that she often brings to school. Her classmates sometimes become impatient with her increasing differences from them.

Austin

Austin is a seventh-grade student who generally enjoys school, his teachers, and his classmates. He is the equipment manager for the boys' basketball team, and he knows that keeping this privileged position depends on working hard in school and behaving appropriately. Austin has Down syndrome, and he also has a partial hearing loss and wears thick glasses. When Austin was in elementary school, he tended to refuse any activity he did not want to do and occasionally had a tantrum. Now, though, he has learned to use words to convey his opinions, and his teachers are impressed with his manners and his commitment to learning. Austin learns English and math in a special education classroom, but he learns science and social studies and participates in art, music, technol-ogy, and other exploratory subjects in the general education setting. Austin's assessment to meet No Child Left Behind testing requirements is called an *alternate assessment*. It consists of an extensive portfo-lio of his work that demonstrates a connection to the grade-level curriculum, and it is scored according to a rubric provided by the State Department of Educa-tion. Austin is proud of the fact that last year he was rated as proficient on all parts of the portfolio. When asked what he is thinking of doing when he grows up, he explains that he wants to work in a nursing home, a place where he already does volunteer work.

Jack

Jack is nineteen years old, and he is a student at Lin-coln High School. He attends classes for part of the day, and then he participates in a vocational training program. Jack takes part in one general education class, an art class that has only nine other students. He is assisted in the class by Ms. Russo, a special educa-tion paraprofessional. Jack has a moderate intellectual disability that is the result of a disorder called *Fragile X syndrome*, but his most significant challenges concern behavior. For example, he tends to be distracted by nearly any small noise or movement in the classroom. When he is upset, he sometimes chews on the neck band of his T-shirt. One thing that disturbs Jack is change in routine such as last week's shortened class schedule on an early-release day. Jack has just begun a new job. He is working two hours per day in the small business of a friend of his family, and his responsibili-ties include making copies, shredding documents, and helping to distribute and organize supplies. With the help of a job coach and this rather structured environ-ment, Jack is quickly learning to work independently. Although Jack does not speak very often, he has communicated that he wants to work in a full-time job after high school. Jack's stepmother and father concur that Jack should work after high school, and they hope he can achieve his goal of living in an apartment. Even so, they are planning for him to live at home at least for the next few years, and they also are meeting with an estate planner to ensure that Jack has what he needs after they die.

For most of the history of public schools, students with intellectual disabilities, also called *mental retardation,* have been characterized primarily by the word *can't*—what they can't do, what they can't learn, what they can't participate in. For example, in my own late-1970s classroom for students with mild intellectual disabilities, no books were provided because of the strongly held belief that these students could not learn to read. As these students became adults, the emphasis on their limitations continued. Except for those individuals who blended into society and shed their disability labels, most people with mental retardation lived with their parents, were placed in residential facilities, or resided under close supervision in group homes with several other adults with disabilities.

> "Contemporary thinking about individuals with intellectual disabilities is positive; it is based on much higher expectations and a world of possibilities, not limitations."

Although the past sometimes still influences professionals in today's schools, contemporary thinking about individuals with intellectual disabilities now is based on much higher expectations and a world of possibilities, not limitations. This has meant rethinking beliefs about these students' academic potential and the priorities they may have for their lives beyond the school years. As you read this chapter, continue to think about your own beliefs about children and adults with intellectual disabilities, including the stigma associated with the term *mental retardation* and reflecting on how your perceptions can influence these students' lives. How do the expectations you set and the enthusiasm you have assist students in reaching their goals?

You will notice that the focus of this chapter is on students with mild or moderate intellectual disabilities or mental retardation.

What Are Intellectual Disabilities?

Contemporary perspectives on intellectual disabilities are a response to past views and practices. You can better understand why today's optimism about these students is so important by reviewing how these students were thought of and treated in the past.

Beliefs about the inherited nature of intellectual disabilities have led to laws being passed to prevent some people from having children. This was called the *eugenics movement.*

Development of the Field of Intellectual Disabilities

Focused study of individuals with intellectual disabilities began earlier than the study of people with most other disabilities. For example, advances in medicine and psychology, as well as the beginnings of urbanization, drew attention to this group even in the early nineteenth century (Hickson, Blackman, & Reis, 1995). In 1866 English physician Langdon Down created a classification system for individuals with intellectual disabilities, describing in detail for the first time the characteristics of children with what became known as *Down syndrome* (Scheerenberger, 1983). By the late nineteenth century, small residential facilities were established for children with intellectual disabilities. The goal was to educate these youngsters so that they could succeed when they returned to their communities as adults. At the same time, the first special classes were being created in public schools. In both settings, optimism prevailed. In fact, one special class supervisor at the turn of the twentieth century estimated that 80 percent of the students with intellectual disabilities who attended were eventually "cured" (Hickson et al., 1995).

Shifting Perspectives

The turmoil in American society at the beginning of the twentieth century led to a radical shift in thinking about individuals with intellectual disabilities. Optimism was replaced by pessimism. Prominent physicians and psychologists theorized that intellectual disabilities—called *mental retardation*—were inherited, that they were accompanied by criminal tendencies, and that allowing people with these disabilities to have children would undermine the strength of American society (Kanner, 1964).

Professionals gradually abandoned efforts to educate these children and adults, and they became satisfied with providing custodial care for them. Children with significant intellectual disabilities were kept at home or sent to an institution, often at the recommendation of a family physician. Children with mild intellectual disabilities attended special classes, and these segregated classes became a means for keeping these students from interfering with the educational progress of other students (Winzer, 1993). Most professionals agree that the early twentieth century was the lowest point in the modern history of education for individuals with intellectual disabilities (Wehmeyer & Patton, 2000).

By the middle of the twentieth century, beliefs were beginning to change (Hickson et al., 1995). First, the research that had suggested all intellectual disabilities were inherited was challenged. Second, statistics indicated that individuals with intellectual disabilities were not predisposed to criminal activities as had been thought. Finally, social reformers were objecting to the poor treatment of these individuals. During this time, comparison studies of students with mild mental retardation in separate classes and general education classes indicated that integration often was more beneficial than segregation. Parent organizations such as the National Association of Parents and Friends of Mentally Retarded Children (now called The Arc) were formed, and these groups advocated for the rights of their children. The deplorable conditions in institutions also were exposed at this time. In 1965 Burton Blatt and Jack Kaplan prepared a photographic essay of the abuse and neglect in these places. Published in 1974, *Christmas in Purgatory* was a wake-up call to professionals. It graphically highlighted the need for radical reform in the treatment of individuals with intellectual disabilities and mental health disorders.

> "Most professionals agree that the early twentieth century was the lowest point in the modern history of education for individuals with intellectual disabilities."

As you know, the 1960s and 1970s were noteworthy for the growing emphasis on the rights of children with disabilities and the litigation that eventually formed the basis for Public Law (P. L.) 94-142, the federal special education law now called IDEA (the Individuals with Disabilities Education Act). It was also during this time that the definition of intellectual disabilities began to change. Most significantly, the approximate IQ cutoff score for being identified as having this disability was lowered from 85 to 70, thus changing significantly the number of students identified.

Recent Changes for Students with Intellectual Disabilities

Even after federal special education law protected the basic rights of students with intellectual disabilities, their parents and other advocates continued to push for improved programs and services. Many of the first court cases addressing inclusive practices were brought by parents of students with intellectual disabilities. *Daniel R. R. v. State Board of Education* (1989) is considered to be the first critical test of inclusion (Yell, 2006); it concerned a student with Down syndrome. In this case Daniel's parents filed suit because their son had been removed from a general education prekindergarten class because of his highly disruptive behavior. The Fifth Circuit Court of Appeals ruled that Daniel's needs were so great that he could not be educated with his peers and that Daniel had sufficient contact with his peers in nonacademic activities.

In *Sacramento City Unified School District v. Rachael H.* (1994), the Ninth Circuit Court of Appeals reached a different decision (Yell, 2006). Rachael, a student with a moderate intellectual disability, had been educated in special education classes for several years, and her

Lipnitzki/Roger-Viollet/The Image Works

Although in the past many children with intellectual disabilities were sent to institutions, professionals and families now stress helping them to reach their potential and function successfully in society.

PROFESSIONAL MONITORING TOOL

Council for Exceptional Children

Standard 1 Foundations
. . . historical points of view

CHECK
Your Learning

At the beginning of the twentieth century, what caused the shift from optimism to pessimism in the education of individuals with cognitive disabilities?

parents requested a general education placement. The school district refused, arguing that Rachael's needs were too significant. The court found that the school district had not demonstrated that Rachael could not be instructed in a general education setting and supported Rachael's parents' request for a more inclusive education.

Definitions of Intellectual Disabilities

As is true for some other students with disabilities, the language that describes students with intellectual disabilities requires clarification (Panek & Smith, 2005). You may already have noticed that the terms *intellectual disabilities* and *mental retardation* are being used interchangeably in this chapter. Here is the explanation why: The term used in IDEA is *mental retardation*, and many (but not all) states still use it. However, this term often is considered offensive and stigmatizing, partly because of the negative connotations assigned to it at the beginning of the twentieth century (Akrami, Ekehammar, Claesson, & Sonnander, 2006; Cuskelly, 2004). Many professionals and parents now use the term **intellectual disabilities.** In fact, in January 2007 the American Association on Mental Retardation (AAMR), the leading professional organization addressing the needs of these individuals throughout the life span, changed its name to the **American Association on Intellectual and Developmental Disabilities (AAIDD).** The second part of the new name—**developmental disabilities**—is a broad term that is usually used in reference to chronic and significant impairments such as cerebral palsy and autism that result in intellectual disabilities.

> "As is true for some other students with disabilities, the language that describes students with intellectual disabilities requires clarification."

You may find that your state uses yet other terms to refer to students with intellectual disabilities. For example, you may hear the term **cognitive impairment** or **cognitive disability** or *mental impairment* or *mental disability.* What are the terms used in your state to describe this group of students? Which terms do you think have the greatest and least stigma associated with them?

Federal Definition

The definition generally used by educators is the one in IDEA. This definition for mental retardation is based on one developed in 1982 by the AAMR. It states that **mental retardation** is

> significantly subaverage general intellectual functioning, existing concurrently with deficits in adaptive behavior and manifested during the developmental period, that adversely affects a child's educational performance. (IDEA 20 U.S.C. §1401 [2004], 20 C.F.R. §300.8[c][6])

This definition illustrates the important fact that the mental retardation designation is assigned only when a student demonstrates both low cognitive ability and significant problems with **adaptive behavior**—that is, the day-to-day skills that are necessary for independence (e.g., self-care, the use of money). The third part of the definition clarifies that the identification of mental retardation is made only if the condition is present by the time the student is eighteen years old—the generally accepted definition of the phrase "during the developmental period." If an adult was injured or experienced an illness that resulted in a significant reduction in intellectual ability, a term such as *cognitive impairment* might be used, but the term *mental retardation* usually would not be applied.

American Association on Intellectual and Developmental Disabilities Definition

In 1992 the AAMR revised its definition on which federal special education law was based. It reaffirmed the use of this new definition in 2002, even though the group has not yet been successful in changing the IDEA definition. This newer definition states the following:

PROFESSIONAL MONITORING TOOL

Council for Exceptional Children

Standard 1 Foundations ... issues in definition and identification

Mental retardation is a disability characterized by significant limitations both in intellectual functioning and in adaptive behavior as expressed in conceptual, social, and practical adaptive skills. This disability originates before age eighteen.

The following five assumptions are essential to the application of this definition:

1. Limitations in present functioning must be considered within the context of community environments typical of the individual's age peers and culture.

2. Valid assessment considers cultural and linguistic diversity as well as differences in communication, sensory, motor, and behavioral factors.

3. Within an individual, limitations often coexist with strengths.

4. An important purpose of describing limitations is to develop a profile of needed supports.

5. With appropriate personalized supports over a sustained period, the life functioning of the person with mental retardation generally will improve. (Luckasson et al., 2002, p. 1)

This definition does not so much contradict the IDEA definition as extend it. Specifically, it stresses the importance of context in considering intellectual disabilities (Gross & Hahn, 2004; Harries, Guscia, Kirby, Nettelback, & Taplin, 2005). Some students are eligible for the designation only while they are in the intensive academic environment of public schools. When they leave school and find employment that does not rely heavily on specific academic skills, the label may no longer apply. The definition also emphasizes strengths and the need for supports for helping individuals to succeed, a dimension that includes assistance in social skills, life skills, and health and medical matters. As you compare the older and newer definitions of intellectual disabilities, would you support adoption of the latter in IDEA? Why or why not?

Prevalence of Intellectual Disabilities

During the 2002–2003 school year, 0.88 percent of all children ages six through twenty-one, or 580,375 students, received special education because they were identified as having mental retardation (U.S. Department of Education, 2004). An additional 0.09 percent, or 58,075 students, in this age group were served with the general label *developmentally delayed,* the alternative federal disability category for students ages three through nine that includes some students with mental retardation.

The prevalence of mental retardation as reported in IDEA dropped off dramatically between the 1970s and 1980s, but it has remained relatively stable for the past decade. Some of the decline in prevalence may be attributable to better differentiation between these students and those with other disabilities, including learning disabilities and autism. However, professionals also acknowledge that the recent stability of the figure reflects the strong stigma associated with mental retardation terminology and the increasing trend to avoid assigning it to students (Hourcade, 2002).

Because the decision to identify an individual as having an intellectual disability involves professional judgment, no single prevalence estimate is considered definitive. For example, the American Association on Intellectual and Developmental Disabilities (Luckasson et al., 2002) estimates that 2.5 percent of the population has this disability. The Arc (2004), an organization for professionals and parents supporting children and adults with intellectual disabilities, estimates prevalence at 3 percent. These data suggest that school-age children with intellectual disabilities are underidentified.

Other Prevalence Considerations

Little research has explored the prevalence of intellectual disabilities in boys versus girls or based on age (Dembro, 2003). Generally, boys are thought to have intellectual disabilities at a slightly higher rate than girls (1.5:1). In addition, some specific syndromes that include intellectual disability (topics addressed later in this chapter) affect boys and girls at different rates.

Standard 1 Foundations
... issues in definition and identification

dimensions of
DIVERSITY

Some disorders that result in cognitive disabilities are linked to gender. For example, Rett syndrome is found only in females. It is characterized by handwringing and deteriorating cognitive ability.

Standard 2 Development and Characteristics of Learners
... typical and atypical development

INTERNET
RESOURCES
www.nads.org
The National Association for Down Syndrome (NADS) provides counseling and support to families of children newly diagnosed with this syndrome. It also advocates for the rights of individuals with Down syndrome and provides news related to this disorder.

The aspect of prevalence and intellectual disability that has received the most attention among educators is the disproportionate representation of African American students, especially boys, in this group (Jones & Menchetti, 2001; Skiba, Poloni-Studinger, Gallini, Simmons, & Feggins-Azziz, 2006). The reasons for this situation include teacher expectations for student classroom behavior and academic performance, racial/ethnic bias, bias in assessment, and risk factors such as living in poverty. Presently, African American students are three times more likely than other students to be identified as having an intellectual disability, based on their overall representation in the population (U.S. Department of Education, 2004). These data indicate that despite widespread attention to disproportionate representation, the issue still exists.

Causes of Mental Retardation

For most students with intellectual disabilities, especially those with mild impairments, the cause of the disability cannot be determined. Hope, the elementary student introduced at the beginning of this chapter, is in this group of students. A mild intellectual disability for which a specific cause cannot be identified is sometimes referred to as **cultural familial retardation**. This term is a remnant of early-twentieth-century thinking in that it implies that intellectual disabilities occur in certain family groups and are related to the ways in which they live.

"For most students with intellectual disabilities, especially those with mild impairments, the cause of the disability cannot be determined."

For students with more significant intellectual disabilities, the causes usually are considered in terms of when they occurred: during the *prenatal* (before birth), the *perinatal* (during or immediately after birth), or the *postnatal* (after birth) period. The following examples illustrate the types of conditions that can lead to intellectual disability and the extent to which scientific knowledge about this disability has progressed.

Prenatal Causes of Intellectual Disabilities

Intellectual disabilities sometimes are caused by factors at play before birth. For example, it may be the result of chromosomal abnormalities such as these:

Down Syndrome Probably the most well known of all the genetic disorders that can result in intellectual disabilities is **Down syndrome (DS).** One in every 733 children is born with DS (National Down Syndrome Society, 2006), and this syndrome occurs in both sexes and across racial/ethnic groups. The cause of DS is clear: Usually, individuals have forty-six chromosomes, twenty-three contributed each by one's mother and father. In individuals with Down syndrome, an extra chromosome is present in the twenty-first chromosome pair, and so the syndrome is sometimes called **Trisomy 21.** Scientists have not yet discovered why this extra chromosome develops, but it is this extra genetic material that causes children with this syndrome to have easily identified characteristics.

When these children are young, they often have poor muscle tone and may be called "floppy" babies. They also have eyes that slant upward and small ears, and their tongues may seem somewhat large for their mouths. About half of these children have vision or hearing impairments, and approximately the same number have heart defects that may require medication or surgery (March of Dimes, 2006). Students with this syndrome usually have mild or moderate intellectual disabilities. Austin, the middle school student described at the beginning of this chapter, has Down syndrome.

Although Down syndrome can occur in any expectant mother, there is a correlation with age. Mothers who are twenty-five years old have a 1 in 1,350 chance of having a baby with Down syndrome. Those who are forty-five years old have a 1 in 28 chance of having a baby with DS (National Institutes of Health, National Institute of Child Health and Development, 2006).

Fragile X Syndrome The most common form of inherited intellectual disability is **Fragile X syndrome,** sometimes called Martin-Bell syndrome. Both men and women may carry the disorder, but only mothers transmit the disorder to their children. This syndrome develops when a mutation occurs in one of the genes in the X chromosome. The mutation, occurring when a gene segment that is repeated in most people about 30 times is repeated from 55 to 200 times, causes the gene to turn off, that is, to stop producing a chemical present in the cells of people who do not have this disorder (Fast, 2003). Fragile X syndrome is seen in approximately 1 in every 1,200 males and 1 in every 2,500 females (National Institutes of Health, National Institute of Child Health and Development, 2006). Males with this disorder usually have significant intellectual disabilities (Roberts et al., 2005); females usually have much milder impairments.

Individuals with Fragile X syndrome tend to have long faces, large ears, and poor muscle tone, but generally they are healthy. They often display characteristics similar to students with attention deficit–hyperactivity disorder (ADHD), including distractibility, and they may share some characteristics with students who have autism, including hypersensitivity to certain stimuli (e.g., the sound of a doorbell, the feel of certain types of clothing) and a tendency to say or do the same thing over and over again (Symons, Clark, Roberts, & Bailey, 2001). Students with this syndrome also are likely to become anxious when routines are changed, and they often have poor social skills. Jack, described in the chapter opening, has Fragile X syndrome.

Prader-Willi Syndrome **Prader-Willi syndrome** is much less common than Down syndrome and Fragile X syndrome, occurring in about 1 of every 15,000 babies (Wattendorf & Muenke, 2005). It is caused by any of several types of mutation on chromosome 15 (e.g., the father's chromosome is missing in the child; the mother contributes both chromosome 15s instead of one coming from the father). It occurs equally in boys and girls and occurs in individuals from any race/ethnicity.

Children who have Prader-Willi syndrome may have mild or moderate intellectual disabilities, and some have abilities in the low-average to average range (Prader-Willi Syndrome Association, 2003). Research on the specific cognitive characteristics of these individuals is just beginning (Bertella, Girelli, Grugni, Marchi, Molinari, & Semenza, 2005).

These children typically are happy as toddlers, and their behavior is similar to that of their peers. As they reach school age, though, they begin to have significant behavior problems, including stubbornness, problems switching from one activity to another, and resistance to changes in routines. However, the primary characteristic of this disorder is insatiable appetite and compulsive eating, and this symptom generally begins between the ages of two and four. Students with this disorder may steal food or eat discarded food, and educators working with these students must ensure that all food is kept locked away. Obesity occurs in 95 percent of these students if food intake is not carefully controlled. Families who have children with Prader-Willi syndrome often are under a great deal of stress because of the need to provide constant control and extensive behavior interventions (ERIC Clearinghouse on Disabilities and Gifted Education, 2003).

The technical information in the preceding paragraphs may leave you thinking that most intellectual disabilities are caused by chromosomal problems. This is not the case. There are many other prenatal causes of mental retardation, including those described in the following sections.

Fetal Alcohol Syndrome The potentially harmful impact of maternal alcohol consumption on the unborn child has been known for many years, but it was not until 1973 that the term **fetal alcohol syndrome (FAS)** was first used. The prevalence of FAS generally is believed to be significantly underreported at 0.33 cases per 1,000 babies born; some studies have reported the prevalence at 2.2 cases per 1,000 babies born (University of South Dakota Center for Disabilities, 2002). Some experts have

INTERNET RESOURCES
www.fragilex.org/home.htm
The National Fragile X Foundation provides support to families and professionals regarding Fragile X syndrome, and it supports research regarding this disorder. The website includes information on characteristics, education, interventions, and life planning, as well as discussion boards for parents and others.

Ellen B. Senisi

*F*etal alcohol syndrome (FAS) is a completely preventable cause of intellectual disabilities.

proposed that as many as two-thirds of all students receiving special education services may be affected by this disorder, or its less severe form, **fetal alcohol effect (FAE)**. FAS is considered the leading cause of intellectual disabilities and the only one that is clearly preventable (Burd, 2004; Miller, 2006), but it must be remembered that not every student with FAS has an intellectual disability.

> *"FAS is considered the leading cause of intellectual disabilities and the only one that is clearly preventable."*

Students with fetal alcohol syndrome usually are somewhat small and slower than other children in their development. Their eyes may be small with drooping eyelids, the groove between the upper lip and nose may be absent, and the lower part of the face may seem flat. These students often have mild or moderate intellectual disabilities, and they also are likely to have very short attention spans and hyperactivity, learning disabilities, and poor coordination (Ryan & Ferguson, 2006).

Phenylketonuria **Phenylketonuria (PKU)** is an inherited metabolic disorder that leads to intellectual disabilities if it is untreated. It affects 1 out of every 15,000 babies. PKU occurs when the body is unable to produce the chemicals needed to convert other toxic chemicals into harmless products. Children inherit PKU only if both parents carry the defective gene that causes it, and it affects boys and girls equally. PKU is mentioned here because you have undoubtedly seen a warning about it: If you look at the small print on a diet soft drink can, you will see a warning to "phenylketonurics" that the product contains phenylalanine, the chemical they cannot metabolize. All states now mandate that newborns be tested for PKU.

The treatment of PKU can begin even before a baby is born; when a mother known to carry this gene controls her dietary intake of phenylalanine, prenatal harmful effects can largely be avoided. Treatment for the child begins as soon as the disorder is detected, and it consists of a carefully planned diet low in foods containing phenylalanine (National Institutes of Health, 2006). For example, high-protein foods such as meat, fish, and poultry are not allowed. Although it was once believed that the special diet could be discontinued around age six, lifelong control of diet is the current recommended practice (National Institutes of Health, 2006). When the diet is followed and chemical levels in the blood carefully monitored, students with this disorder experience no significant effects on intellectual ability or learning.

Toxoplasmosis **Toxoplasmosis** is an infection caused by a parasite, and more than sixty million people in the United States carry it (Centers for Disease Control and Prevention, 2003), including 10 to 15 percent of women of childbearing age (fifteen years to forty-five years old). It usually is harmless because the body's immune system prevents it from causing illness. However, an expectant mother who becomes infected with the parasite for the first time can pass it on to her unborn child. The baby may seem fine at birth, but an intellectual disability or blindness may develop later in life. It is important to know that this parasite is spread through cat fecal matter. Thus, expectant mothers are cautioned to have someone else clean the litter box.

Perinatal Causes of Mental Retardation

In some instances a problem that occurs during or immediately after the birth of a child leads to an intellectual disability. For example, premature babies weighing less than 3.3 pounds have a 10 to 20 percent risk of having an intellectual disability (Beers & Berkow, 2003). Birth injury is another category of causes of intellectual disabilities during the perinatal period. For example, if a baby is deprived of oxygen as she is born or if the infant is hurt by the incorrect use of forceps or procedures followed during birth, an intellectual disability may result.

Postnatal Causes of Mental Retardation

Children who are born without disabilities sometimes develop an intellectual disability as a result of an accident or illness that occurs during childhood. Examples include the following:

■ *Encephalitis.* Inflammation of the brain, or encephalitis, can be caused by any viral infection. Vaccinations have reduced the chances of most children getting certain viral infections (e.g., measles, mumps, chickenpox), but this disease also can be carried by certain types of mosquitoes and animals that have rabies. In some cases, encephalitis results in intellectual disabilities.

■ *Lead poisoning.* You already have learned that students exposed to lead as young children are at higher risk for developing learning disabilities, emotional and behavior disorders, and ADHD. Lead poisoning can lead to intellectual disabilities as well. It is estimated that nearly one-half million children ages one through five have raised levels of lead in their blood (Centers for Disease Control and Prevention, 2003a). Even though lead-based paint was banned in 1978, it is the primary source of childhood lead exposure and is found in more than four million buildings in which young children live. Like fetal alcohol syndrome, lead poisoning is a completely preventable cause of intellectual disabilities.

"Even though lead-based paint was banned in 1978, it is the primary source of childhood lead exposure and is found in more than four million buildings in which young children live."

■ *Brain injury.* Any event that causes injury to the brain can be a cause of intellectual disabilities in children. Examples include falls from bicycles or playground equipment, auto accidents, near drownings, child abuse, and severe malnutrition.

Does it seem that the causes of intellectual disabilities are a little overwhelming? Remember that the preceding discussion includes only a few of all the causes and that advances in medical technology are providing additional information every year. These advances someday may help prevent some types of intellectual disabilities from ever occurring and minimize the impact of those that cannot be prevented.

What Are the Characteristics of Individuals with Intellectual Disabilities?

As you read about the causes of intellectual disabilities, you learned some of the specific characteristics associated with individuals who have well-known syndromes and disorders. In this section the emphasis is on a more general picture of the cognitive, academic, social, behavior, emotional, and physical/medical characteristics of this group of students.

Cognitive and Academic Characteristics

A student is identified as having mental retardation only if his IQ score places him at approximately two standard deviations or more below the mean or average score of 100. And even though IDEA does not draw these distinctions, in traditional classification systems individuals are grouped based on the extent of their cognitive impairment:

Mild mental retardation	IQ = 55–69
Moderate mental retardation	IQ = 40–54
Severe mental retardation	IQ = 25–39
Profound mental retardation	IQ = below 25

What does all this mean? Perhaps you have seen a diagram like the one presented in Figure 8.1, called a *bell-shaped curve.* It demonstrates how these concepts relate to one another. The average IQ score is considered 100. Most people—approximately 68 percent of them—have an IQ score that falls between one standard deviation (i.e., 15 points) below the mean and one standard deviation above the mean, or between 85 and 115. As you can see from the figure, the IQ scores for students with intellectual disabilities fall significantly below this range.

Keep in mind that IQ scores are approximations that guide professionals in making decisions about students' needs, but the scores should not by themselves dictate decisions regarding students. A student with an IQ slightly above 70 could be identified as having an intellectual

dimensions of
DIVERSITY

Based on population data, Hispanic students are underrepresented in the category of intellectual disabilities. If a risk of 1.0 means that the proportion of students is exactly what would be predicted, these students are represented at the 0.6 level, just over half of the number expected.

Figure 8.1

Bell-Shaped Curve for IQ Scores

This figure illustrates the approximate distribution of IQ scores across the entire population. The traditional classification system for intellectual disabilities is noted. Sixty-eight percent of people have an IQ that is considered average—that is, between 85 and 115.

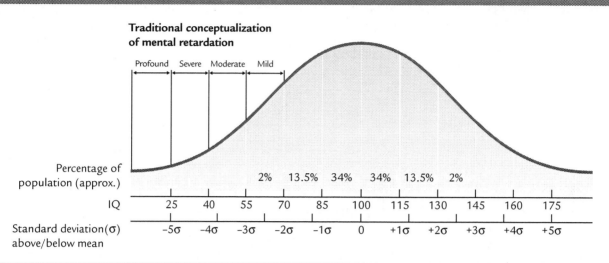

disability if he was experiencing many problems in adaptive skills. Likewise, a student with a score slightly below 70 might not be identified if she seemed to be functioning well.

Although some variation of this classification system of mild, moderate, severe, and profound is used in most states, it has bothered professionals for many years because of its emphasis on limitations and its tendency to relate specific scores to highly stigmatizing labels. In 1992 the American Association on Mental Retardation proposed an alternative classification system based on the **levels of support** individuals with intellectual disabilities may need. Figure 8.2 provides a summary of this support–need approach to thinking about and planning for individuals with intellectual disabilities, one that classifies students based on whether they need intermittent, limited, extensive, or pervasive support. This system was praised because it deemphasized reliance on IQ scores in program planning and stressed assisting individuals to reach their potential (Polloway, Smith, Chamberlain, Denning, & Smith, 1999). Regardless, the system has not been widely adopted. Only four states use this approach for classifying students with this disability (Denning, Chamberlain, & Polloway, 2000); most other states use the older classification system.

Cognitive Functioning

The cognitive characteristics of students with intellectual disabilities have a significant impact on several dimensions of cognitive functioning (Bergeron & Floyd, 2006), including the following:

■ *Memory.* In some respects, students with intellectual disabilities have cognitive functioning difficulties similar to those of other students about whom you have already learned. One example concerns working memory. Do you recall that students with ADHD have difficulty with working memory, or the ability to remember what needs to be done and how much time there is to do it? Students with intellectual disabilities also experience these problems. They are likely to forget what they are supposed to do, particularly if a task involves many steps. However, technology is helping to address this dilemma. The Technology Notes box explains

PROFESSIONAL MONITORING TOOL

Council for Exceptional Children

Standard 1 Foundations . . . issues in definition and identification

Figure 8.2

AAIDD Classification System Based on Levels of Support Needed

Level	Support Needed
Intermittent	Supports provided on an as-needed basis. Characterized by episodic nature, person not always needing the support(s), or short-term supports needed during life span transitions (e.g., job loss or an acute medical crisis).
Limited	An intensity of supports characterized by consistency over time and time limited but not of an intermittent nature; may require fewer staff members and cost less than more intense levels of support (e.g., time-limited employment training or transitional supports during the school-to-adult period).
Extensive	Supports characterized by regular involvement (e.g., daily) in at least some environments (such as work or home) and not time limited (e.g., long-term home living support).
Pervasive	Supports characterized by constancy, high intensity, and provision across environments; of a potential life-sustaining nature. Pervasive supports typically involve more staff members and intrusiveness than do extensive or time-limited supports.

Source: Luckasson, R., et al. (2002). *Mental retardation: Definition, classification, and systems of support* (10th ed., p. 152). Washington, DC: American Association on Mental Retardation. Reprinted with permission.

how personal digital assistants (PDAs) are being used to help these students overcome limitations in working memory.

▓ *Generalization.* The ability to learn a task or idea and then apply it in other situations is called **generalization.** When a student learns in language arts or English to use adjectives to make her writing more interesting and then uses adjectives when writing an essay in a social studies class, generalization has occurred. Students with intellectual disabilities have difficulty with generalization of academic tasks, of behavior expectations, and in social interactions. For example, if a student who tends to speak loudly is being taught to keep his voice at an acceptable classroom level, the skill may need to be taught in general education classrooms, in the music room, and in the cafeteria.

▓ *Metacognition.* Another difficulty for many students with intellectual disabilities is metacognition, or the ability to "think about thinking" (Erez & Peled, 2001). Students with intellectual disabilities are most successful when they are not expected to make judgments about what to do next; otherwise, they may struggle. For example, in a community setting, an adolescent with an intellectual disability might be successful riding a bus each day to go to a job, but the day that a detour requires him to get off in a different location, only a block away from the usual stop, he might get confused and not know how to find his way to that stop or how to get assistance.

▓ *Motivation.* Some students with intellectual disabilities share another characteristic with students with learning disabilities. They experience problems with motivation and learned helplessness—that is, the tendency to give up easily. For students with intellectual disabilities, however, learned helplessness may not be a result of frustration with the task at hand. It sometimes develops because professionals and classmates, in attempts to be helpful, are too eager to offer assistance. Some students soon learn that if they simply wait, someone will help out.

PROFESSIONAL MONITORING TOOL

Council for Exceptional Children

Standard 2 Development and Characteristics of Learners . . . similarities and differences among individuals

Enhancing Student Independence with Personal Digital Assistants (PDAs)

When students with intellectual disabilities are learning a new task, they will learn it more easily if it is broken down into small steps. In addition, they need assistance remembering what the steps are and the order in which they should occur. In the past, a person provided this support. For example, in teaching students the requirements of a job, a teacher or job coach would provide the necessary assistance.

Technology is changing that. Visual Assistant is part of a suite of software tools from AbleLink Technologies for PDAs. Visual Assistant combines digital pictures along with custom-recorded audio messages to provide step-by-step instructional support. That is, students can learn by looking at the pictures, listening to the instructions, and doing the task without having someone else present to guide them.

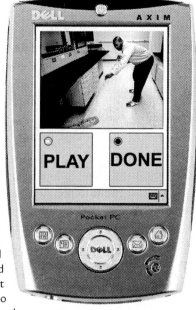

Davies, Stock, and Wehmeyer (2002) studied the use of Visual Assistant with students ages eighteen to twenty-one who were learning vocational skills. These researchers identified assembling pizza boxes and packaging software as two job-specific tasks. They trained ten individuals to use PDAs and then provided instruction on the two vocational skills. The results of the study clearly demonstrated the effectiveness of the technology: Participants were able to complete both vocational tasks accurately. Davies and his colleagues also found that the young men and women who participated in the study clearly enjoyed using the PDAs, that they could complete their work without needing a job coach, and that the software allowed the prompting system to be tailored to the ability level and skills of each person.

Millions of individuals, from school children to professionals, now carry PDAs to remind them of what to do and when. The argument made by the research community and consumers is that there is no reason individuals with intellectual disabilities should not have access to these same tools that can maximize strengths and minimize weaknesses.

Courtesy of Ablelink Technologies

Source: Based on Davies, D. K., Stock, S. E., & Wehmeyer, M. L. (2002). Enhancing independent task performance for individuals with mental retardation through use of a handheld self-directed visual and audio prompting system. *Education and Training in Mental Retardation and Developmental Disabilities, 37,* 209–218.

▨ *Language.* As you might expect, many students with intellectual disabilities have delays in the development of language. For example, it may take longer for them to learn concepts such as *up/down* and *over/under*. These students also may struggle with words that are abstract in meaning and benefit when professionals can make those words more concrete. Here is an example: A middle school student with an intellectual disability was in a social studies class learning about democracy, a very abstract concept. By using discussions and examples, the student was able to learn what democracy means. When other students wrote essays on the subject, she compiled pictures and described them to her classmates. For example, she held up a picture of a protest rally and explained that in a democracy people can say things that other people do not like and the people saying the things cannot be put in jail for saying them. No one doubted that she grasped the essential meaning of democracy.

■ *Academic skills.* Students with intellectual disabilities usually have to work harder and practice longer than other students in order to learn academic skills (Bertella, Girelli, Grugni, Marchi, Molinari, & Semenza, 2005). In times past, assumptions were made about the so-called ceilings that these students would reach in learning. Now, however, professionals are balancing the realistic understanding that learning is difficult for these students with the conviction that they may learn more than anyone ever thought they could—if they are only given the opportunity. For example, Cole, Waldron, and Majd (2002) report that when students with mild intellectual disabilities are educated in general education classrooms with peers, they often make more academic progress than students who are taught in special education classes.

Social, Behavior, and Emotional Characteristics

The social, behavior, and emotional characteristics of students with intellectual disabilities can vary as much as those of students without disabilities (Freeman, 2000). Stereotypes that assign specific characteristics to particular groups of children generally are not accurate unless a specific behavior is associated with a particular disorder, such as those you read about earlier in the chapter.

Social Characteristics

Many students with intellectual disabilities have difficulties in social relationships (Addeduto et al., 2006). They tend to be less accepted by their peers and more likely to be rejected by them, although inclusive practices may help students to be more positive about their peers with disabilities (Krajewski & Hyde, 2000; Krajewski, Hyde, & O'Keefe, 2002). Students with intellectual disabilities also have few friends outside school (Geisthardt, Brotherson, & Cook, 2002).

What are the reasons for these students' social difficulties? First, many students with intellectual disabilities have immature behaviors that make other students want to avoid them. Second, their ways of dealing with social situations may be inappropriate (Farmer, 2000). For instance, a student with an intellectual disability may walk up to a group of students engaged in conversation and elbow his way in; those students then may form a negative perception of him. Finally, students with intellectual disabilities may have difficulty picking up subtle social cues, and so they may misinterpret other students' actions (Leffert, Siperstein, & Millikan, 2000). One way that school professionals measure the social relationships among students in their classrooms, including those with intellectual disabilities, is to use sociograms as explained in the Positive Behavior Supports.

Adaptive Behavior Characteristics

To be identified as having an intellectual disability, a student must display deficits in adaptive behavior. These are some of the skills that are included in the area of adaptive behavior:

■ *Communication*—the ability to exchange thoughts, messages, or information with other people through speaking, sign language, or other means

■ *Self-care*—the ability to tend to personal hygiene, eating, and other related tasks

■ *Social skills*—the ability to interact appropriately with others

■ *Home living*—the ability to manage the day-to-day tasks of living in an apartment or house

■ *Leisure*—the ability to use free time productively

■ *Health and safety*—the ability to take precautions and act in ways that do not endanger oneself or others

■ *Self-direction*—the ability to make and implement decisions

■ *Functional academics*—the reading, writing, math, and other skills needed for independence

Using Sociograms to Gather Information about Student Interactions

One concern about students with disabilities in inclusive settings is their acceptance by peers. You can get a sense of the patterns of friendships and social interactions in a classroom by using a *sociogram*, a teacher-made survey intended for this purpose. Students respond to teacher-provided items such as "List the two classmates with whom you would most like to sit," "Write the name of the person with whom you would enjoy working on a project," and "If you were going on a vacation, which of your classmates would be nice to have along, and why?" The responses are then compiled to create a social snapshot of the class group.

How to Make and Use Sociograms

1. Devise one or several questions depending on the ages and abilities of students. State questions in easy-to-understand language. Word questions to be consistent with the information you wish to obtain (e.g., who to assign as field trip partners; who is unpopular and in need of social skills instruction).

2. Have students write their answers to your questions. Allow and encourage your students to make their choices privately. Clearly explain any limitations on choices (e.g., number of choices, classmates only). Some students may need assistance writing down their responses.

3. On a class list, tally next to each student's name the number of times she was selected by another student.

4. You can analyze the data is several ways. One way is to make a large diagram of concentric

rings so that it looks like an archery target. Have one more ring than the greatest number of times any student was chosen. Start outside the last ring and number the spaces from the outside toward the inside starting with zero. Write each student's name inside the ring space corresponding to the number of times he or she was chosen. Draw arrows from each student to the student(s) they selected.

5. A simple strategy is to draw a bar graph, in which one bar represents each student and the number of times she was selected.

6. Survey your results to assess popularity and interaction preferences. Of course, you should keep this information confidential.

In the sample below, ten students were asked who they would like to sit next to. What does the chart tell you about student social status?

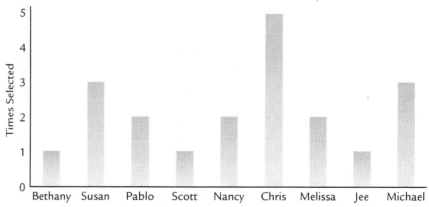

Source: McIntyre, T. (2003). Sociograms. Retrieved September 24, 2003, from www.behavioradvisor.com. Reprinted by permission of the author.

- *Community use*—the ability to identify and access services and activities in the neighborhood or area

- *Work*—the ability to obtain and keep employment

In very young children, adaptive behavior might include learning to crawl and then walk and learning to speak. In elementary school, adaptive behavior includes taking turns, following directions, and moving safely around the school and its grounds. For secondary school students, adaptive behavior includes going to the mall, dining out with friends, changing classes at school, and preparing for employment. Students with mild intellectual disabilities may experience delays in a few areas of adaptive behavior. Students with more significant disabilities are likely to have difficulties in many of these domains.

Students with Intellectual and Developmental Disabilities

Additional Behavior Characteristics

Some types of intellectual disabilities are related to specific behaviors. Prader-Willi syndrome, with its compulsive eating, is one example. Other students with intellectual disabilities do not display extraordinary behaviors. Rather, they need rewards and consequences much like those needed by other students, perhaps with a greater emphasis on the use of specific rewards (e.g., stickers, small prizes) used in a very systematic way. A few students may have self-injurious behaviors such as pulling their hair out or biting others. When such behaviors are present, the services of a behavior specialist will likely be needed to design interventions to reduce or eliminate the behaviors.

Emotional Characteristics

A relatively new topic being explored in relation to school-age students with intellectual disabilities is these students' mental health (Dudley, 2005). Researchers have found that students with intellectual disabilities experience more loneliness than students without disabilities but that these differences diminished as students entered adolescence (Heiman & Margalit, 1998). Clearly, valuing individuals with intellectual disabilities includes understanding that they experience the same emotions as others and that they have mental health needs (U.S. Department of Health and Human Services, 2001; Lorenzi, Horvat, & Pellegrini, 2000).

Physical and Medical Characteristics

Most students with mild intellectual disabilities do not have any extraordinary medical conditions. However, they have been found to be less physically fit than other students, and this concern has led to an increased emphasis for these students to learn good health habits and engage in physical activities (Hoge & Dattilo, 1999).

However, as a student's cognitive impairments become more pronounced, the likelihood of having serious physical problems and medical conditions needing intervention increases. Examples were provided earlier in the descriptions of specific causes of intellectual disabilities; for example, children with Down syndrome likely will have vision or hearing loss or heart problems requiring surgery. For educators, knowing about students' health and medical needs is important for several reasons. First, if a student's medical condition is fragile or changing, educators need to know whether an emergency might occur and how to respond. Second, if a student should be wearing glasses or using a hearing aid or another medical device, educators need to be prepared to monitor this. Finally, some students may miss significant amounts of school because of surgery or illness; in these cases, professionals are responsible for working with parents to minimize the impact on student learning.

John Birdsall/The Image Works

As students with intellectual disabilities approach adulthood, the emphasis in their education usually shifts toward learning important job skills.

Research Notes

When students with moderate intellectual disabilities were taught functional vocabulary words by embedding them in a variety of classroom activities in general education, they were successful in learning the vocabulary and remembering it over time (McDonnell, Johnson, Polychronis, & Risen, 2002).

How Are Intellectual Disabilities Identified?

For students with intellectual disabilities to receive special education services, they must go through the formal process of identification. For some students, this will have occurred when they are very young, even as infants, using assessment methods designed just for that age group. Other students are identified when they enter kindergarten and cannot manage the academic, social, and other expectations of the school setting, and yet others are identified sometime during the elementary school years.

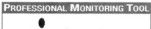

PROFESSIONAL MONITORING TOOL

Council for
Exceptional
Children

Standard 8 Assessment
. . . use and limitations of
assessments

PROFESSIONAL MONITORING TOOL

Council for
Exceptional
Children

Standard 8 Assessment
. . . use assessment information
in making decisions

Assessment

For students who may have intellectual disabilities, assessment focuses on intellectual functioning and adaptive skills, as stressed in the definitions presented earlier. However, medical
and other information also is assessed as appropriate.

Assessment of Intellectual Functioning

You already have learned that one common test used to assess intellectual functioning in
students being considered for special education services is the Wechsler Intelligence Scale for
Children (WISC–IV) (Wechsler, 2003). Another test sometimes used is the Stanford–Binet
(Roid, 2003). These tests tend to measure a student's
overall abilities and predict school achievement.
They are individually administered only by professionals specially trained to do so.

You should keep in mind that no single test can
measure all aspects of intelligence. Moreover, intelligence tests tend to ignore what some people consider
key components of intelligence such as creativity and
humor. Most professionals also acknowledge that no
single, universally accepted definition of *intelligence* exists. And so, although intelligence tests
and the scores they produce are integral to the procedures of special education, they should be
treated as valuable information, not as a prescription of a student's abilities and limitations.

> *"No single test can measure all aspects
> of intelligence. Moreover, intelligence
> tests tend to ignore what some people
> consider key components of intelligence,
> such as creativity and humor."*

Assessment of Adaptive Behavior

The assessment of adaptive behavior is completed through interviews or surveys with parents,
teachers, and others and with direct observation of the student. The goal is to obtain an accurate
description of how well the student is functioning across school, home, and community settings.

One common assessment instrument used for this area is the AAMR Adaptive Behavior
Scale (2nd edition) (Lambert, Nihira, & Leland, 1993). It is available in a school form and a
form for individuals in residential settings or community settings. This instrument considers a student's abilities to independently perform daily-living skills that are age appropriate
and situation appropriate. It also evaluates inappropriate behaviors, including self-injurious
behaviors (e.g., biting oneself when anxious). A teacher or other professional completes the
scale for a student who has been referred, rating her adaptive behaviors.

Another measure of adaptive behavior is the Vineland Adaptive Behavior Scales (Spar-
row, Balla, & Cicchetti, 1985). This instrument is based on interviewing, and it must be administered by a psychologist, social worker, or other appropriately trained professional. The
scales address communication, daily-living, socialization, and motor skills, and they include
an assessment of motor skills for children younger than six years old and an optional behavior
assessment for children older than five.

On these and other adaptive behavior instruments, a student's current level of functioning is compared to that of typical children. The student's score provides an estimate of
whether he is functioning at the expected level, above the expected level, or below it.

Assessment of Medical Factors

For students with medical considerations, school team members may seek input from appropriate medical professionals concerning medications being taken, health risks for or limitations needed on physical activities, chronic conditions that school professionals should be
aware of, and anticipated medical procedures that may affect school attendance or performance. These factors may be found to be integral to students' disabilities.

Eligibility

The decision to identify a student as having an intellectual disability must be based on the assessment information that has been gathered. The essential questions that are asked include these:

1. *Does the student's intelligence, as measured on a formal individual assessment, fall at least 2 standard deviations below the mean? That is, is the student's measured IQ approximately 70 or below?* The federal definition of *mental retardation* refers to significantly subaverage intellectual functioning, and the IQ scores mentioned earlier represent the operational definition of that term. However, no cutoff score is considered absolute, and students with scores slightly above 70 might still be considered in this disability category.

2. *Does the student display deficits in adaptive behavior?* For this decision, team members review data from the adaptive behavior scales used in the assessment as well as observational data and anecdotal information offered by teachers, parents, and others. In many ways, answering this question relies on making a judgment call. Although the scales provide scores that indicate a student's functioning level in the adaptive domain, the team must consider the school and home context and the student's overall success in each. If clear and persistent deficits are noted, the decision is straightforward. However, for some students whose skills are marginal, discussion might be needed about the scores obtained versus observed student functioning. As with intelligence measures, a test score is considered a guideline.

3. *Do the student's characteristics adversely affect educational performance?* Federal special education law is premised on the adverse effect of disabilities on student learning and behavior, and so the team must consider this question as well as the others.

If the multidisciplinary team finds that the student meets the criteria to be identified as having an intellectual disability and would benefit by receiving special education, the remaining special education procedures are followed, and an individualized education program (IEP) is prepared so that the student receives an appropriate education. Some of the options for education are outlined in the following section.

How Do Learners with Intellectual Disabilities Receive Their Education?

Students with intellectual disabilities access the same sets of services in the same settings as other students with disabilities. However, because of the nature of their special needs and the importance of both early intervention and transition from school to adult life activities, their education often includes some specialized options.

Early Childhood

Young children who have clearly recognizable disorders that include an intellectual disability usually are identified as needing special services shortly after birth, and these babies may begin their education during the first few months of life. For these very young children, services often are based in the home and have an emphasis on helping family members learn how best to teach their children. Both parents and early childhood professionals view this type of service as highly valuable in fostering children's development and learning and increasing parent confidence in working with their young children (Dunst & Bruder, 2002). This type of early intervention usually includes an early interventionist who consults with the family, but it also could involve a physical therapist, speech/language pathologist, and other specialists. Services for these infants and toddlers may include medical and health professionals as well (Beirne-Smith, Ittenbach, & Patton, 2002).

These very young children move into preschool programs at age three, where they may be joined by children who recently have been identified as having developmental delays or other disabilities. Preschool programs have been demonstrated to have strongly positive effects on the language skills, motor development, and preacademic skill development of children with intellectual disabilities (e.g., Berglund, Eriksson, & Johansson, 2001; Roberts, Hatton, & Bailey, 2001; T. Smith, Groen, & Wynn, 2000). Both professionals and families continue to strongly support such programs, and attention on them has shifted to refining the services

Research Notes

In a qualitative study, Gallagher, Floyd, Stafford, Taber, Brozovic, and Alberto (2000) found that siblings of students with intellectual disabilities viewed their brothers and sisters in terms of their abilities, wanted them to be around children without disabilities, and saw themselves as models for them. A surprising finding was siblings' lack of knowledge about and involvement in school inclusion.

offered (Guralnick, 2000) and respecting the different early intervention preferences of families from specific cultural groups (Weisner, 1999).

Elementary and Secondary School Services

Students with intellectual disabilities in elementary, middle, and high school are entitled to receive their education in the least restrictive environment just like other students with disabilities (Katisyannis, Zhang, & Archwamety, 2002). However, if you review the information included in Figure 8.3, you can see that only a small proportion of students identified with this disability spend the majority of their time in general education classrooms. In fact, the most common setting for these students is a special education classroom for more than 60 percent of the day.

When students with intellectual disabilities are in general education classrooms with their peers, the extent to which they participate in exactly the same activities and the amount of support they need depends on the student's level of functioning (Fox, Farrell, & Davis, 2004). In one first-grade classroom, Jasmine—who has a moderate intellectual disability—was participating in a review of consonant blends. The chart being used contained nearly two dozen blends, but when it was Jasmine's turn to pronounce a blend and include it in a word,

PROFESSIONAL MONITORING TOOL

Council for Exceptional Children

Standard 5 Learning Environments and Social Interaction . . . supports needed for integration

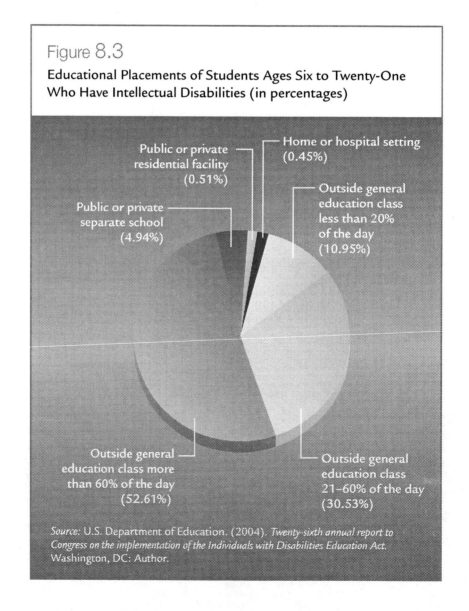

Figure 8.3

Educational Placements of Students Ages Six to Twenty-One Who Have Intellectual Disabilities (in percentages)

Public or private residential facility (0.51%)

Home or hospital setting (0.45%)

Public or private separate school (4.94%)

Outside general education class less than 20% of the day (10.95%)

Outside general education class more than 60% of the day (52.61%)

Outside general education class 21–60% of the day (30.53%)

Source: U.S. Department of Education. (2004). *Twenty-sixth annual report to Congress on the implementation of the Individuals with Disabilities Education Act.* Washington, DC: Author.

Students with Intellectual and Developmental Disabilities

Working with Students with Intellectual Disabilities in Inclusive Classrooms

Sandy is a special education teacher. She has been working with fourth- and fifth-grade students with intellectual disabilities as they learn in the general education setting. Here is her view on including these students.

I knew that I wanted to be a teacher as soon as I started my first college experience with preschoolers in Puerto Rico, my home. That was the first time I had an opportunity to work with children. I have to admit, I used to think, "Children should be able to accomplish whatever it is the teacher assigns them to do." But then I had my own children, and both of my children have special needs. Then it became personal. My own children began to struggle . . . and I was no longer an "outsider." I had my own experience with how hard it was for my children in school, and I decided that I wanted to become a special education teacher.

I've just recently completed my teacher education program and started teaching, and I love seeing how the children who have been identified with mental retardation and other special needs are able to accomplish so much

in the inclusive classrooms. Many times the reason they are able to do so much is due to our collaboration—the fact that I am able to work with them, along with the general education teacher. We are able to give them the help they

"I am always amazed at the children's ability!"

need, and they are able to accomplish as much as their classmates without disabilities.

I am always amazed at the children's ability! For example, we were working on some difficult math problems using division. The students with mental retardation were actually demonstrating that they understood how to do the problems before some of their classmates! Ms. Reynolds, the special education teacher, had taught the children a problem-solving process that helped

them see the problem in a different way and understand how they could use a different approach. The great thing was that after this strategy worked so well with these children, all the children in the classroom were taught the strategy, so all the children benefited.

I have to say that I am in an inclusive school—everybody at this school, from the office staff to the principal to all the teachers, is involved with all the children. It really does give true meaning to the saying, "It takes a village to raise a child." The teachers in the classrooms appreciate all the assistance that the special education teachers, the interns, and other support staff provide to all the children, and everyone here values working together as a team so that all students learn. I always feel welcome and appreciated. And I know from being at this school that inclusion works!

she always was given the blend *fr*, the one that happened to be at the beginning of her family name, *Franklin*. No special accommodations were needed.

Some students need alternative activities that are based on the general education curriculum. For example, in a sixth-grade social studies class the students were studying cultures, and they had reached the study of ancient Egypt. As part of the unit students were given the assignment of creating a magazine that ancient Egyptians would have wanted to read. Some students applied their new knowledge to produce magazines that contained references to Egyptian recreation, politics, and religion. Chase, a student with a moderate intellectual disability, created a picture magazine that incorporated artifacts from ancient Egypt for which he would see references in the normal course of life, including pharaohs and pyramids. Sandy Oyola is an enthusiastic supporter of inclusive practices for these students, and her experiences are presented in the Firsthand Account on this page. As a teacher and the mother of two children with special needs, her perspective is especially valuable.

Other students with intellectual disabilities are supported in general education settings through the use of paraprofessionals (Broer, Doyle, & Giangreco, 2005), but many students spend at least part of the day receiving specialized academic instruction in a special education setting (Burcroff, Radogna, & Wright, 2003). For example, in Ms. DeCuir's classroom

PROFESSIONAL MONITORING TOOL

Council for Exceptional Children

Standard 7 Instructional Planning
. . . identify areas of general curriculum and accommodations

of middle school students who take an alternate assessment, the goal of the math program is to assist students to learn the skills they will need in order to shop, order in a restaurant, and possibly work in a fast-food restaurant. For some students the concept of a budget and saving money also is a priority. This is part of a **life skills curriculum,** a plan for students' education that stresses skills they need throughout life. In several lessons, the middle school students review coins and paper currency using real coins and facsimiles of bills, and they practice at their own skill levels how to make change, an **applied academic skill.** On Friday, Ms. DeCuir plans to take the students to the Dollar Store so they can make small purchases and put their skills into action. The outing will conclude with a stop at a fast-food restaurant; students will practice ordering food items based on how much money they have. The outing is part of **community-based instruction**—that is, experience in applying skills learned in the classroom within the larger context of the community in which they live.

High school students are more likely than younger students to be educated primarily in special education settings, although in some communities inclusion is emphasized (Doré, Dion, Wagner, & Brunet, 2002; Williamson, McLeskey, Hoppey, & Rentz, 2006). Andrew, a student with a mild intellectual disability, exemplifies a blended approach to education. As a sophomore he decided to take the introductory Spanish class. Why? He lives in a community with many Spanish-speaking residents and wanted to know about their language. No Spanish instruction was available in a special education class. With a strongly supportive Spanish teacher, Andrew learned basic Spanish. However, Andrew's English and math classes were taught by special education teachers. Three afternoons each week Andrew went to a local computer repair shop with his **job coach** Ms. Hickman. There he learned how to install motherboards and other computer components. Ms. Hickman's role was to analyze the skills Andrew needed, help him learn them, and ensure that he could carry out his responsibilities independently.

A few students with intellectual disabilities attend separate schools or live in residential facilities that include academic programs. Usually, these are students who have complex medical needs requiring the on-call availability of nursing or medical staff, or they are students who have very serious behavior problems in addition to intellectual disabilities. In some regions of the United States, the separate schools for students with moderate intellectual disabilities that were built around the time the first federal special education law was passed are still in place. They are becoming less and less common, though, as access to the general education curriculum and emphasis on an academically and socially integrated education have become priorities.

Inclusive Practices

Despite the fact that the parents of children with intellectual disabilities were leaders in the educational movement that greatly increased inclusive practices, the preceding discussion indicates that this goal has been only partially achieved. Why are so many students with intellectual disabilities still separated for instruction?

The answer to this question is complex (Hall, 2002; Stodden, Galloway, & Stodden, 2003; Wilson, 1999). One factor affecting the education of these students is traditional thinking. Many educators still believe that the best instructional arrangement for these students, particularly as they move from elementary to middle and high school, is a special education classroom. Many high school special education teachers for students with mild intellectual disabilities have asked, "Why would I support putting my students into classrooms where they don't know what is being taught and can't keep up with the pace? They need the practical skills that I give them." Their concern for their students is understandable and their advocacy for their education is important, especially given the current climate of accountability and the resulting pressure on secondary teachers to ensure students are successful on high-stakes tests.

However, the belief that only special educators can give the students what they need and that the entire high school curriculum is irrelevant for these students is troublesome (Wehmeyer, 2003). It reflects the thinking of the past and raises another point: Inclusive practices do not mean that a student's only option is to attend general education classes for the entire school day without necessary supports. For example, in some high schools part of the move toward inclusiveness is a peer-buddy program in which students without disabilities receive an elective credit to assist students with cognitive and other disabilities in their general education classes (Copeland et al., 2002). This highly successful arrangement has many benefits: Students with intellectual disabilities receive the support they need to succeed in general education classes, general education teachers sense that the problem of not being able to get to all the students who need assistance is being addressed, and the peer-buddies are exploring career options related to special education.

Parents also play an important role in considering inclusive practices as they relate to students with intellectual disabilities. For example, most parents of young children with intellectual disabilities see their children in the context of a larger world, not only in the context of schools and disabilities. They want their children to have normal experiences, and their perspectives on the best educational options often have to do with the quality of the relationships they have with school professionals (Bennett, Lee, & Lueke, 1998). Evidence suggests that the parents of older students are influenced by their child's current educational placement (Hodapp, Freeman, & Kasari, 1998): They tend to be satisfied with the type of education currently being provided. However, the type of disorder also may influence parents. Parents of children with Down syndrome tend to favor inclusive practices more than parents of other children with intellectual disabilities (Hodapp et al., 1998).

"Parents' perspectives on the best educational options often have to do with the quality of the relationships they have with school professionals."

More and more questions are being raised about appropriate educational options for students with intellectual disabilities (Browder, Wakeman, Spooner, Ahlgrim-Delzell, & Algozzine, 2006; Clayton, Burdge, Denham, Kleinhart, & Kearns, 2006), and some of the factors prompting these questions are reviewed in the section on issues later in this chapter. As educators create additional options for successful inclusion (e.g., Carter, Hughes, Guth, & Copeland, 2005; Maroney, Finson, Beaver, & Jensen, 2003), the ways in which students with intellectual disabilities receive their education are sure to change. The Inclusion Matters summarizes a procedure for helping teachers to think inclusively.

PROFESSIONAL MONITORING TOOL

Council for Exceptional Children

Standard 4 Instructional Strategies
. . . strategies that promote transitions

Transition and Adulthood

As students with intellectual disabilities reach adolescence, emphasis usually shifts to helping them make a successful transition from school to adulthood. Some students will leave school at about age eighteen with their peers. Others are entitled to receive services through age twenty-one. For students with mild intellectual disabilities, transition may emphasize learning tasks that foster independence, including planning and using a household budget, searching for and finding employment, using resource tools such as the phone book and Internet, and developing hobbies and recreational skills. For students with more significant intellectual disabilities, the same types of preparation may be emphasized but on a somewhat more limited basis. Instead of budgeting, for example, math activities may focus on making wise choices about using spending money. The vehicle through which this type of planning occurs is the transition plan that is required by federal special education law, and it is a collaborative effort on the part of parents, the student, and professionals (Frank & Sitlington, 2000). The importance of transition planning for these students and the concept of **self-determination**—that is, students' rights to make plans that reflect their wishes, not only the ideas of professionals and parents—is addressed in detail in the final section of this chapter as a critical issue for the field.

Remember that some students with intellectual disabilities will never again be identified as such once they leave school (Black & Rojewski, 1998). They will blend into their communities, get by with assistance from family and friends, and lead happy and productive lives. Other students will need structured support throughout their lives. They may work in entry-level jobs in businesses (e.g., copy assistant in an office, assembly line worker) or schools (e.g., housekeeping staff), or they may work in a specialized setting (e.g., a business that employs people with disabilities to assemble materials for other businesses). Many will live independently, but some will live with family or with other individuals with disabilities with assistance provided. Most importantly, the plans these students and their families have for their futures should guide the types of transition services they receive (Lindsey, Wehmeyer, Guy, & Martin, 2001).

CHECK
Your Learning
What types of specialized programs are offered to students with intellectual disabilities in special education classes? What are examples of the skills these programs emphasize?

Funding for secondary and postsecondary vocational education programs is provided through the Carl D. Perkins Act. Some students with mental retardation can receive training for postschool employment through these programs.

SUCCEEDing in Inclusive Classrooms

Many students with mild disabilities, including those with mild intellectual disabilities, are spending more and more time learning with their classmates in general education classrooms. Understandably, teachers may have questions about how to help all the students in their classrooms succeed, and they need innovative ways to help them make important decisions for maximizing students' learning. SHE WILL SUCCEED is an acronym that you can use for this purpose or share with general education teachers with whom you work.

S *Show concern for students with special needs.* Remember to set a positive tone in the classroom and to focus on student strengths. Clearly convey to students that you care about them as individuals.

H *Have faith in yourself and your students with disabilities.* Students with mental retardation often have learned helplessness. They do not believe that their efforts to learn are connected to success in learning. You can help them learn to expect to succeed and to recognize that their efforts lead to rewards.

E *Examine your classroom.* Review your curriculum, classroom rules, instruction, materials, and overall environment to ensure that all are designed to enhance student learning.

W *Write down student strengths and limitations.* Know how to use student strengths and work to help students overcome their limitations.

I *Include skills, learning preferences, and behaviors specific to your classroom.* Try to match student strengths and limitations in the context of your classroom and your strengths and limitations as a teacher. Think about your textbooks, the type of homework you usually assign, your teaching style, and even the physical arrangement of the classroom.

L *Line up student and classroom characteristics as those that facilitate, provide barriers, or are neutral for students' learning successes.* Assess the strengths and limitations you listed above. Label each as a facilitator, barrier, or neutral factor related

to students' learning. For example, if you frequently ask students to write lengthy answers, a facilitator for students might be their skills at using computer word processing software, and a barrier might be their slow speed in completing such lengthy tasks.

L *List one to three classroom characteristics you could modify and skills that you could teach.* Perhaps you could require somewhat less writing on some assignments. Perhaps you could teach students to use a word prediction program that would help them complete writing tasks more efficiently.

S *Select and implement accommodations and goals.* As you implement the ideas you have generated, you should be prepared to make adjustments based on student responses.

U *Use effective teaching principles to teach goals.* When teaching new skills, be sure to use effective strategies, including task analysis.

C *Collaborate with others as needed.* When professionals work together, they generate more ideas and resolve more difficulties. Two heads are better than one.

C *Change accommodations and instruction as necessary* and

E *Evaluate results.* Gather data about the effectiveness of accommodations and adjust them if they are not having the desired impact on student learning.

E *Exit here* or

D *Do it again.* If students are making appropriate progress, teachers may want to gradually withdraw the amount of supports provided. If challenges are being encountered, it may be time to reassess the plan.

Source: Prater, M. (2003). She will succeed: Strategies for success in inclusive classrooms. *Teaching Exceptional Children, 35*(5), 58–64. Copyright © 2003 by the Council for Exceptional Children. Reprinted with permission.

What Are Recommended Educational Practices for Students with Intellectual Disabilities?

PROFESSIONAL MONITORING TOOL

Council for Exceptional Children

Standard 4 Instructional Strategies
. . . strategies to facilitate maintenance and generalization of skills

A number of instructional strategies that are effective for teaching students with intellectual disabilities already have been introduced in this chapter. Strategies such as planning for generalization and making abstract concepts more concrete are essential to these students' education. Likewise, some students need a life skills curriculum and functional academics. Others need to participate in the general education curriculum. All of these options illustrate the diversity of recommended instructional practices. Also important are other strategies—for example, direct instruction and behavior interventions such as clear rules, schoolwide behavior plans, and the use of contracts.

Here, the focus is on two additional strategies: task analysis and peer-mediated instruction. Both are important across elementary, middle, and high school settings and across special education and general education classrooms.

Task Analysis

Universal design for learning (UDL) and differentiation can be applied to teaching students with intellectual disabilities. For example, you have learned that students with intellectual disabilities experience difficulty with metacognition. To succeed, they often need to have their assignments and activities clearly outlined and presented to them so that they do not have to make judgments about what to do next or whether other options should be considered. The instructional strategy for ensuring this type of very systematic learning—and one that enables you to make appropriate decisions about planning instruction—is called **task analysis.** Think about how complex most school tasks are. Working on the computer involves turning it on, finding and loading the correct program, launching that program, following directions to complete the work, saving it, printing it, exiting the program, and shutting down the computer. You may complete such a task with ease, but for many students with intellectual disabilities such a task is daunting. In task analysis, the professional's responsibility is to break any task or activity—from following classroom rules to using musical instruments—into small steps and then teach those steps to students. By guiding students to learn each small step of the process and then assisting them to put the steps together, teachers can help these students master more and more complex tasks. The Specialized Instruction on the next page outlines the steps for using task analysis and includes examples of its application.

> *"In task analysis, the professional's responsibility is to break any task or activity into small steps and then teach those steps to students."*

Once task analysis has been completed, students with intellectual disabilities may need to practice the component steps for a task more than other students. For academic work, a computer with drill-and-practice software (e.g., for math facts or for consonant sounds) will make the amount of practice available almost limitless. For activities such as following classroom routines or moving around the school, peers, paraprofessionals, or volunteers might be able to assist.

Peer-Mediated Instruction

Another way of making learning accessible to all students is to use *peer-mediated instruction,* in which peers teach peers. Doing so can involve cooperative-learning strategies that bring together student groups of three, four, or even more students (Jenkins, Antil, Wayne, & Vadasy, 2003). Another peer-mediated instructional approach is **peer tutoring,** which is especially effective for students with intellectual disabilities (Spencer & Balboni, 2003). Peer tutoring is an approach to instruction in which students are partnered, provided with instructional materials that they are to learn, and expected to help each other in accomplishing the learning goal.

There are several types of peer tutoring. One approach pairs older students who are struggling to learn with younger students. Another approach partners high-achieving students with struggling learners in their classrooms. More recently, an alternative approach has been identified. Called *classwide peer tutoring (CWPT),* this approach assumes that peer tutoring should be reciprocal—that all participating students should have opportunities to be both the teacher and the learner (Maheady, Mallette, & Harper, 2006). For students with intellectual disabilities, a growing body of research is demonstrating that they can successfully participate in these programs and that their learning is enhanced. Further, students without

PROFESSIONAL MONITORING TOOL

Council for Exceptional Children

Standard 7 Instructional Planning
. . . use task analysis

CHECK Your Learning

What is *task analysis*? No matter what your role is in schools, how can task analysis help you in working with students with cognitive disabilities?

PROFESSIONAL MONITORING TOOL

Council for Exceptional Children

Standard 4 Instructional Strategies
. . . select and use strategies according to characteristics

Using Task Analysis

Task analysis often is helpful in teaching students with intellectual disabilities. You teach each small step to the student, and then help the student to put the steps together, which is sometimes called *chaining* them. Chaining can be forward—where you help the student to do the first step, then you do the rest; then you help the student to do the first two steps, and you do the rest; and so on. Chaining also can be backward—where you complete all the steps except the last one, and the student does only that step; then you complete all the steps except the last two, and the student does those two steps; and so on. Whether you choose forward or backward chaining to teach skills to students depends on the students' abilities and the type of task. For example, teaching classroom routines might be best taught using forward chaining. Teaching students to put the proper heading on their papers might best be accomplished through backward chaining.

The following examples illustrate the use of task analysis for two life skills, one for younger students and one for older students: tying shoes and getting ready for a foods lab. Would you choose forward chaining or backward chaining for each?

Tying Shoes

1. Pinch the laces.
2. Pull the laces.
3. Hang the ends of the laces from the corresponding sides of the shoe.
4. Pick up the laces in the corresponding hands.
5. Lift the laces above the shoe.
6. Cross the right lace over the left one to form a tepee.
7. Bring the left lace toward you.

8. Pull the left lace through the tepee.
9. Pull the laces away from one another.
10. Bend the left lace to form a loop.
11. Pinch the loop with the left hand.
12. Bring the right lace over the fingers and around the loop.
13. Push the right lace through the hole.
14. Pull the loops away from one another.

Getting Ready for Foods Lab

1. Put on your hair net.
2. Gather your books and items together.
3. Take those materials to the shelves in the back of the room.
4. Place your materials in the assigned section.
5. Go to the closet and select an apron.
6. Put on the apron.
7. Go to your desk and wait quietly for the instructor to start class.

Task analysis can be used for many life skills, but it also can be used to help you think about teaching academic or organizational skills. What steps might you include in a task analysis of writing a sentence or getting ready to leave the classroom at the end of the instructional period?

Source: McIntyre, T. (2003, October). Task analysis. Retrieved October 10, 2003, from http://maxweber.hunter.cuny.edu/pub/eres/EDSPC715_MCINTYRE/TaskAnalysis.html.

---

disabilities develop more positive views of their peers with special needs when peer tutoring is carefully implemented.

You can learn the fundamentals of developing a peer-tutoring program in the Specialized Instruction on the next page. As you reflect on this instructional approach, consider these questions: Why might peer tutoring be particularly effective in raising all students' achievement? How might peer tutoring help to address the social, emotional, and behavioral characteristics of students with intellectual disabilities?

What Are the Perspectives of Parents and Families?

Some parents of students with intellectual disabilities—parents whose children have disorders that can be medically identified—may learn about their children's likely needs even before they are born. Other parents—often those whose children have mild intellectual disabilities that are not the result of a specific cause—may suspect that their children are not

Peer Tutoring

Peer tutoring has been studied for many years as an effective way to enhance student learning. For students with intellectual disabilities, peer tutoring can be a means of facilitating inclusion, improving academic achievement, fostering positive relationships with classmates, and encouraging positive student behavior (Utley, 2001). Here are the steps involved in setting up a peer tutoring program (Fulk & King, 2001):

1. Explain the purpose of peer tutoring to students and give a rationale for using it. Stress the idea of increased opportunities for practice and on-task behavior.

2. Stress collaboration and cooperation rather than competition.

3. Select the content and instructional materials for tutoring sessions.

4. Train students in the roles of tutor and tutee. Students need to learn specific procedures for
   - feedback for correct responses (for example, teach students to say, "That's correct. Good answer!").
   - error correction (for example, teach students to say, "That's not correct; the correct answer is _____. I'll ask the question again . . .").
   - score-keeping (for example, have students use tally marks on a scorecard for correct answers).

5. Model appropriate behaviors for tutor and tutee. Demonstrate acceptable ways to give and accept corrective feedback.

6. Provide sample scripts for students to practice roles. Divide the class into practice pairs and teams.

7. Let pairs practice roles of tutor and tutee as you circulate, providing feedback and reinforcement of appropriate tutor and tutee behavior.

8. Conduct a follow-up discussion with the class regarding constructive and nonconstructive tutor and tutee behavior. Answer any student questions.

9. Let pairs switch roles and practice new roles as you circulate and provide additional feedback and reinforcement, repeating the follow-up discussion.

Once students know both the tutor and tutee roles, you can assign partners that may be kept for several weeks. Generally, peer tutoring is most effective with information that has clear correct or incorrect answers, particularly for younger students, and so you should select materials carefully for tutoring.

Peer tutoring is very much a strategy that addresses the concept of universal design for learning. It can help educators reach their students in a way that demonstrates value for every class member.

Source: Fulk, B. M., & King, K. (2001). Classwide peer tutoring at work. *Teaching Exceptional Children, 34*(2), 49–53. Copyright © 2001 by the Council for Exceptional Children. Reprinted with permission.

---

keeping up developmentally with other youngsters, but they may not hear the phrase *mental retardation* or *intellectual disability* until their children begin school. No matter when parents and family members learn about their children's disabilities, the role of professionals is to foster collaboration by engaging parents as partners in planning for the children's education.

Parent Experiences and Acceptance

Laurie recently shared her experience in learning that her unborn child would have Down syndrome:

> I had been having some problems, and I had been ordered to have bed rest. I was seeing my doctor every week, and he had ordered extra tests from a specialist. The results of those tests were due at any time on the day that I had an appointment to see my doctor. I was sitting on the examining table, half-dressed in one of those awful open gowns. My doctor had just left after finishing his examination of me. He walked back in and announced, "Your baby has Down syndrome. You're so far along that you'll have to decide right away if you want to keep it." And then he walked out. I sat there, stunned at the news, at the implication that I would ever think of giving up my baby, and at my doctor's total disregard for my dignity or my feelings—his lack of respect for me as a person. I called my husband—he came and got me. We cried some, and then we started the process of adjusting our dreams and educating ourselves.

Students with Intellectual and Developmental Disabilities

Robin Nelson/PhotoEdit

Most families of children with intellectual disabilities think of their children in terms of their personalities and contributions to the family, not their disability label.

Christopher was born a short time later, and he could not be loved more. His parents are active members of a support group, and they speak about their experiences to others.

Are you thinking that this story must have happened many years ago? In fact, it occurred very recently, when doctors are supposed to know better how to discuss such complex topics with parents. Imagine how the doctor's insensitive words to these parents affected their views. Do you think their initial experience might influence the way they approach school professionals? How?

Parents' Reactions to Having a Child with an Intellectual Disability

Many professionals have written about parents' responses to having a child with an intellectual disability, and you can read about one parent's reaction in the Firsthand Account on the next page. Some authors claim that parents may experience any or all of the classic stages of grief—denial, blame, fear, guilt, mourning, withdrawal, rejection, and acceptance (e.g., Prout & Prout, 2000). Others dismiss this set of responses as too simplistic to accurately capture the tremendous diversity of parent reactions and the factors that may influence reactions (e.g., Singh, 2000; Stoneman & Gavidia-Payne, 2006). For example, the amount of support offered by grandparents can affect parents' abilities to respond to their children with intellectual disabilities (Sandler, 1998). In cases where grandparents can provide emotional support, assume some child care responsibilities, and help in day-to-day activities such as getting to medical appointments, the family benefits greatly (Seligman, Goodwin, Paschal, Applegate, & Lehman, 1997).

"The amount of support offered by grandparents can affect parents' abilities to respond to their children with intellectual disabilities."

Two additional examples of factors that affect parents' reactions to their children with intellectual disabilities are religious participation and culture. Hughes (1999) studied the faith-related beliefs and practices of families with children with intellectual disabilities. She found that prior to the birth of a child with special needs, 44 percent of the parents had strong religious conviction, but that percentage rose to 91 percent after having the child. Further, mothers and fathers who were active in their place of worship had more positive perceptions of their children than other parents. Cultural mores make the differences among families even clearer. Although Western culture views disability as a chronic physical phenomenon that needs fixing, some other cultures view disability as a spiritual phenomenon that is time

PROFESSIONAL MONITORING TOOL

Council for Exceptional Children

Standard 3 Individual Learning Differences
. . . variations in beliefs, traditions, and values

Welcome to Holland

Emily Perl Kingsley is the mother of now-adult son, Jason, who has Down syndrome. She is an Emmy Award–winning writer for the children's program Sesame Street *as well as the author of more than twenty children's books. She speaks frequently about her experiences as the mother of a child with a moderate intellectual disability. Her essay captures the feelings of many parents.*

I am often asked to describe the experience of raising a child with a disability—to try to help people who have not shared that unique experience to understand it, to imagine how it would feel. It's like this . . .

When you're going to have a baby, it's like planning a fabulous vacation trip—to Italy. You buy a bunch of guide books and make your wonderful plans. The Coliseum. The Michelangelo David. The gondolas in Venice. You may learn some handy phrases in Italian. It's all very exciting.

After months of eager anticipation, the day finally arrives. You pack your bags and off you go. Several hours later, the plane lands. The stewardess comes in and says, "Welcome to Holland."

"Holland?!?" you say. "What do you mean Holland? I signed up for Italy! I'm supposed to be in Italy. All my life I've dreamed of going to Italy."

But there's been a change in the flight plan. They've landed in Holland and there you must stay.

The important thing is that they haven't taken you to a horrible, disgusting, filthy place, full of pestilence, famine, and disease. It's just a different place.

So you must go out and buy new guide books. And you must learn a whole new language. And you will

> "When you're going to have a baby, it's like planning a fabulous vacation trip."

meet a whole new group of people you would never have met.

It's just a different place. It's slower paced than Italy, less flashy than Italy. But after you've been there for a while and you catch your breath, you look around . . . and you begin to notice that Holland has windmills . . . and Holland has tulips. Holland even has Rembrandts.

But everyone you know is busy coming and going from Italy . . . and they're all bragging about what a wonderful time they had there. And for the rest of your life, you will say "Yes, that's where I was supposed to go. That's what I had planned."

And the pain of that will never, ever, ever, ever go away . . . because the loss of that dream is a very, very significant loss.

But . . . if you spend your life mourning the fact that you didn't get to Italy, you may never be free to enjoy the very special, the very lovely things . . . about Holland.

limited and worthy of acceptance (Park & Turnbull, 2001; Warger, 2001). In families that hold the latter set of beliefs, discussions of adjustment may not even be appropriate. More important may be the issue of professionals' acceptance and responsiveness to the family perspective (Geenen, Powers, & Lopez-Vaasquez, 2001).

Parents' Concerns

Although nearly all parents want their children with intellectual disabilities to have a normal life (Harry, Rueda, & Kalyanpur, 1999), the meaning of *normal* differs for families based on several factors. One important consideration is the extent of the child's cognitive impairment. Children with mild impairments may be similar enough to their siblings that parents adjust their expectations but do not have extraordinary concerns (Hannah & Midlarsky, 2005). However, parents may have many questions about their children with moderate or severe intellectual disabilities. Another factor affecting parents' concerns is age: Parents of young and school-age children are likely to worry about developmental and medical issues as well as

In 2002 the Council for Exceptional Children division that addresses the needs of students with cognitive disabilities changed its name from the Division on Mental Retardation and Developmental Disabilities to the Division on Developmental Disabilities and Autism, thus dropping the increasingly rejected *mental retardation* language.

behavior problems (Baroff & Olley, 1999). Parents of adolescents express concern about those problems, too, but they also begin thinking about what their child will do and how their child will live after graduation. As the parents of children with intellectual disabilities themselves face aging, they become concerned with the possibility of keeping an adult child at home, the need to arrange for someone to look after their child after they die, and the necessity of providing for the child financially (Lustig & Akey, 1999; Thorp, 2002).

> *"Culturally determined beliefs about the nature, cause, and appropriate treatment for disabilities strongly affect the types of concerns parents express."*

One other influence on parents' concerns relates directly to the discussion about acceptance: parent culture. Parents from Western cultures sometimes ask, "When will my child grow out of this?" or "When will my child be cured?" Parents from cultures that emphasize acceptance would never think to ask such questions. Similarly, the latter parents could not conceive of their child's siblings refusing to care for him or her after the parents die, but parents in Western cultures may with good reason spend considerable time negotiating such care (Harry et al., 1999). In other words, culturally determined beliefs about the nature, cause, and appropriate treatment for disabilities strongly affect the types of concerns parents express.

Professionals' Interactions with Parents of Children with Mental Retardation

When all the information about families of students with intellectual disabilities is presented in a single picture, it is one that suggests your responsibility as a professional is to frame your interactions from the perspective of the family. Some of the parents you encounter will have been working with the special education system for years, and they will likely have far different needs than those parents who have just learned of their child's disability. Some parents will seem unconcerned about their children's long-term progress; others will fret about it even during the elementary school years. Your first priority should be to listen so that you learn about the parents' points of view. Next, you should check to be sure that your understanding of the parents' needs for their child is accurate. Finally, you should remember that whatever type of service you provide—whether general education, special education, or a related service—your goal is to base your work on the priorities of the students and families, even when they are not consistent with your own.

What Trends and Issues Are Affecting the Field of Intellectual Disabilities?

Despite the advances in understanding the causes of intellectual disabilities and the characteristics of students with this disability, the field still faces significant issues. Two of the most compelling are (1) the expectations for students with intellectual disabilities in the high-stakes testing environment of today's schools and (2) the rights of individuals with intellectual disabilities to make their own decisions about their lives.

Students with Intellectual Disabilities in Today's Schools

Public schools today are being shaped by the provisions of the federal No Child Left Behind Act (2001) and its emphasis on accountability. Higher expectations are being set for all students, but some professionals question the implications for students with mild or moderate intellectual disabilities.

Which Curriculum?

One question concerns the curriculum that is appropriate for students with intellectual disabilities. In the past these students often followed a curriculum that was different from that of typical learners. It usually emphasized life skills and adaptive behavior, and it could be offered in a special education classroom. Skills such as counting money and personal care (e.g., brushing teeth) were not simply occasional topics for elementary students; they were of central concern. As students got older, cooking tasks and household chores (e.g., changing bed linens, doing laundry) were emphasized. Increasingly, however, most students with intellectual diabilities are being expected to learn in the same curriculum as other students, whether in a general education or a special education setting.

Some see this change as positive, enabling students to have true educational access and to learn as much of that curriculum as possible. Proponents of this thinking argue that it is unethical for professionals to decide that students with intellectual disabilities should not have the same learning opportunities as other students. They maintain that although some variations in activities and assignments will be needed, these students are capable of learning far more than those supporting alternative curricula have assumed. Opponents argue that many topics in the general education curriculum simply are not important for students with intellectual disabilities, especially when viewed in the context of all the survival skills these students need to learn before adulthood. These critics contend that students with intellectual disabilities, even mild cognitive impairments, too often attend general education classes where they understand little of the instruction, even when accommodations are provided. The content is too abstract; the pace is too fast.

The Dilemma of High-Stakes Testing

A discussion of curriculum expectations can be related directly to the accountability for that curriculum as measured on high-stakes tests. As you learned, few students with disabilities can be exempt from such tests, and some students with mild intellectual disabilities are being expected to complete them.

Some professionals applaud this strong initiative to ensure that high standards are maintained for all students with disabilities. They point to student success stories and argue that over time, as an increasing number of students with intellectual disabilities access the general

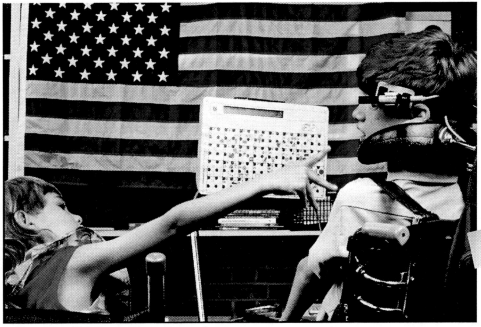

Will and Deni McIntyre/Photo Researchers

*A*ssistive technology enables some students with intellectual disabilities to communicate more readily with others and participate fully in school and neighborhood activities.

PROFESSIONAL MONITORING TOOL

Council for Exceptional Children

Standard 10 Collaboration
. . . assist individuals in becoming active participants
Standard 4 Instructional Strategies
. . . procedures to increase self-management and self-reliance

education curriculum from the beginning of their school careers, more and more students will learn more and more of that curriculum. Opponents to the current requirements for high-stakes testing tell stories as well. They describe tearful children being asked to take tests that are beyond their capabilities. They contend that few students with intellectual disabilities should participate in high-stakes testing and that legislation demanding their participation does not make it correct. Critics point out that in some communities, students with disabilities are blamed for causing schools' failure to achieve federally mandated goals of adequate yearly progress. Finally, some professionals support the participation of all students in assessment, but they strongly support using tests that are appropriate for the students' levels of learning (Council for Exceptional Children, 2003).

As you read about the No Child Left Behind Act and the focus on accountability in your professional preparation courses, keep both of these perspectives in mind. Think about the possibilities of helping more students to master the core curriculum as well as the pitfalls of setting standards at too high a level. How can these two points of view be reconciled?

Self-Determination: The Potential, Promises, and Practices

The topic of self-determination was mentioned as becoming particularly important for students with intellectual disabilities as they make the transition from school to adulthood (Jones, 2006). It is included here as an issue, not because of professional sentiment about its importance but because of the difficulties in making the concept of self-determination a reality in the transition process (Schwartz, Jacobson, & Holburn, 2000).

Perceptions of Parents and Teachers

Parents' views of self-determination seem to be unequivocally positive: They strongly believe that their nearly adult children should be directly taught self-determination skills and fully participate in transition planning (Grigal, Neubert, Moon, & Graham, 2003; Lee, Palmer, Turnbull, & Wehmeyer, 2006). However, it also has been reported that parents do not seem to deliberately assist their children to use self-determination skills (Thoma, Rogan, & Baker, 2001). For example, they do not seem to know how to go about preparing their children to participate in their IEP meetings, which offer natural opportunities for self-determination.

One question related to self-determination is the extent to which teachers are familiar with the concept. When Grigal and her colleagues (Grigal et al., 2003) surveyed teachers, they were surprised to find that teachers rated themselves as only slightly

"Parents' views of self-determination seem to be unequivocally positive."

knowledgeable about self-determination and how to go about teaching it to students. Other researchers have obtained similar results (e.g., Wehmeyer, Agran, & Hughes, 2000). Some teachers have indicated that they are highly supportive of self-determination, but when asked how they incorporate it into students' IEPs, many noted that they did not directly address it (Agran, Snow, & Swaner, 1999; Field & Hoffman, 2002).

Implementation of Practices That Foster Self-Determination

As some professionals have been exploring the beliefs of parents and teachers regarding self-determination, others have been reviewing their own practices. For example, when Zhang and Stecker (2001) interviewed teachers about self-determination, the teachers reported that students had a low level of participation in transition meetings, particularly in activities that were implemented after the meetings. Observational studies support this view. Thoma and her colleagues (Thoma et al., 2001) observed at transition IEP meetings for students with intellectual disabilities and found that while students were physically present, the adults in the meetings talked about the students rather than with the students. The adults also tended to ignore ideas expressed by the students during the planning process.

Self-determination skills can be taught beginning in elementary school, but they are particularly important as students make the transition from school to adulthood. Here are some activities that foster self-determination.

Professionals' Activities: Before Developing a Transition Plan

- Listening to the student/family about their future vision regarding the student's life after high school
- Identifying the student's interests and preferences
- Identifying the student's needs
- Incorporating the student's family's needs, interests, and preferences into a draft transition service plan

Professionals' Activities: During Transition Planning Meetings

- Helping the student identify available choices
- Facilitating the student in making his or her own decisions
- Allowing the student to take charge of some or all parts of the transition planning meeting
- Providing the student/family opportunities to review the developed transition plan

- Providing the student/family sufficient time for asking questions
- Responding to the student/family questions
- Having the student and/or family sign the transition plan after they understand and agree with the plan

Students' Activities

- Before the meeting, talking with teacher and/or parents in order to be prepared
- Before and during the meeting, expressing ideas about preferences
- During the meeting, actively participating in discussions
- After the meeting, meeting with school personnel to discuss the transition plan
- During the academic year following the meeting, asking questions about the plan and wanting to know about progress related to the plan

Source: Zhang, D., & Stecker, P. M. (2001). Student involvement in transition planning: Are we there yet? *Education and Training in Mental Retardation and Developmental Disabilities, 36,* 293–303. Reprinted with permission.

Clearly, the positive impact of teaching students to act on their own behalf is that they will be able to advocate for themselves throughout life (Palmer & Wehmeyer, 2003). Further, programs have been developed to teach specific self-determination skills to students (Zhang & Stecker, 2001). What remains are questions about how to prepare teachers and other professionals to teach these skills to students and how to ensure that students have opportunities to practice them (Steere & Cavaiuolo, 2002). The Professional Edge contains some important aspects of self-determination that can be addressed as part of transition.

SUMMARY

The treatment of children and adults with intellectual disabilities, called *mental retardation* in IDEA, has been strongly influenced by societal views. The late-nineteenth century was a period of optimism, the early twentieth century was one of pessimism, and the current era can be characterized as one of rising expectations and a focus on abilities instead of limitations. Although the causes of most students' intellectual disabilities are unknown, some prenatal causes (e.g., chromosomal abnormalities, toxoplasmosis, alcohol use), perinatal causes (e.g., lack of oxygen, low birth weight), and postnatal causes (e.g., illness, brain injury) have been identified. Students with intellectual disabilities usually have a cognitive functioning level at least two standard deviations below the mean of 100 on an IQ test, and they have significant problems in carrying out the day-to-day life activities, referred to as *adaptive behavior.* They also may have an array of physical and health problems.

All the procedures outlined in IDEA must be followed in identifying students as having intellectual disabilities, with the emphasis on assessing intelligence level and adaptive behavior. Students identified as having intellectual disabilities are likely to receive a significant amount of their education in special education classrooms, although parents and other advocates continue to promote a more inclusive education for them. Because of these students' characteristics, instructional strategies are recommended that stress repetition, small increments of learning, and the use of concrete materials, as are peer-learning strategies such as cooperative learning and peer tutoring. Assisting students to prepare for independence after school also is stressed.

Parents of children with intellectual disabilities may learn of their children's special needs before the school years. Their ability to adapt and to normalize family functioning often relies on their system of supports. Two issues facing the field today are students' participation in high-stakes testing and other accountability systems in today's public schools and the options available for these individuals in adulthood.

BACK TO THE CASES

Hope

As a rising sixth-grader, Hope will transition to the local middle school next year. Her school is just one of three feeder schools for this middle school. You and her family are concerned that while she will have support for inclusion in the sixth grade, she will have an increasingly difficult time making and keeping friends in this larger school environment. The middle school special education teacher has suggested peer tutors or Best Buddies for Hope. Hope's parents want your advice. Which would you recommend to the parents? (See CEC Standard 3 and INTASC Principles 2.01, 5.04, and 5.05.) Be sure to explain why your selection will best meet Hope's individual needs.

Austin

Austin is a student who has significant needs, but also significant potential to be successful. He clearly enjoys school and is achieving both academic and social goals. However, in his middle school he spends a significant part of each day in a special education classroom. As you know, professionals disagree on whether a student like Austin is best educated in a general education or a special education environment. Based on this chapter, additional readings, and any personal experiences you have had, how would you react to a suggestion that Austin spend more time in general education next year? (See CEC Standard 9 and INTASC Principles 9.01 and 9.02.)

Jack

Jack's transition from school to the adult world is under way. His parents are engaged in planning for his future after they have died, and his job coach is helping Jack meet his goal for employment. However, Jack continues to experience difficulty with behavior and interpersonal relationships at school. Both of these issues may have a negative effect on his successful transition into the work world. What role should school personnel take to help Jack? (See CEC Standard 5 and INTASC Principles 7.01 and 7.07.) Be sure to include responsibilities for the paraprofessional and both the general and special educators.

KEY TERMS AND CONCEPTS

Adaptive behavior
American Association on Intellectual and Development Disabilities (AAIDD)
Applied academic skills
Cognitive disability
Cognitive impairment
Community-based instruction
Cultural familial retardation
Developmental disabilities

Down syndrome (DS)
Fetal alcohol effect (FAE)
Fetal alcohol syndrome (FAS)
Fragile X syndrome
Generalization
Intellectual disabilities
Job coach
Levels of support
Life skills curriculum

Mental retardation
Peer tutoring
Phenylketonuria (PKU)
Prader-Willi syndrome
Self-determination
Task analysis
Toxoplasmosis
Trisomy 21

REVIEW, DISCUSS, APPLY

1. The early twentieth century is considered a low point in the history of educating individuals who have intellectual disabilities. How are the events and decisions from that era still influencing the perceptions and treatment of these individuals today? (Learning Objective 1)

2. How are the IDEA and AAIDD definitions of mental retardation similar? Different? What are the implications for educators of the assumptions that are included in the AAIDD definition? (Learning Objective 2)

3. Some causes of intellectual disabilities in children are preventable. What role should educators play in helping to eliminate these causes? (Learning Objective 2)

4. Explain the traditional and AAIDD systems of classifying intellectual disabilities. What are the advantages and drawbacks of each? How can each help you as a professional educator in your work with students with intellectual disabilities? (Learning Objective 3)

5. Review Figure 8.1. The lower range of average intelligence, which is part of the definition of learning disabilities, generally is considered to be an IQ of 85 or so. Mild intellectual disability generally is identified at an IQ of 70 or so. These ranges indicate that a group of students whose intellectual abilities are in the 71 to 84 IQ range are not eligible for services. Whose responsibility is it to provide assistance to these students who struggle to learn? Should they have been included in IDEA? (Learning Objective 3)

6. What areas of functioning are included in the assessment of adaptive behavior? How do professionals assess adaptive behavior in order to determine whether a student has mental retardation? (Learning Objective 4)

7. How might the No Child Left Behind mandates related to increased achievement and high-stakes testing be influencing educators' perceptions of inclusive practices for students with intellectual disabilities? (Learning Objective 5)

8. What is *self-determination*? Why is self-determination an important yet somewhat controversial topic in considering best practices for students with intellectual disabilities? (Learning Objective 6)

9. Why might the experiences of families with children with intellectual disabilities be somewhat different from those of families with children with learning disabilities, ADHD, and emotional and behavior disorders? (Learning Objective 7)

10. How should the positive trend of raising expectations for students with intellectual disabilities be balanced against some educators' concerns that the current requirements for academic achievement for these students are too high? How can high academic expectations and the need for vocational preparation be reconciled? (Learning Objective 8)

mylabschool
Where the classroom comes to life!

Go to Allyn & Bacon's MyLabSchool (www.mylabschool.com) and enter Assignment ID SPV8 into the Assignment Finder. Watch the video *Mental Retardation,* in which the parents and teachers of Carlyn, a preschooler with developmental delays, discuss her experiences and successes in an integrated preschool program.

Question: Consider the information presented in this chapter about early childhood education and inclusive practices for students with developmental delays, including the Firsthand Account. How did Carlyn benefit from being included with her general education peers? You may also answer the questions at the end of the clip and e-mail your responses to your instructor.

2

Students with Emotional and Behavior Disorders

Students with Emotional and Behavior Disorders

Ellen B. Senisi/The Image Works

learning objectives

- Define emotional and behavior disorders (EBD), explain their prevalence and causes, and outline the development of the EBD field.

- Describe characteristics of individuals with emotional and behavior disorders.

- Explain how emotional and behavior disorders are identified.

- Outline how students with emotional and behavior disorders receive their education.

- Describe recommended educational practices for students with emotional and behavior disorders.

- Explain the perspectives and concerns that parents and families of students with emotional and behavior disorders may have.

- Identify trends and issues influencing the field of emotional and behavior disorders.

Kayla

Kayla is a first-grade student who has just been identified as having an emotional disability. She is a complex child, one who is sometimes charming and agreeable and sometimes rude and obstinate. She has a history of being extraordinarily aggressive: She was dismissed from two private preschool programs for hitting and biting other children, and in kindergarten she frequently threatened her classmates. When asked to complete school tasks such as coloring or printing, she often loudly refuses, sometimes engaging in a tantrum by lying on the floor, crying, and kicking her feet. Kayla has been in counseling since her parents divorced when she was four years old, and her pediatric psychiatrist is considering the use of medication to help Kayla function successfully in school, at home, and in other settings. Kayla's mother freely discusses the fact that she simply does not know what to do with Kayla. She observes that Kayla does not follow directions at home and does not really have any neighborhood friends. In the self-contained special education classroom, Kayla is working on using words to express her anger instead of acting out, and she is in a highly structured program that stresses rewards for appropriate behavior. She is slightly below grade level academically, but sometimes her achievement level is difficult to judge because of her frequent behavior incidents.

Garrett

Garrett is a challenge for his teachers, and they are very concerned about his well-being. Garrett's physical appearance is consistent with his emotional response to others: He is a somewhat overweight sixth-grader, large for his age, with a noticeably pale complexion and long, thin, often dirty hair plastered to his scalp. His face is expressionless, and he often sits motionless for long periods. Unless coaxed, he does not speak in class or for that matter in the halls or the cafeteria. His special education teacher describes him as always being in "emotional neutral"; he does not laugh at jokes or other students' antics and he does not appear to be motivated by any system of rewards that school personnel have designed for him, even with his input. His general edu-

cation teachers comment that he does not participate in class discussions or activities; that he does not complete in-class or homework assignments; and that he seems content to simply sit, almost as though he is letting all the instruction and interactions of middle school classes roll right over him. Academically, Garrett is barely passing his core classes, but his teachers are not sure that this is an accurate reflection of his ability. Garrett lives with his grandmother, who is his legal guardian. She is reluctant to come to school to discuss Garrett's problems. She describes Garrett as well behaved and much less of a burden to raise than his older brother. She explains that Garrett spends most of his time at home in his room, watching television, mentioning only that he is not much help with household chores.

Carlos

Carlos has had a difficult life. His father was killed before he was born, and his mother has serious alcohol and drug problems. He spent much of his childhood in six different foster homes. Of his three older siblings, two are in state prison. Carlos was retained in first grade and again in fifth grade, and his clearest memories of elementary school include feeling dumb and fighting classmates who called him names. While in middle school, Carlos was arrested for setting fires in neighbors' trash cans; after that he attended an alternative school for students with significant behavior and academic problems. According to Carlos, the school was "like prison, with guards all over the place and someone always in your face." He completed his first year of high school in his neighborhood in a self-contained program for students with emotional disabilities, but he missed thirty days of school that year. Carlos began his sophomore year but dropped out last month. Asked why, he describes high school as a waste of his time. He also admits that he had a shouting match with a security guard and was probably going to be suspended again anyway. Carlos has been arrested twice since he began high school: once for stealing a car and once for shoplifting. He has no specific plans for getting his high school diploma. When asked what type of job he would like to have, he brightens and says that he would like a job where he would sit at a desk and have a secretary to take his calls and greet his visitors.

Of all the school-age students who have disabilities, few can be as puzzling as those who have emotional and behavior disorders. As you can tell from the vignettes about Kayla, Garrett, and Carlos, these students defy simple description, and at times it is difficult to understand how they can be grouped into a single disability category. When compared to other students with disabilities, these students are more likely to have attended multiple schools, and they are four times more likely to have been suspended or expelled from school (Wagner, Kutash, Duchnowski, Epstein, & Sumi, 2005). Their teachers often report that they feel unprepared to work with them (Wagner et al., 2006). These students pose unique challenges to school personnel because they often need structure and therapeutic intervention strategies that are difficult to provide. At the same time, successful outcomes for students with emotional and behavior disorders rely on those interventions.

What Are Emotional and Behavior Disorders?

The study of emotional and behavior disorders has gone on for centuries. Contemporary practices for students in public school have their foundation in the work of early physicians and psychologists and their efforts to treat adults with mental illness.

Development of the Field of Emotional and Behavior Disorders

Fascination with insanity and mental illness can be found throughout history (Kauffman & Landrum, 2006). Early treatment usually was harsh and included imprisonment, starvation, and the use of restraints such as chains and straitjackets. Humane treatment of adults with mental illness began to emerge at the beginning of the nineteenth century, but it was not until the very late nineteenth century that emotional problems in children were considered a valid topic for study. G. Stanley Hall was one of the first psychologists to specialize in the study of these children, publishing a two-volume book on adolescent psychology in 1904.

Several factors made it challenging to study children with emotional and behavior disorders (Winzer, 1993). First, no consistent set of terms existed to describe these children. Their disorders were called such intimidating names as *dementia praecox, catatonia, paranoia, childhood schizophrenia,* and *juvenile insanity.* Second, in many cases mental illness and mental retardation were still confused and addressed as though a single disorder. Third, professionals were reluctant to openly admit that children could have mental illness because this view contradicted the long-held perspective that only adults were affected. Mental illness also was still sometimes associated with evil or satanic possession, making it seem unethical to assign this diagnosis to children.

Even as the field of special education in public schools began to evolve with the advent of compulsory schooling early in the twentieth century, children with emotional and behavior disorders generally were considered ill; thus, their treatment was considered the responsibility of physicians and psychologists, not teachers and other education professionals (Coleman & Webber, 2002). However, some professionals were focusing attention on these children's needs and beginning to develop services for them. For example, the American Orthopsychiatric Association was founded in 1924 with the purpose of studying and disseminating information on childhood mental illness. The very first pediatric psychiatric hospital was opened in Rhode Island in 1931.

During this era, three schools of thought developed (Cullinan, 2002). The first was called the *functional approach,* and it proposed that a relationship existed between personality traits and mental illness. For children, this approach led to the *mental hygiene movement,* the belief

> "Even as the field of special education in public schools began to evolve with the advent of compulsory schooling early in the twentieth century, children with emotional and behavior disorders generally were considered ill."

INTERNET RESOURCES
www.samhsa.gov
At the website of the Substance Abuse and Mental Health Services Administration, an agency of the U.S. Department of Health and Human Services, you can find information on many topics of interest, including descriptions of children's mental health disorders, strategies for the prevention of school violence, and strategies to share with parents.

PROFESSIONAL MONITORING TOOL

Council for Exceptional Children

Standard 1 Foundations
. . . historical points of view

that helping children develop mental health and positive personality traits would prevent later mental illness. The second school of thought was called the *organic approach*. Advocates of this perspective theorized that all mental illness was caused by neurological dysfunction or disease. The final school of thought, **behaviorism,** followed the other two. Behaviorists believed that emotional or behavior problems were learned and could be addressed by teaching other more appropriate behaviors to those who were mentally ill. All three of these schools of thought still influence interventions for students with emotional and behavior disorders, as you will see later in this chapter.

From the late 1930s through the 1950s, professionals worked to classify the various types of emotional and behavior disorders they observed in children (Coleman & Webber, 2002). In addition, leaders in the field developed education programs for these youngsters, but the programs usually were carried out in private schools or hospitals. These programs reflected the three schools of thought concerning the development of mental illness: some stressing the need to address children's personality development (functional approach), others compensating for neurological disorders (organic approach), and yet others stressing instruction in appropriate behaviors (behaviorism). However, in the 1960s strong criticism was leveled at the continued medical focus for treating these students, and schools gradually began to take responsibility for them. By the time Public Law (P.L.) 94-142 was passed in 1975, students with emotional and behavior disorders were without question being educated in public schools.

> *"From the late 1930s through the 1950s, professionals worked to classify the various types of emotional and behavior disorders they observed in children."*

Since the passage of federal special education laws, professionals in the area of emotional and behavior disorders have been researching factors that cause these disorders, studying effective interventions, and striving to ensure that all students who have these disorders are identified and served appropriately. These topics are addressed later in this chapter.

Definitions of Emotional and Behavior Disorders

The very language used to describe the students about whom this chapter is written requires explanation. For example, the Individuals with Disabilitites Education Act (IDEA) uses the term *emotional disturbance (ED)* to identify this population. Many professionals in the field object to that term, noting that it carries a strong negative connotation. They advocate for the alternative, **emotional and behavior disorder (EBD),** the term used throughout this chapter. However, other terms also are assigned to describe this group of students, including *emotionally disabled (ED), behavior disordered (BD), emotionally impaired (EI),* and *seriously emotionally disturbed (SED).* What terminology is used in your state to describe this disability?

Like the language used to describe students with emotional and behavior disorders, the definition of this disability category is somewhat controversial. Two definitions are most often considered: (1) the federal definition included in IDEA and (2) the definition proposed by the National Mental Health and Special Education Coalition.

Federal Definition

As noted, the term used in IDEA for emotional and behavior disorders is **emotional disturbance (ED),** which the law defines as

> a condition exhibiting one or more of the following characteristics over a long period of time and to a marked degree that adversely affects a child's educational performance:
>
> **a.** An inability to learn that cannot be explained by intellectual, sensory, or health factors.
> **b.** An inability to build or maintain satisfactory interpersonal relationships with peers and teachers.

Although the link between television violence and violent behavior in children is still being debated, the American Psychological Association and other professional groups have found that television violence can cause children to become less sensitive to others' pain and suffering, more fearful, and more likely to behave in aggressive or harmful ways.

Council for Exceptional Children

Standard 1 Foundations . . . issues in definition and identification

      c. Inappropriate types of behavior or feelings under normal circumstances.

      d. A general pervasive mood of unhappiness or depression.

      e. A tendency to develop physical symptoms or fears associated with personal or school problems.

The term includes schizophrenia. The term does not apply to children who are socially maladjusted, unless it is determined that they have an emotional disturbance. (IDEA 20 U.S.C. §1401 [2004], 20 C.F.R. §300.8[c][4])

For a student to qualify for services through this definition, three sets of factors must be taken into account: First, the student's problem has to occur for a long period of time, to a marked degree, negatively affecting educational performance. Second, only students meeting the five listed criteria are considered to have this disability. Third, like the definition of learning disabilities, this definition contains an exclusionary clause; that is, some students are explicitly prohibited from being identified as having emotional disturbance. Students who are **socially maladjusted** (i.e., those who intentionally act out or break rules) are not considered to have this disability unless they also meet one of the other criteria.

National Coalition on Mental Health and Special Education Definition

Almost since the passage of P.L. 94-142, professionals have criticized the federal definition of emotional and behavior disorders. A group of thirty professional organizations joined together as the National Coalition on Mental Health and Special Education to lobby for change. They contended that the federal definition had several significant problems (Forness & Knitzer, 1992). First, they argued that the five criteria in the definition were not supported by research. Second, they noted that the reference to educational performance too narrowly focused on academic learning, excluding the important but indirect social curriculum of education.

A third criticism of the federal definition was particularly significant. The coalition maintained that the exclusionary clause concerning social maladjustment was unnecessarily confusing and that the intent was to exclude only juvenile delinquents, not all students with this disorder. They illustrated this point by describing students with **conduct disorders,** which are emotional and behavior problems involving aggression, destruction of property, lying or stealing, or serious rule violation (e.g., running away). The coalition reported that conduct disorder is the most common type of social maladjustment, that most states include social maladjustment in their educational definition of emotional disabilities, and that this group of students in fact makes up the largest single group of students included in this category. The coalition proposed this alternative definition (Forness & Knitzer, 1992, p. 14):

> The term emotional or behavioral disorder means a disability characterized by behavioral or emotional responses in school so different from appropriate age, cultural, or ethnic norms that they adversely affect educational performance. Educational performance includes academic, social, vocational, and personal skills. Such a disability
>
>   a. is more than a temporary, expected response to stressful events in the environment;
>
>   b. is consistently exhibited in two different settings, at least one of which is school-related; and
>
>   c. is unresponsive to direct intervention in general education or the child's condition is such that general education interventions would be insufficient.

> Emotional and behavioral disorders can co-exist with other disabilities. This category may include children or youth with schizophrenic disorders, affective disorders, anxiety disorders, or other sustained disorders of conduct or adjustment when they adversely affect educational performance in accordance with section (i).

As you compare the two definitions, what do you notice? Do you think the coalition definition enhances your understanding of this disorder? Although the coalition was not successful in getting this definition incorporated into federal law, professionals who work in

CHECK
Your Learning

How are the IDEA definition of emotional disturbance and the definition of emotional and behavior disorders by the National Mental Health and Special Education Coalition similar and different?

this field generally prefer the latter definition and use it to guide their work, contending that it does not violate the federal definition but rather provides a clearer basis for school practice.

Other Considerations in Defining Emotional and Behavior Disorders

One more topic should be mentioned before concluding this discussion. Because children's emotional and behavior disorders are a focus of treatment in the medical and mental health fields as well as the educational field, the disorders also have been defined by medical professionals. The *Diagnostic and Statistical Manual of Mental Disorders* (fourth edition, text revision) (*DSM-IV-TR*) (American Psychiatric Association, 2000), contains a classification system and definitions of emotional disorders among children. This classification system, which refers to these conditions as **mental disorders,** includes disorders that you have probably heard of but that are not explicitly defined in special education law. Examples include conduct disorders such as **oppositional defiant disorder (ODD), mood disorders** such as depression, and eating disorders such as anorexia nervosa. Brief explanations of these and other *DSM-IV-TR* disorders are outlined in Figure 7.1.

Figure 7.1

Examples of Emotional and Behavior Disorders from a Medical Perspective

Unlike the general definition of emotional and behavior disorders in IDEA, the definition provided by the medical community has identified many specific disorders. These are included in the *Diagnostic and Statistical Manual of Mental Health (DSM-IV-TR)* where they are referred to as *mental disorders*. The following list includes examples of mental disorders that educators would consider emotional and behavior disorders:

- *Anxiety disorders.* An anxiety disorder occurs when a student experiences an overwhelming sense of fear or dread. One example is obsessive–compulsive disorder (OCD) in which the student cannot stop worrying excessively about a specific concern (e.g., germs). Other examples include phobias such as fear of specific items (spiders) or certain activities (going to school), and posttraumatic stress disorder (PTSD) in which the student re-lives in nightmares or flashbacks a traumatic event that was witnessed.

- *Disruptive behavior disorders.* This category includes three types of disorders:

  1. *Attention deficit–hyperactivity disorder (ADHD)* is characterized by inattention, a high level of activity and impulsivity, or a combination of these.

  2. *Oppositional defiant disorder (ODD)* is diagnosed when a student is defiant with adults and vindictive or blaming with peers to an excessive degree over a long period of time.

  3. *Conduct disorder* is diagnosed when a student fights, bullies, displays cruelty to animals or people, or otherwise repeatedly breaks serious rules.

- *Eating disorders.* The most common eating disorder is *anorexia nervosa*, in which the student believes she is overweight and refuses to eat, even when near starvation.

- *Mood disorders.* Also called *affective disorders*, this group includes depression (discussed elsewhere in this chapter) and bipolar disorder (also called *manic depression*), in which the student's moods swing from extreme highs (manic) to extreme lows (depression).

- *Tic disorders. Tics* are involuntary, rapid, stereotyped movements of specific muscle groups. A student with tics may blink his eyes or repeatedly sniff. The most well-known tic disorder is *Tourette syndrome*, which ranges from mild to severe and includes both facial and other physical tics as well as vocal tics (often barking or profanity).

Prevalence of Emotional and Behavior Disorders

Controversy over the definition of emotional and behavior disorders and differences across school, medical, and mental health settings related to who is considered emotionally and behaviorally disordered contribute to uncertainty in estimating the prevalence of this disability. According to the federally collected IDEA data (U.S. Department of Education, 2004), 480,187 students ages six to twenty-one received special education services as emotionally disturbed during the 2002–2003 school year, making this the fourth-largest disability category. This group of students comprised slightly more than 8 percent of all students receiving special education and less than 1 percent of all students in schools, a prevalence rate that has remained consistent for more than a decade. African American students are overrepresented in this category of disability. They are 2.25 times more likely than students in all other racial/ethnic groups combined to receive special education services for this disability (U.S. Department of Education, 2004).

Data on prevalence from schools is only one source of information concerning this group of youngsters. Prevalence estimates using data from mental health clinics, private practitioners, and other community sources indicate that many more children and youth have emotional and behavior disorders than are recognized in schools. These estimates often range from 5 to 20 percent (Cullinan, 2002). This probably occurs because many children receive counseling or services in those settings even though they do not meet IDEA eligibility criteria. Among professionals in the field, the latter estimates are considered more accurate, with many authors suggesting that 3 to 6 percent of school-age children have some type of significant emotional or behavior disorder (Blanchard, Gurka, & Blackman, 2006).

Prevalence by Gender

As with both learning disabilities and ADHD, far more males than females are diagnosed as having emotional and behavior disorders. Although precise statistics are not available, researchers estimate that these disorders are found in boys three or more times more often than in girls (Wagner et al., 2005). Some professionals argue that these differences are inflated because of basic differences in teachers' reactions to students. They hypothesize that teachers are more likely to rate the same behavior displayed by boys and girls as more disturbing in boys. Further, they suggest that as boys move into adolescence, they tend to increase their acting-out behaviors while girls tend to turn inward. The boys' behaviors are more disturbing to teachers, and so boys are more likely to be identified as having these disorders.

Causes of Emotional and Behavior Disorders

Emotional and behavior disorders include a wide variety of complex problems, and seldom can any single, clear cause be identified for them. Two types of factors contribute to the development of emotional and behavior disorders: biological factors and psychosocial factors.

Biological Factors

As is true for learning disabilities and attention deficit–hyperactivity disorder, research suggests that at least some emotional and behavior disorders are the result of a physiological problem. One consideration in this category is genetics and whether these disorders are inherited. In at least some instances, research supports this possibility. For example, between 20 and 60 percent of children who have depression, a disorder recently receiving considerable attention, have at least one parent who has this disorder. Similarly, children with one parent who has schizophrenia, another adult mental illness, are much more likely than other children to develop this disorder by early adulthood (Sullivan, 2005). The rate is even higher if both parents have schizophrenia. As with learning disabilities and attention deficit–hyperactivity disorder, data such as these come from studies of siblings, especially twins, raised apart.

---

dimensions of DIVERSITY

Hispanic students (risk ratio of 0.4) and Asian students (risk ratio of 0.2) are significantly underrepresented as having emotional and behavior disorders, particularly when compared to students who are African American (risk ratio of 1.4) (U.S. Department of Education, 2004).

PROFESSIONAL MONITORING TOOL

Council for Exceptional Children

Standard 2 Development and Characteristics of Learners . . . typical and atypical development

---

A second area examined as a biological influence is brain injury. Children whose mothers abused alcohol or drugs during pregnancy are more likely than other children to develop emotional and behavior disorders. Brain injury also can be related to environmental toxins. Again, children diagnosed with lead poisoning or exposed over time to other chemicals in their homes and neighborhoods are at risk for developing these disorders. Poor nutrition is yet another factor that can affect neurological development and contribute to the development of emotional and behavior disorders. Finally, some children have neurologically based emotional disabilities as a result of an accident (e.g., falling from a bicycle) or illness (e.g., high fever).

PROFESSIONAL MONITORING TOOL

Council for
Exceptional
Children

Standard 2 Development and Characteristics of Learners . . . effects of environmental milieu

Psychosocial Factors

Children are influenced in their psychological and social development by the people around them, the events they experience, and their living conditions. Collectively, these are considered **psychosocial factors.** The U.S. Surgeon General (U.S. Department of Health and Human Services, 1999) outlines the following psychosocial factors as contributing to the development of emotional and behavior disorders in children:

▨ *Chronic stress.* Some children grow up in home and community settings characterized by stress. Perhaps the child's parents frequently fight, sometimes physically assaulting each other. Perhaps the family does not have enough income for even a marginal existence, and so there are frequent moves to avoid eviction or periodic stays in a homeless shelter. In some families with many children, even caring parents simply cannot divide their attention among everyone needing it, and this functions as a stressor for the children competing for that attention. Finally, chronic stress may come from the community—for example, when shootings, drug dealing, and gang activities are daily occurrences.

▨ *Stressful life events.* A second group of psychosocial factors includes intense life events. Two of the most common examples are the death of a parent or primary caregiver and divorce. However, other stressful life events also can affect children. One common example is when children witness violence in homes or their communities.

▨ *Childhood maltreatment.* Reports on television and in newspapers are a constant reminder that child abuse is a very real health concern in the United States. According to the National Clearinghouse on Child Abuse and Neglect Information (2006), in 2004 approximately 872,000 children were victims of abuse or neglect. Most professionals consider this figure to

INTERNET RESOURCES

www.ccbd.net
The Council for Children with Behavior Disorders is a division of the Council for Exceptional Children. Its website includes a discussion forum, links to professional materials and conferences, and the organization's policy statements on topics related to students with emotional and behavior disorders.

Tony Freeman/PhotoEdit

Children who live in extreme poverty are at risk for developing emotional and behavior disorders.

Students with Emotional and Behavior Disorders

45

PROFESSIONAL MONITORING TOOL

Council for
Exceptional
Children

Standard 2 Development and
Characteristics of Learners
. . . role of families in supporting
development

be a significant underestimate of the situation. When children are abused or neglected, in 79 percent of cases the perpetrator is one of the parents. Children who are physically or psychologically abused are at greater risk of developing emotional or behavior disorders.

■ *Additional family factors.* Other family problems also can influence youngsters and possibly cause emotional and behavior disorders. For example, research suggests that when a parent is depressed, he or she may lack the motivation and energy to use effective childrearing practices, and the children in the household thus will be at risk. Peers may also play a role; if extreme sibling rivalry develops, emotional problems can result.

Making Sense of the Factors Contributing to Emotional and Behavior Disorders

Clearly, many different factors, alone or in combination with others, can lead to emotional and behavior disorders. The current thinking is that biological and psychosocial factors probably interact. That is, some children may have a genetic predisposition to have a disorder, and when they live in a situation that includes one or more of the other risk factors, they are more likely to develop a disorder. A related line of thinking addresses **correlated constraints.** It proposes that when children's lives are permeated with risk factors, those factors collectively promote maladaptive behavior patterns and subsequently constrain the development of positive adjustment (Farmer, Quinn, Hussey, & Holahan, 2001).

However, you should keep in mind that children tend to have **resilience;** that is, they tend to be able to recover and not experience long-term harm from brief episodes of stress or single negative experiences (Brooks, 2001). And so many children, even those who might be at risk for developing emotional disabilities, do not experience these disorders. Resilience is explained more fully in the Professional Edge on the next page.

PROFESSIONAL MONITORING TOOL

Council for
Exceptional
Children

Standard 2 Development and
Characteristics of Learners
. . . similarities and differences of
individuals

What Are the Characteristics of Individuals with Emotional and Behavior Disorders?

The characteristics of students with emotional and behavior disorders vary so much that it is almost impossible to provide a comprehensive list. Instead, in this section you will learn about some of the most common behavior and emotional, social, and cognitive and

Although most students identified as having emotional and behavior disorders tend to be aggressive, some students turn their emotions inward.

Mary Steinbacher/PhotoEdit

Students with Emotional and Behavior Disorders

46

The Promise of Resiliency

Resiliency is the ability to bounce back from adversity, frustration, and misfortune. Research suggests that when schools, families, and communities help to build resiliency in children, those children are capable of becoming healthy, competent adults, in spite of the life stresses they may experience (Minnard, 2002). Here are some ways that you can foster resiliency in students:

1. Practice unconditional positive acceptance. When begun from an early age, unconditional positive regard increases the likelihood of positive social development.

2. Establish close, supportive relationships. In addition to parents, educators and other professionals help children develop trust.

3. Communicate high but realistic standards. Students need to know that you expect their best and that you believe they can achieve it.

4. Be sure that students know the important rules and limits. Depending on age, students should be involved in developing the rules.

5. Use warm, positive instruction and as little criticism as possible.

6. Focus on frequent, concrete praise. By telling students what they are doing right, you are helping to clarify expectations and increasing the likelihood that appropriate behavior will be repeated.

7. Help children learn how to persist in reaching their goals by clearly identifying a goal, deciding why it is important, thinking about the best ways to reach the goal, and taking action.

8. Celebrate efforts. Acknowledge efforts and successes. This helps students to develop confidence.

9. Provide opportunities for children to delay gratification. This builds a sense of control and confidence. It also helps students to decrease impulsiveness.

10. Teach students survival and life skills including assertiveness, conflict resolution, refusal skills, stress management, coping techniques, and decision making.

11. Develop students' competencies based on their interests, increasing the complexity of student activities to enhance their self-esteem.

12. Be aware of gender differences. Research suggests that boys often respond to structure, organization, and rules to a greater degree than girls do. Girls may need more support to take risks.

13. Arrange for students to participate in service activities. When students give of themselves, they can develop confidence, self-esteem, and feelings of accomplishment.

14. Motivate students with stories about characters who have risen above adversity to find their own paths to success and achievement.

15. Share your humor. Humor is an effective coping strategy, and when students observe adults responding to challenges with humor and a willingness to try again, they will do the same.

Source: Janas, M. (2002). Twenty ways to build resiliency [electronic version]. *Intervention in School and Clinic, 38*(2), 117–121. Copyright © 2002 by Pro-Ed, Inc. Reprinted with permission.

---

academic qualities of these learners. As you read, think about the message in the Firsthand Account from Ashley Moran, who teaches students identified as having emotional and behavior disorders. Her message provides insights into the uniqueness of these students and the importance of educators' understanding them.

Behavior and Emotional Characteristics

The behaviors of students with emotional and behavior disorders often are not completely different from those of other students. Rather, they occur more often, with more intensity, and for a longer time. Further, the behaviors of these students cover an entire spectrum. One of the most common ways of conceptualizing these behaviors is to think of them as being either internalizing or externalizing. **Internalizing behaviors** are those characterized as withdrawn or directed inward. Garrett, the sixth-grader described at the beginning of this chapter, exhibits internalizing behaviors. Additional examples of these behaviors can be found in Figure 7.2. Not surprisingly, because students with internalizing behaviors often do not disrupt the classroom, their needs can be overlooked by busy educators unless they are particularly vigilant.

More than one million children come into some type of contact with the juvenile justice system each year. As many as 60 to 75 percent of these youths have mental health disorders. However, more than 50 percent of incarcerated youth avoid recidivism (i.e., being a repeat offender) if they are provided with highly structured, intensive, and long-term treatment programs that teach them specific skills such as anger management and self-control (National Mental Health Association, 2003).

My First Year of Teaching Students with Emotional and Behavior Disorders

Ashley Moran just completed her first year of teaching in the Durham, North Carolina, area. Here are her perspectives on working with students with emotional and behavior disorders.

Becoming a teacher was exciting—at first. I had thought about all the wonderful, and not so wonderful, teachers I had when I was in school. I can say that one teacher made me love history, and one gave me a fear of math that I still have today. But most of all, my teachers gave me the love of learning, and I wanted to give that to other children. I was in for a surprise: Children are not the same as when I was in school fourteen years ago, but I wanted to save the world anyway.

When I made the decision to be a teacher, I had never taken a class in education. I decided to quit my job in the business sector and go to graduate school to get a master's degree in special education. I remember sitting in my first exceptional children's graduate class. I would hear all the stories that teachers would share, and I would think to myself, "If she feels that way, she does not need to be in the classroom; maybe she's the problem."

The following semester I took a position at a charter school in a nearby county. The position had been created over the winter holiday break. A number of students were so disruptive in this school that teachers had

threatened to leave if these students were not somehow better taught. So, I became the new BED (behavioral and emotional disorders) teacher. My class consisted of eight students in the intermediate grades.

The first day, I collected my students and told them that they would now be

> *"I realize that BED class was my birth as a teacher, and it made me stronger."*

my students. These students had not been told that they would be placed in a new class. We had a long first day. We started off with a lot of questions about why they were placed in this class. I explained to my students that their behavior had them placed in this class, and it was up to them to find ways to improve their behavior.

I gave all the students journals to write down their thoughts. They were told that this was their journal, and without question, when they felt themselves feeling angry, instead of becoming disruptive in class, to write their thoughts in that journal. Little did I know that these kids were calling me

everything they could spell that was a four-letter word!

This was only my first week as a new BED teacher. I remember going home and not eating because the children had so worn me out those days. I have to honestly say that I did not know what I was doing. I hadn't finished my training, and I did not have enough support from my administrator to help me over my stumbling blocks. Sometimes I felt it was all out of control.

What I would say to a new teacher who wants to go into teaching, especially special education, is to visit many different schools to see how different teachers teach classes for students with behavior problems. Take what you feel is good from these classroom visits and incorporate those things with your style.

I realize that BED class was my birth as a teacher, and it made me stronger as a person as well as a teacher. I can't even explain how much I learned about what my students needed or how important I was to them. Now I plan to finish my graduate work and eventually pursue a law degree to advocate for these children who cannot speak for themselves, but also for those new teachers who often face too many challenges in their classrooms.

Externalizing behaviors are those characterized as directed toward others; when students display these behaviors, they generally bother both teachers and other students. Kayla and Carlos, the other students whose stories began this chapter, both display externalizing behaviors. They are aggressive, they violate school rules and commit crimes, and they might be described as acting out. As you might expect, students with externalizing behaviors are very likely to be identified by their teachers as needing assistance, particularly if they exhibit two or more externalizing behaviors (Carlson, Tamm, & Gaub, 1997). Figure 7.2 includes examples of externalizing behaviors.

Figure 7.2

Examples of Internalizing and Externalizing Behaviors for Students with Emotional and Behavior Disorders

Students with emotional and behavior disorders may display two types of behaviors that cause concern. *Internalizing behaviors* are characterized by withdrawal, and *externalizing behaviors* are characterized by acting out. Here are examples of both types of behavior.

Internalizing Behaviors

- Exhibits sad affect, depression, and feelings of worthlessness
- Cannot get mind off certain thoughts, ideas, or situations
- Cannot keep self from engaging in repetitive and/or useless actions
- Suddenly cries, cries frequently, or displays totally unexpected and atypical affect for the situation
- Complains of severe headaches or other somatic problems (stomachaches, nausea, dizziness, vomiting) as a result of fear or anxiety
- Talks of killing self—reports suicidal thoughts and/or is preoccupied with death
- Shows decreased interest in activities that were previously of interest
- Is excessively teased, verbally or physically abused, neglected, and/or avoided by peers
- Shows signs of physical, emotional, and/or sexual abuse

Externalizing Behaviors

- Displays recurring pattern of aggression toward objects or persons
- Argues excessively
- Forces the submission of others through physical and/or verbal means
- Is noncompliant with reasonable requests
- Exhibits persistent pattern of tantrums
- Exhibits persistent patterns of stealing, lying, and/or cheating
- Frequently exhibits lack of self-control and acting out behaviors
- Exhibits other specific behavior(s) that intrudes on other people, staff, self, or the physical environment to an extent that prevents the development or maintenance of satisfactory interpersonal relationships

Source: Kentucky Department of Education and Department of Special Education and Rehabilitation Counseling at the University of Kentucky. (1999, December). Behavioral examples. Retrieved August 14, 2003, from www.state.ky.us/agencies/behave/EBD%20TA%20Manual/beexaman.html.

Thinking about students having internalizing or externalizing behaviors is a convenient way to illustrate the diversity of these individuals, but such a simple framework can be misleading. In fact, a single student may display both types of behaviors. For example, Hector is a middle school student who usually keeps to himself. He may even be the victim of others' bullying. However, Hector may suddenly lash out at other students, hitting and cursing about what may seem to an observer to be a minor incident—for example, a classmate bumping into his desk.

Emotional Characteristics

Students' behaviors often are indicators of their emotions. Some students identified as having emotional disturbance experience anxiety as the result of excessive fears. They may be afraid of going to school, afraid of enclosed spaces or other specific types of physical environments (e.g., stairways), afraid of potential catastrophic events (e.g., hurricanes or terrorist attacks), or afraid of becoming ill. Fears such as these are intense and quite real to the students.

It is estimated that approximately 5 percent of children and adolescents in the United States have depression (American Academy on Child and Adolescent Psychiatry, 2004). These young people are at high risk for physical illness, interpersonal difficulty, substance abuse, and suicide. Unless educators, family members, and medical professionals recognize the symptoms of depression, the condition may go unrecognized. The risk of depression is approximately equal for boys and girls during childhood, but during adolescence girls are twice as likely as boys to develop this disorder.

Symptoms of Depression

These symptoms of depression occur in clusters and persist for more than two weeks:

- Frequent sadness, tearfulness, crying
- Hopelessness
- Decreased interest in activities, or inability to enjoy previously favorite activities
- Persistent boredom, low energy
- Social isolation, poor communication
- Low self-esteem and guilt
- Extreme sensitivity to rejection or failure
- Increased irritability, anger, or hostility
- Difficulty with relationships
- Frequent complaints of physical illnesses such as headaches and stomachaches
- Frequent absences from school or poor performance in school
- Poor concentration
- A major change in eating and/or sleeping patterns
- Talk of or efforts to run away from home
- Thoughts or expressions of suicide or self-destructive behavior

Treatment for Depression

The treatment for students who are depressed usually includes some type of counseling or psychotherapy, medication, and home and school interventions. The therapy component of treatment is intended to help youngsters develop a more positive, less distorted view of themselves and the world. Antidepressant medication in recent years has been shown to be safe and effective for use with children, but it remains somewhat controversial. Home and school interventions might include talking with students and helping them to identify and build on their strengths, creating opportunities for students to feel special and the focus of adult attention, and encouraging all students to report bullying or other serious student behavior (Cash, 2001).

Sources: National Institute of Mental Health (2003), Depression in children and adolescents: A fact sheet for physicians. Retrieved August 12, 2003, from www.nimh.gov/publicat/depchildresfact.cfm; and American Academy of Child and Adolescent Psychiatry (2004), The depressed child. Retrieved October 15, 2006, from http://aacap.org/page.ww?section=Facts+for+Families&name=The+Depressed+Child.

Research Notes

McConville and Cornell (2003) studied the correlation between middle school students' attitudes toward aggressive behavior and their actual behavior. They found that students who had positive attitudes toward aggression were more likely than other students to report hitting, kicking, pushing, threatening, and bullying their classmates. These results were consistent across seven months.

Other students with emotional and behavior disorders may feel anger. They may respond to your request for them to complete an assignment by refusing to work at all. They may perceive that a classmate who smiles at them is making fun of them. They may run from the classroom when corrected for using profanity. Often when students feel such anger, they display it through the externalizing behaviors of aggression (e.g., hitting, spitting, fighting).

Yet other students have very low self-esteem. They see only their negative characteristics instead of their positive traits, and they may describe themselves as worthless. When such feelings are chronic, these students may be identified as having **depression,** a mental illness that goes beyond having an occasional bad day or being sad about a life event such as the death of a pet (National Institute of Mental Health, 2006). Students who have a chronic illness, those who live in an abusive home, and those who witness a traumatic event are at risk for developing depression. The symptoms of depression in children and approaches to treating it are discussed in the Professional Edge on this page.

If you understand the symptoms of depression in children and are vigilant as you interact with students, you can play an important role in urging parents to seek assistance for their children and in alerting counselors and other school professionals about students who may have this mental illness. Sadly, when children's depression is untreated it can lead to suicide, the sixth-leading cause of death among children ages five to fourteen and the third-

After unintentional injuries and homicide, suicide is the third-leading cause of death among young people fifteen to twenty-four years old and the sixth-leading cause of death for children five to fifteen years old (National Mental Health Association, 2006). Suicide rates for children and adolescents have nearly tripled since 1960.

Educators can play an important role in recognizing the signals that may indicate a student is a high risk for suicide, which include the following:

- Belief that a person goes to a better place after dying
- Tendency to be impulsive (i.e., acting before thinking about consequences)
- Tendency to be a perfectionist
- Family history of suicide attempts
- Hopelessness, feeling that things will never get better

Verbal and Behavior Clues

Here are specific verbal and behavior clues that should cause you to seek assistance for a student identified as high risk for suicide:

Verbal Clues	Behavior Clues
"I shouldn't be here."	Talking or joking about suicide
"I'm going to run away."	Giving possessions away
"I wish I were dead."	Being preoccupied with death or violence in television, movies, drawings, books, playing, or music
"I'm going to kill myself."	Displaying risky behavior such as jumping from high places, running into traffic, and self-cutting
"I wish I could disappear forever."	Having several accidents resulting in injury, including close calls
"If a person did _____, would he or she die?"	Being obsessed with guns and knives

"The voices tell me to kill myself."	Previously having suicidal thoughts or attempts
"Maybe if I died, people would love me more."	
"I want to see what it feels like to die."	

Tips for School Professionals

Here are things that you can do if you suspect a student is at high risk for suicide:

- Most importantly, know the warning signs.
- Know the school's responsibilities. The courts have held schools liable for not warning parents in a timely fashion or adequately supervising the suicidal student.
- Encourage students to confide in you. Let students know that you are there to help, that you care. Encourage them to come to you if they or someone they know is considering suicide.
- Refer students immediately. You should escort a student you suspect is suicidal to the appropriate person, possibly the principal, psychologist, counselor, or social worker.
- Help to form a school crisis team and participate on it. If educators are prepared in advance, they are better able to respond to students' crises.
- Advocate for the child. If an administrator or other professional minimizes the warning signs, represent the student's interests until you are satisfied the student is safe.

Sources: Suicide Awareness Voices of Education (2003, August), Suicide: Identifying high risk children and adolescents. Retrieved August 12, 2003, from www.save.org/Identify.shtml; and National Association of School Psychologists (2001), A national tragedy: Preventing suicide in troubled children and youth, tips for parents and schools. Retrieved August 12, 2003, from www.nasponline.org/NEAT/syouth.html.

---

leading cause of death among young adults ages fifteen to twenty-four (National Institute of Mental Health, 2003). Most students who commit suicide give clear signals before they take their lives, and you should be alert to these warning signs. They are outlined in detail in the Professional Edge on this page.

Social Characteristics

Students with emotional and behavior disorders experience significant challenges in establishing and maintaining social relationships with peers and adults. For example, in one large study teachers rated students who were receiving special education services for emotional disabilities and also those not labeled as having emotional and behavior disorders (Cullinan, Evans, Epstein, & Ryser, 2003). The identified students were rated as having significantly more relationship problems than other students. This was true for both boys and girls, and it was

PROFESSIONAL MONITORING TOOL

Council for Exceptional Children

Standard 5 Learning Environments and Social Interactions . . . strategies for crisis prevention

What Social Skills Do Students Need to Succeed in General Education Settings?

For students with emotional and behavior disorders to succeed in general education settings, they must have the social skills that are seen as essential by general education teachers. Lane, Pierson, and Givner (2004) surveyed 240 middle and high school teachers; they identified the following social skills as most essential:

- Responds appropriately to aggression from peers
- Politely refuses unreasonable requests
- Responds appropriately to teasing by peers
- Accepts peers' ideas for group activities
- Receives criticism well
- Attends to instructions
- Controls temper with peers
- Listens to classmates when they present work
- Controls temper with adults
- Complies with directions

- Responds appropriately to peer pressure
- Initiates conversations with peers
- Introduces self to new people without being told to do so
- Appears confident in social interactions with opposite-sex peers
- Invites others to join in activities
- Gives compliments to members of the opposite sex

Many of these skills are the precise ones that may be particularly challenging for students with emotional and behavior disorders. What does this tell you about the preparation necessary for including students with these disabilities in general education settings? What is your role in preparing students to have these skills?

Source: Lane, K. L., Pierson, M. R., & Givner, C. C. (2004). Secondary teachers' views on social competence. *Journal of Special Education, 38,* 174–186.

INTERNET RESOURCES
www.nmha.org
The National Mental Health Association website includes pages on topics just for students, parents, and educators. For example, there are tips for all three groups about bullying. Other topics are building respect for diversity and appreciating differences in people.

true for both African American and Caucasian students. In fact, professionals generally agree that lack of social skills is one of the primary reasons that students are identified as having emotional and behavior disorders (Jones, Dohrn, & Dunn, 2004).

Some students have problems in their social interactions because they live in situations in which adults and other children model inappropriate social skills (Christie, Jolivette, & Nelson, 2000). For example, if the expectation in a student's home is that children should be quiet, that student may not know how to join peers in a game or activity or to ask a teacher for assistance. The message for educators is this: When students do not have the social skills necessary for them to interact effectively with peers and adults, they need to be taught those skills. Having appropriate social skills will help students throughout their lives (Jolivette, Stichter, Nelson, Scott, & Liaupsin, 2000). An example of teaching social skills in a general education environment is included in the Inclusion Matters.

Cognitive and Academic Characteristics

The first step in understanding the cognitive and academic characteristics of students with emotional and behavior disorders is to recognize the guidelines that are used in identifying these students. If a student's cognitive ability is below a certain level—usually an IQ of about 70—he generally will be considered to have an intellectual disability and any behavior problems he displays will be thought of as secondary to or caused by his primary disability. The student generally will not be identified as having an emotional or behavior disorder. Thus, you might think that students with emotional and behavior disorders could have a cognitive ability from a low-average to a gifted range because there is no direct relationship between intelligence and emotional problems. Although this is true, most of these students have been found to have low-average to average intellectual ability (Vaughn, Levy, Coleman, & Bos, 2002).

The academic difficulties that students with emotional and behavior disorders experience are significant. They have the lowest grade-point averages and highest dropout rates of students in any disability category (Sutherland, Wehby, & Gunter, 2000). Many authors have documented that students with emotional and behavior disorders fail to achieve in school and that their academic problems occur across subject areas. For example, Nelson, Benner, Lane, and Smith (2004) examined the academic achievement of a sample of students with emotional and behavior disorders spanning kindergarten through twelfth grade. They found that the students had significant academic problems across all content areas.

"The academic difficulties that students with emotional and behavior disorders experience are significant."

The Question of Cause and Effect

Many professionals have considered this question: Do emotional and behavior disorders cause academic problems, or do students' chronic and significant academic problems cause emotional and behavior disorders? No clear answer to this question can be found. However, it is likely that both parts of the question contain some truth. Because of emotional difficulties, some students cannot adequately focus on schoolwork. At the same time, repeated failure in schoolwork contributes to some students' emotional and behavior disorders. What is most important for educators to keep in mind is that effective services for these students address both academic and emotional and behavior needs.

Emotional and Behavior Disorders and Comorbidity

Many students with ADHD also have other disabilities. The same point must be made for students whose primary disability is emotional disturbance. Many students who are identified as having an emotional or behavior disorder have comorbid, or additional, disabilities (National Institute of Mental Health, 2006). Some also have a learning disability, and others have ADHD. In addition, many of these students have more than one emotional or behavior disorder—for example, both depression and a disruptive behavior disorder. For school professionals, recognizing comorbid disorders is essential so that all the needed interventions can be implemented to help the student succeed.

How Are Emotional and Behavior Disorders Identified?

Before special education services are considered for students with emotional and behavior disorders, professionals already have tried to assist them in many ways. General education teachers usually implement behavior reward systems and other strategies that have been successful with other students. In most schools educators also request input from a prereferral team. If that team, working with the general education teacher, is not able to adequately address a student's needs, then a referral is made to determine whether an emotional or behavior disorder exists, whether special education services are needed, and whether those services would benefit the student.

Assessment

Although the areas of assessment for emotional and behavior disorders are similar to those for learning disabilities and mental retardation, the emphasis for the former is on emotional, behavior, and social concerns. As for all students, the assessment must address all pertinent aspects of student functioning, use multiple measures, and be nondiscriminatory.

PROFESSIONAL MONITORING TOOL

Council for Exceptional Children

Standard 2 Development and Characteristics of Learners . . . educational implications of exceptionalities

According to the Youth Risk Surveillance that is conducted by the Centers for Disease Control and Prevention, youth drinking is decreasing in the United States. However, of the ninth- through twelfth-graders surveyed in 2005, 43 percent had had a drink on at least one day in the month prior to the survey and 25 percent admitted to episodic heavy drinking.

PROFESSIONAL MONITORING TOOL

Council for Exceptional Children

Standard 2 Development and Characteristics of Learners . . . similarities and differences among individuals

dimensions of
DIVERSITY

Although minorities represent approximately 25 percent of the population, less than 10 percent of mental health providers are minorities (American Psychological Association, 2000). This underrepresentation contributes to the fact that individuals from minority groups are not as likely as others to access mental health services.

Formal Assessments

Several types of formal assessments may be completed to help professionals decide whether a student has an emotional or behavior disorder. First, rating scales may be used to determine the nature and extent of a student's problems. For example, the Scale for Assessing Emotional Disturbance (SAED) (Epstein & Cullinan, 1998) is a norm-referenced instrument that can be completed by teachers in just a few minutes. It includes a subscale for each dimension of the federal definition: inability to learn, relationship problems, inappropriate behavior, unhappiness or depression, and physical symptoms or fears. An additional subscale addresses social maladjustment. Other rating scales that are to be completed by professionals and parents include the Behavior Assessment System for Children (BASC-2) (Reynolds & Kamphaus, 2004) and the Behavior Rating Profile (BRP-2) (Brown & Hammill, 1990).

In addition to assessments regarding emotional and behavior factors, cognitive ability and achievement levels also are measured. An intelligence test such as the Wechsler Intelligence Scale for Children–IV (WISC–IV) (Wechsler, 2003) usually is administered to decide whether a student's cognitive level might be affecting her emotions and behavior. An achievement test such as the Woodcock–Johnson Psychoeducational Battery–III (Tests of Achievement) (Woodcock, McGrew, & Mather, 2001) helps the team decide the extent to which the emotional and behavior disorders are affecting the student's educational performance.

Classroom Assessments

An essential part of an assessment for emotional and behavior disorders is systematic observation in the classroom, lunchroom, physical education class, and other school and possibly home environments. Professionals need to see exactly what students do or do not do in a variety of activities and settings, they need to analyze what might trigger inappropriate behavior, and they need to consider the context in which the student is expected to function—the level of structure in the classroom, the number of adults with whom the student interacts, and so on. Rating scales measure what teachers, parents, and others perceive the student is doing. *Observations* of actual behavior provide confirmation of those perceptions and more detail about the student's strengths and problems.

Classroom assessments also can include curriculum-based measurements that demonstrate how the student is achieving in day-to-day schoolwork in core academic areas. This information supplements the standardized achievement data gathered as part of the formal assessment.

Other Assessment Strategies

Several other assessment strategies usually are included in deciding whether a student has an emotional or behavior disorder. A family history is obtained by interviewing parents and other key family members; this information can help to explain whether genetic and/or environmental factors might be affecting the student. The developmental history of the student in question, also obtained through parent interviews, provides professionals with information on whether the problem has been evident for some time or has recently emerged. For example, a family might be asked whether their child tended to dislike adult attention as an infant or toddler, whether the child began speaking at a later rather than an earlier age, and whether the child played with other children in age-appropriate ways.

In many cases a psychologist or counselor also will interview the student who is being assessed. Using nonthreatening approaches, these professionals seek to hear from the student his perspective on what is occurring and the reasons for his problems. Think about this component of assessment. What information might be obtained directly from the student that would not otherwise be considered?

Medical Information If a student is under the care of a physician or psychiatrist, school professionals, with parental permission, will request pertinent information from those medical professionals. For example, a student might be taking a medication related to depression, and

In 2003 juveniles accounted for 15 percent of all arrests and 16 percent of arrests for violent crimes (Snyder, 2005).

school professionals need to know this information. Alternatively, a student might be receiving intensive therapy from a private clinic. Again, school professionals need this information so that it can be considered in their evaluation of the student.

Strengths-Based Assessment Most of the assessments for emotional and behavior disorders are designed to discover details about the student's problems and to thoroughly explore the nature and severity of those problems. However, most professionals also advocate assessing student strengths and assets. **Strengths-based assessment** refers to measuring students' social and emotional strengths, the characteristics that give them confidence, and the traits that help them cope with adversity. Epstein (2002) has developed a strengths-based assessment instrument, the Behavioral and Emotional Rating Scale (BERS–2nd edition) which gathers information on interpersonal strength, family involvement, intrapersonal strength, school functioning, and affective strength. Why is it particularly important to include strengths-based assessment information in the evaluation process for students with emotional and behavior disorders?

> *"Most professionals also advocate assessing student strengths and assets.""*

Eligibility

Once assessment data have been gathered, the multidisciplinary team, including the parents, meets to make the critical decisions regarding eligibility.

PROFESSIONAL MONITORING TOOL

Council for Exceptional Children

Standard 8 Assessment
. . . use assessment information in making decisions

Eligibility Criteria

The team must address the following questions in deciding whether a student has an emotional or behavior disorder and should receive special education:

1. *Does the student have one or more of the characteristics in the definition of emotional disturbance?* If you refer back to the federal definition of this disability earlier in this chapter, you will see that the characteristics include unexplained difficulties in learning, unsatisfactory interpersonal relationships, a pervasive mood of unhappiness, and physical symptoms associated with personal or school problems. If a student is to receive special education, one or more of these characteristics must be documented through the information that has been gathered.

2. *Do the student's characteristics, as assessed, adversely affect educational performance?* Special education services are designed only for students whose education is being limited by their disabilities. Professionals look at cognitive ability and achievement data to make this decision. For students with emotional and behavior disorders, the concern is whether the emotional or behavioral difficulties prevent them from learning at a level consistent with their ability.

3. *Can social maladjustment be eliminated as the sole cause of the student's behavior problems?* As you have learned, the federal definition of emotional disturbance contains an exclusionary clause: If a student is socially maladjusted and no other emotional disability exists, she is not eligible for services. Recall, though, that many states do not use this clause in their definitions, and so for those states this question would not be necessary.

If the multidisciplinary team answers yes to the preceding questions, the student is identified as having an emotional and behavior disorder and can begin to receive services if it is determined they would be beneficial. However, if the team's decision is that a disability does not exist or that the student is not eligible for special education services, the members might decide to recommend that a Section 504 plan be prepared to provide support to the student. Alternatively, they may assist the general education teachers working with the student to design intervention programs to address the emotional or behavior problems that prompted the initial referral.

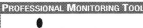

PROFESSIONAL MONITORING TOOL

Council for Exceptional Children

Standard 8 Assessment
. . . screening and classification procedures

How Do Learners with Emotional and Behavior Disorders Receive Their Education?

Because students with emotional and behavior disorders typically are capable of learning the same curriculum as their peers without disabilities, you might think that they are likely to be in general education settings. However, this often is not the case. These students are educated in the entire range of educational environments outlined in federal law—from general education through part-time special education to self-contained classes to separate educational facilities and homebound services. In fact, some data suggest that they are educated in separate settings more than most other students with disabilities (Wagner et al., 2006).

Early Childhood

As you know, young children are not usually assigned specific disability labels. When the disability under consideration is an emotional or behavior disorder, the reluctance to assign a label is particularly strong, for several reasons. One is that when a child is young, judgments about the presence of emotional and behavior disorders are particularly difficult to make because of developmental differences. Another reason is that all the labels related to emotional and behavior disorders are viewed as having a strong negative stigma, one that professionals are uncomfortable assigning to young children.

Despite this uneasiness about labeling, however, professionals have for many years been concerned about the mental health of infants, toddlers, and preschoolers (Egger & Angold, 2006). This concern is based on two related factors. First, professionals are strongly committed to addressing the risk factors discussed earlier in this chapter for young children so that they are less likely to develop emotional and behavior disorders. In particular, professionals focus their efforts on educating young women about the risks associated with prenatal alcohol, nicotine, and drug use; teaching new mothers parenting skills; and improving parent–child relationships. Second, early interventionists know that young children who already are displaying behaviors known to be associated with later serious emotional and behavior disorders must receive intensive intervention at a very early age in order to change the course of their lives (Fox, Dunlap, & Cushing, 2002; Lopes, 2005). Thus, they have developed a number of programs designed to help young children at risk for emotional and behavior disorders as well as their families.

One example of an early intervention program is First Steps to Success (Walker, Stiller, Severson, Feil, & Golly, 1998). In this program entering kindergartners are screened for risk factors related to developing emotional and behavior disorders. With direct and intensive support from a consultant, the teacher implements a highly structured system of classroom rewards designed to encourage appropriate behaviors among high-risk students. The system includes praise for appropriate behaviors, points earned toward rewards, and group and individual privileges. In addition, the consultant works with parents to teach them how to help their children learn school skills. Home–school communication is a critical part of the program. Studies of First Steps to Success indicate that it is highly effective in teaching young children appropriate school behaviors and that the results are lasting (Golly, Sprague, Walker, Beard, & Gorham, 2000; Golly, Stiller, & Walker, 1998).

Elementary and Secondary School Services

Students with emotional and behavior disorders in elementary, middle, and high school receive their education in all the service delivery options described in IDEA, more so than almost any other group of students with disabilities. As shown in Figure 7.3, 28 percent

---

PROFESSIONAL MONITORING TOOL

Council for Exceptional Children

Standard 1 Foundations
. . . issues in definition and identification
. . . issues, assurances, and due process rights
Standard 5 Learning Environments and Social Interactions
. . . effective behavior management strategies

Research Notes

Frey (2002) conducted a study to determine the factors that influenced the recommendations special education teachers made regarding placements for students with emotional and behavior disorders. He found that the teachers who were most confident of their behavior management skills recommended less restrictive placements, including general education. Students with low socioeconomic status were likely to be recommended for more restrictive placements. No placement differences were found based on race/ethnicity.

---

of these students are in general education for 80 percent or more of the school day. Approximately 30 percent of them attend self-contained special education classes, and nearly 18 percent are educated in separate schools or other facilities (U.S. Department of Education, 2004).

Placements for students with emotional and behavior disorders also vary considerably across states. In Nebraska 60 percent of these students are in general education settings at least 80 percent of the day; the data for Vermont are similar. In contrast, Mississippi places more than 56 percent of these students in a special education setting for most of the day, and Louisiana follows closely at 54 percent. Think about the practical and potential lifelong implications for students of these wide differences in placement decisions: If you were a student with an emotional or behavior disorder and lived in Nebraska, you would have a very good chance of being educated beside your peers without disabilities. However, if your family moved to Mississippi, you probably would spend most of the day in a special education classroom, interacting primarily with other students with emotional and behavior disorders, excluded from many of the typical social lessons learned in the general education environment. Do you think such differences should exist? Why or why not?

The types of services students receive may vary somewhat based on the setting in which they are educated. In a general education classroom, a student may be expected to meet most of the same expectations as other students, but the teacher probably will pay closer attention to effective instructional approaches that can reduce inappropriate behavior. In a resource room, students may receive instruction from a highly qualified special educator in a single academic subject such as reading or English, or they may get assistance with organizational skills, general learning and study strategies, and self-management techniques. The special educator in this setting also will manage various types of behavior intervention programs designed to help students display appropriate classroom behavior. In a self-contained special education classroom, a small group of students may spend the day with a single teacher or move as a group among several special education teachers. Students in these classrooms often are working on highly structured point systems that move students through various levels of privileges based on their behavior. For example, leaving the classroom unaccompanied might be a reward earned by displaying appropriate in-class behavior.

For students needing a more restrictive placement, alternatives may include day treatment or residential programs (Gagnon & Leone, 2005). **Day treatment programs** are special schools that include special education in small classes and place a strong emphasis on individualized instruction. They usually also include individual and group therapy, family counseling, vocational training, crisis intervention, positive skill building, and other services such as recreational, art, and music therapy. *Residential programs,* usually attended by students with the most serious or dangerous emotional problems, are just what the name suggests: Students live at these schools, attending classes and participating in therapeutic and recreational activities. The school services may look much like those in a day treatment program.

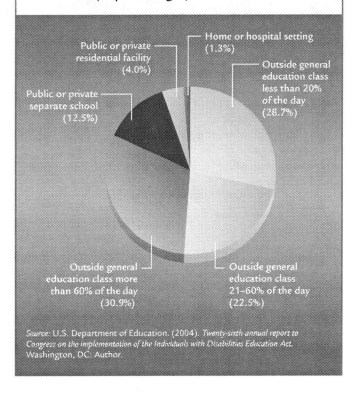

Figure 7.3

Educational Placements of Students Ages Six to Twenty-One Who Have Emotional or Behavior Disorders (in percentages)

Public or private residential facility (4.0%)

Public or private separate school (12.5%)

Home or hospital setting (1.3%)

Outside general education class less than 20% of the day (28.7%)

Outside general education class more than 60% of the day (30.9%)

Outside general education class 21–60% of the day (22.5%)

Source: U.S. Department of Education. (2004). *Twenty-sixth annual report to Congress on the implementation of the Individuals with Disabilities Education Act.* Washington, DC: Author.

INTERNET RESOURCES
http://cecp.air.org
The Center for Effective Collaboration and Practice is a federally funded effort to bring together professionals at the federal, state, and local levels to facilitate the production, exchange, and use of knowledge about effective practices for students with emotional and behavior disorders. The center's website includes information on critical issues (e.g., juvenile justice), opportunities for discussions, and resources for developing behavior intervention plans.

David Young-Wolff/PhotoEdit

Increasingly, professionals are stressing that very early and intensive intervention is essential for improving outcomes for students with emotional and behavior disorders.

CHECK
Your Learning

Why is the inclusion of students with emotional and behavior disorders considered challenging? Under what circumstances can inclusion be successful for these students?

Inclusive Practices

Given the data about educational placements for students with emotional and behavior disorders, it is clear that inclusive practices are an issue for these students (Johns & Guetzloe, 2004; Visser & Stokes, 2003). In fact, the debate about inclusion for students with emotional and behavior disorders has been particularly contentious. Coleman and Webber (2002) have identified these areas of concern:

1. *Curriculum.* With today's academic standards, general education classrooms establish high expectations for students. This pressure may cause students with emotional and behavior disorders to develop further problems. At the same time, these classrooms often do not emphasize social skills development, anger management, and other topics that may be crucial for students with emotional disabilities. Unless these concerns are directly addressed, students may be inadvertently set up for failure.

2. *Social rejection.* Students with emotional and behavior disorders often have difficulty making friends, or they make friends with students who have similar problems. Just as important, general education teachers are more negative about students with these disorders than about any other group of students with disabilities. They often note that they feel ill prepared to work with these students (Wagner et al., 2006). As a result they often do not have a sense of ownership for the students or feel responsible for their success or failure (Guetzloe, 1999). This concern implies that teachers need professional development to learn how to support students in the social domain.

"Students with emotional and behavior disorders often have difficulty making friends, or they make friends with students who have similar problems."

3. *Mental health treatment.* Students with emotional and behavior disorders often need comprehensive services that include a strong mental health component in addition to academic supports. Although general education classrooms address academic and social domains, they are not structured to incorporate mental health services, such as counseling. However, it should be noted that the provision of mental health treatment can be problematic in any school setting, whether inclusive or more restrictive.

Two important points should be made in thinking about the inclusion of students with emotional and behavior disorders. First, the concerns just mentioned are based on the assumption that inclusion is mostly about where students sit. The view expressed here is that inclusion is about welcoming all students to their learning community—that is, their school. Thus, in inclusive schools students with emotional disabilities might spend a small part of the day in a general education classroom, or they might have the option of leaving that classroom if it becomes too stressful. In addition, students without disabilities might tutor students with emotional and behavior disorders in the special education classroom, and they might also serve as buddies for these students. In other words, students can be included even if they do not sit in a general education classroom for the entire day.

Second, with careful planning and preparation, school professionals are succeeding in supporting students with emotional and behavior disorders in their general education classrooms (Heineman, Dunlap, & Kincaid, 2005). For example, one group of researchers provided staff development for school professionals in the best practices for supporting students with emotional disabilities in general education settings (Shapiro, Miller, Sawka, Gardill, & Handler, 1999). By providing this training and offering intensive consultation designed to help the general educators problem solve about specific students and implement the interventions they had learned, inclusionary practices were successful for these students. Thus, to say that inclusion for students with emotional and behavior problems is not possible is an overstatement: It is more accurate to say that it requires strong administrative support; a plan for implementation that addresses academic, behavioral, and emotional needs; and attention to enhancing the knowledge and skills of general education teachers as well as other school professionals.

Transition and Adulthood

The outcomes for students with emotional and behavior disorders have been disappointing (Ackerman, 2006). For example, it is estimated that between 21 and 64 percent of students with these disorders drop out of high school (Scanlon & Mellard, 2002). Although some of these students later earn their high school diplomas through GED programs, those who do not are especially at risk for poor adult outcomes. In addition, students with emotional and behavior disorders have difficulty finding and keeping jobs (Carter & Wehby, 2003).

Most professionals agree that improving outcomes for students with emotional and behavior disorders is quite feasible (Carter, Lane, Pierson, & Glaeser, 2006). The key is to translate the knowledge base for effective interventions into widespread practice. For example, students with these disorders should be served through family-centered approaches that coordinate school and community assistance (Burns, Hoagwood, & Maultsby, 1998). Better access to mental health services for students and their families is needed. These students should be taught specific skills that will help them pursue postschool options. An example is anger management, a skill described in the Specialized Instruction on the next page. Focused transition programs with measurable goals that provide vocational training and on-the-job training also can help outcomes (Corbett, Clark, & Blank, 2002) as can specific training in self-determination skills (Carter et al., 2006). Finally, better training for school professionals is necessary so that all the other elements of transition can be implemented.

What Are Recommended Educational Practices for Students with Emotional and Behavior Disorders?

A strong base of research has developed over the past twenty-five years that can guide school professionals in their work with students with emotional and behavior disorders. Effective practices include prevention, collaboration, procedures required by IDEA, and specific interventions.

The Importance of Prevention

Because of highly publicized incidents of school violence and research demonstrating poor outcomes for students with emotional and behavior disorders, the prevention of emotional and behavior disorders has in recent years become one of the highest priorities among school and community agencies concerned about children (Masia-Warner, Nangle, & Hansen, 2006; U.S. Department of Health and Human Services, 1999).

Early Intervention

Prevention has several components. As you have read, one component is early intervention. Professionals agree that if early interventions could be implemented with young children who are at risk for developing behavior disorders, some children would not experience later problems. This type of early intervention may address young children's behavior. It also may address the development of their language and other communication skills because of the evidence already discussed suggesting that one factor that may contribute to the development of emotional and behavior disorders is the frustration that results from poor communication skills (Benner, Nelson, & Epstein, 2002).

Specialized Instruction

Teaching Anger Management Skills

Students with behavior disorders often experience difficulty managing their anger, and without intervention they respond by physically attacking others, using profanity, or breaking or throwing things. However, research has demonstrated that students can be taught anger management strategies that help them to reduce their anger and to display anger more appropriately (e.g., Presley & Hughes, 2000).

A variety of anger management programs have been developed for middle and high school students. The content of these programs usually includes recognition that anger is normal, understanding of individual responses to anger, identification of anger triggers, awareness of degrees of anger, tools for anger management—cognitive and behavioral—and practice of anger management strategies.

The accompanying figure illustrates an anger log used by students in middle and high school after they had completed an anger management program. In what types of situations might such a log be helpful for students in monitoring and refining their anger management skills? How might general and special education teachers, counselors, psychologists, social workers, school administrators, and other professionals collaborate to help students apply anger management skills?

Source: Kellner, M. H., Bry, B. H., & Colletti, L. A. (2002). Teaching anger management skills to students with severe emotional or behavioral disorders. *Behavioral Disorders, 27,* 400–407. Reprinted by permission of the Council for Children with Behavioral Disorders.

Final Anger Log

Name _____ Date _____

What was your trigger?
- ❏ Somebody started fighting with me.
- ❏ Somebody teased me.
- ❏ Somebody insisted I do something.
- ❏ Somebody took something of mine.
- ❏ Somebody did something I didn't like.
- ❏ Other _____

Where were you when you got angry? ❏ School ❏ Neighborhood ❏ Home ❏ Other _____

How angry were you?	1	2	3	4	5
	not angry	mildly angry	moderately angry	really angry	burning mad

		How did you handle your anger?	How will you handle your anger next time?
Inappropriate responses	Yelling	❏	❏
	Throwing something	❏	❏
	Cursing	❏	❏
	Threatening someone	❏	❏
	Breaking something	❏	❏
	Hitting someone	❏	❏
	Other _____	❏	❏
Appropriate responses			
Physiological tools	Counting to 10, 20, 30	❏	❏
	Taking deep breaths	❏	❏
	Relaxing my muscles	❏	❏
	Other _____	❏	❏
Thinking tools	Using self-think/self-statement	❏	❏

Write down what you thought or said to yourself.

_____

_____

Behavioral tools	Talking it out	❏	❏
	Ignoring it	❏	❏
	Going for a run	❏	❏
	Walking away	❏	❏
	Other _____	❏	❏

Did you make your anger work for you?
- ❏ Yes I stayed in control, respected people and property, and had positive results.
- ❏ No I lost control, hurt people or property, and/or had negative results.

How did you handle the situation?	1	2	3	4	5
	poorly	not so well	OK	well	great

Source: Reprinted from Kellner, M. H. (2001). *In control: A skill-building program for teaching young adolescents to manage anger* (p. 91). Champaign, IL: Research Press. Reprinted with permission.

Positive Behavior Supports

Another focus for prevention in elementary and secondary schools involves implementing schoolwide **positive behavior supports (PBS)**. Schoolwide PBS includes these elements (U.S. Department of Education, 2003):

1. An approach to discipline that is agreed on by all the administrators, teachers, and other professionals in the school

2. A positive statement of the purpose of the PBS

3. A small number of rules for students and staff, worded in positive ways

4. Clear procedures for teaching behavior expectations to students

5. A set of procedures for encouraging students to display appropriate behaviors

6. A set of procedures for discouraging inappropriate behaviors and rule breaking

7. A clear plan for monitoring the schoolwide PBS and for evaluating its effectiveness

Mary Kate Denny/PhotoEdit

In schools using PBS, all students and teachers are clear about the expectations for behavior in all common use areas of the school—hallways, gym, cafeteria, and so on. Students are rewarded for knowing and following these rules. In addition, behavior expectations are set at the classroom level. That is, teachers arrange the physical space of the classroom, establish expectations with students, and arrange rewards tailored to the specific group of students. For students whose behavior is not addressed with these schoolwide and classroom strategies, often a team meets and creates an individualized behavior plan using the procedures for functional behavior assessment and behavior intervention plans outlined in the next section. The specific elements of this alternative to traditional, more punitive school behavior management approaches are outlined in the Positive Behavior Supports on the next page.

Research on the effects of schoolwide PBS is encouraging. Professionals in schools using this approach report that they are more effective and that they are motivated to continue using PBS (Oswald, Safran, & Johanson, 2005; Sprague et al., 2001). In middle school this approach has led to an increased use of rewards for students by teachers, decreased aggressive behavior by students, and decreased discipline referrals (Metzler, Biglan, Rusby, & Sprague, 2001). Students also improved in their perception of school safety. Why do you think that schoolwide PBS can have such positive effects?

*P*ositive behavior supports that are schoolwide, classwide, and individual can assist students with emotional and behavior disabilities to succeed in inclusive settings.

PROFESSIONAL MONITORING TOOL

Council for Exceptional Children

Standard 5 Learning Environments and Social Interactions
. . . classroom management theories and strategies
. . . modify environments to manage behaviors

The Effectiveness of Collaboration

A second element of effective practice for students with emotional and behavior disorders is *collaboration*. For students with emotional and behavior disorders, however, collaboration takes on an added dimension. Professionals have increasingly come to agree that because the needs of students with emotional and behavior disorders are so complex and addressed by so many different agencies and organizations, the only way to ensure effective services is to create systems for effective interagency collaboration—that is, collaboration that spans school and nonschool agencies (Anderson, 2000). These agencies might include the school, a community mental health agency, a family social services agency, the juvenile justice system, a state hospital or other residential facility, and so on.

Many examples of this type of interagency collaboration have now been documented, and collectively they are sometimes referred to as **wraparound services** (Duckworth et al., 2001). Most of these collaborations are based on a **system of care** (Stroul, 1996), an approach to interagency collaboration based on a coordinated network of service providers that is child

Students with Emotional and Behavior Disorders

Behavior Supports

Implementing a Positive Behavior Support Program

These questions can help you to understand how PBS is implemented at the individual, classroom, and school levels.

Question	Individual	Classroom	Schoolwide
Who should be involved in the process and how?	Must include student, parents, teacher, and other direct support providers, but may include friends, extended family, administration, specialists, and community members	Must include teacher, administration, and paraprofessionals, but may include related service providers, specialists, student/parent representatives, and other teachers	Must include administration, grade-level, and discipline specific representatives, but parents, community members, and students are recommended participants
How do we identify the variables affecting student behavior?	Identification of contexts (setting, events, antecedents) and functions (maintaining variables) of individual student behavior (e.g., obtained via functional behavioral assessment)	Inventory of classroom features and management (including disciplinary procedures) and identification of problematic routines that affect the behavior and academic performance of students in the classroom(s)	Multilevel site analysis (incorporate classroom, individual students), surveys, observations, patterns in discipline referrals, and organizational features that affect all of the students in a school
How do we identify and implement effective strategies?	• Modifying the circumstances associated with the problem behaviors (e.g., difficult tasks) • Teaching replacement behaviors (e.g., asking for breaks) • Providing functional consequences for behavior (e.g., earning free time) • Addressing lifestyle supports (e.g., peer buddy, medical evaluation)	• Modifying classroom management structure (e.g., rules, routines, arrangement of physical environment) • Modifying instructional methods to engage participation and address social–personal skills • Implementing rewards and in-class discipline methods (e.g., time-out)	• Redesigning the school environment (e.g., increased supervision) • Establishing, teaching, and rewarding adherence to schoolwide expectations • Implementing a continuum of consequences for infractions • Addressing staff incentives and organizational changes (e.g., revised policies and procedures)
What systems will be used to measure desired outcomes?	Increases/decreases in specific target behaviors, including development of skills to replace problem behaviors, and quality of life changes (e.g., improved relationships, participation in integrated activities)	Increases in academic engagement (e.g., assignment completion, grades) reductions in disruptive behavior and enhanced classroom functioning (e.g., fewer referrals, time-outs, more rewards/points earned)	Improvements in overall social and academic environment (e.g., grades, attendance, school climate); fewer discipline referrals and crisis procedures as well as diminished need for individual plans

Source: Heineman, M., Dunlap, G., & Kincaid, D. (2005). Positive support strategies for students with behavioral disorders in general education settings. *Psychology in the Schools, 42,* 779–794.

PROFESSIONAL MONITORING TOOL

Council for Exceptional Children

Standard 10 Collaboration
. . . collaborate with school personnel and community members

and family centered, community based, and sensitive to cultural diversity. The system of care approach is guided by these principles:

1. Children with emotional disabilities should have access to a comprehensive array of services that address their physical, emotional, social, and educational needs.

2. Children with emotional disabilities should receive individualized services in accordance with their unique needs and potential and guided by individualized service plans.

Students with Emotional and Behavior Disorders

Robin Nelson/PhotoEdit

In a system-of-care approach, school, community, and family collaborate to design services that enable students with emotional and behavior disorders to succeed.

3. Children with emotional disabilities should receive services within the least restrictive, most normative environment that is clinically appropriate.

4. The families and surrogate families of children with emotional disabilities should be full participants in all aspects of the planning and delivery of services.

5. Children with emotional disabilities should receive services that are integrated with linkages between child-serving agencies and programs and mechanisms for planning, developing, and coordinating services.

6. Children with emotional disabilities should be provided with case management or a similar mechanism to ensure that multiple services are delivered in a coordinated and therapeutic manner and that they can move through the system of services in accordance with their changing needs.

7. Early identification and intervention for children with emotional disabilities should be promoted by the systems of care in order to enhance the likelihood of positive outcomes.

8. Children with emotional disabilities should be ensured a smooth transition to the adult service system as they reach maturity.

9. The rights of children with emotional disabilities should be protected, and effective advocacy efforts for children and youth with emotional disabilities should be promoted.

10. Children with emotional disabilities should receive services without regard to race/ethnicity, religion, national origin, sex, physical disability, or other characteristics, and services should be sensitive and responsive to cultural differences and special needs.

In essence, the system of care approach is based on the understanding that collaboration among families, professionals, and community services is the most effective way to address the multiple and complex needs of students with emotional and behavior disorders.

Requirements for Interventions in IDEA

IDEA requires that school professionals use very systematic procedures to document the behavior problems that students display, to analyze the reasons those behaviors occur, and to develop and systematically implement interventions intended to reduce inappropriate behaviors while increasing appropriate behaviors. Two specific procedures—functional behavior assessment (FBA) and behavior intervention plans (BIP)—are required for all students with disabilities who experience behavior problems, regardless of whether their identified disability involves emotional disturbance. For example, Dora is a student with an

Educators should remind themselves to tell students what they are doing that is right. By saying "Thanks for putting your assignment in the in-box," "It was very nice of you to apologize when you bumped into Jerry," and similar comments, you help students understand your expectations. This is much more effective than simply telling students what not to do.

Some students with emotional and behavior disorders can be helped by proximity control. In this simple technique, a professional observing student misbehavior moves toward the student in a nonthreatening manner, often making direct eye contact, with the intent of getting the student to stop the behavior in question.

PROFESSIONAL MONITORING TOOL

Council for
Exceptional
Children

Standard 1 Foundations
. . . laws, policies, and ethical principles regarding behavior management

Research
Notes

Are functional behavior assessments and the resulting behavior intervention plans effective? Van Acker, Boreson, Gable, and Potterton (2005) examined FBAs and BIPs from trained professionals. They found that those who had at least two days of intensive training on these topics were most successful in using these procedures.

intellectual disability. When she gets upset, she slaps the teacher and other students. The team making educational decisions for Dora would need to complete a functional behavior assessment and a behavior intervention plan for her. However, these procedures are particularly applicable to students with emotional and behavior disorders.

Functional Behavior Assessment

When a student misbehaves, school professionals are faced with the challenge of finding an effective way to respond. **Functional behavior assessment (FBA)** is a multidimensional problem solving strategy for analyzing the student's behavior within the context of the setting in which it is occurring. The purpose is to decide the function of the behavior and a way to address it (Barnhill, 2005; Erickson, Stage, & Nelson, 2006).

FBA is based on two assumptions (Ryan, Halsey, & Matthews, 2003). The first is that challenging behavior occurs in context; that is, it is influenced by the setting in which it occurs. Thus, the setting must be considered when trying to change a behavior. The second assumption underlying FBA is that challenging behavior serves a function for the student. Educators need to identify that function in order to change the behavior. Functional behavior assessment involves these five steps:

1. *Identify the problem behavior.* Carefully describe the behaviors in observable ways and prioritize them. For example, instead of stating that Tate sulks when work is assigned, the team would specify that when Tate is given a written assignment by the general education teacher, he puts his head down on his desk, covers his face, and does not respond to teacher requests that he begin his work.

2. *Describe in detail the settings in which the behavior occurs.* In the example of Tate, the setting of concern is the general education classroom. The team might further note that Tate is seated in the front of the room, that the class includes twenty-seven other students, and that the desks are arranged in rows with aisles.

3. *Gather information about the behavior using interviews, rating scales, observation, review of student records, and other techniques.* One common observation technique is called an ABC approach. ABC stands for *antecedents* (what comes immediately before the behavior that causes it to happen), *behaviors*, and *consequences* (what happens as a result of the behavior). For Tate, the antecedent is his teacher giving him an assignment. The behavior is what Tate does. The consequence is that his teacher asked him to do the work several times and then sent him with a discipline referral to the office. One other element might be considered: setting events. These are things that may have happened earlier in the day that could be affecting the situation. For Tate, a setting event might be his working in the evenings at a fast-food restaurant and not getting enough sleep.

4. *Review the data.* The team would examine the observational data; they probably would also have information from the teacher, from Tate, and possibly from Tate's parents. They might compare what was observed to Tate's perception of his behavior and to his teacher's views (Kinch, Lewis-Palmer, Hagan-Burke, & Sugai, 2001).

5. *Form a hypothesis about the function of the behavior based on the data gathered.* If you were going to make an educated guess about what function Tate's behavior is serving, what would you say? One reasonable hypothesis is that Tate's behavior is his way of avoiding difficult assignments. By refusing to do the work, he gets sent to the office and does not have to complete the assignments. In other situations, behaviors could serve other functions (Frey & Wilhite, 2005), such as the following:

- For some students, behaving inappropriately is a way to get adults to pay attention to them, something they may crave.
- For other students, behaving inappropriately may be a means for ending a social interaction with a classmate.

- For yet other students, behaving inappropriately may help them to get items or activities that they want (e.g., having a tantrum results in being taken to the special education classroom, where the student can play with colored chalk on the blackboard).

What other functions can you think of that behaviors might address?

Behavior Intervention Plan

Based on the hypothesis the team makes, the next task is to create a **behavior intervention plan (BIP),** which is a set of strategies designed to address the function of the behavior in order to change it (Wright-Gallo, Higbee, Reagon, & Davey, 2006). For Tate, the team decided to change the antecedent by arranging for Tate temporarily to be partnered with a classmate whenever lengthy written assignments were given. In addition, the team designed a *contract.* A contract is a behavior intervention strategy that clearly spells out expectations, rewards, and consequences for students, as illustrated in the Positive Behavior Support. For Tate, the contract rewarded him for completing work. It also included an extended deadline so that he can work on such assignments in parts. The setting event of working in the evenings is one that the team decided it would not be able to address. Data were gathered to determine whether the assignment partner and contract with rewards and extended time were effective. In this case, the BIP was successful. If it had not been, the team would have been responsible for reanalyzing the information they had gathered about the problem, possibly looking for additional information and designing another intervention. The new intervention also would be evaluated to check its effectiveness.

> *"The expectation today for students experiencing behavior problems is to teach them appropriate behaviors that will help them succeed not only in school but also later in life."*

The expectation today for students experiencing behavior problems is to teach them appropriate behaviors that will help them succeed not only in school but also later in life. Negative consequences, or punishment, although not eliminated completely, usually are employed only in partnership with positive behavior supports and only if no other effective approaches can be found.

Examples of Classroom Interventions

In addition to interventions that are incorporated into the FBA and BIP procedures, general education teachers, special education teachers, and other professionals working with students with emotional and behavior disorders can use a wide variety of strategies to enhance student learning while fostering appropriate behaviors. For example, many students need assistance in recording their assignments, in remembering when assignments are due, and in dealing with the mechanics of completing them, including checking spelling and grammar. Others may benefit by learning how to more responsibly use technology, the topic of the Technology Notes.

Peer-Mediated Instruction

Many students with emotional and behavior disorders have as a goal to learn to participate in groups with other students without disruption. Some teachers use peer tutoring or cooperative learning to accomplish this goal. In peer tutoring each student works with one other student to practice math facts, review vocabulary, or complete another instructional task. One student is the tutor, or the student responsible for acting as the peer teacher; the other student is the tutee, or the student answering the questions. In one successful peer-tutoring approach, called *reciprocal tutoring*, both students take both roles in a single tutoring session.

In cooperative learning, students work in groups of three or four. They have a specific task to complete, play assigned roles (e.g., notetaker), and take accountability for the learning.

Behavior Supports

Behavior Contracts

f a student has serious behavior problems, the team will decide to include in the individualized education program (IEP) goals and objectives related to improving appropriate behavior. To accomplish behavior goals, a behavior contract sometimes can be used. Behavior contracts can address a wide array of behaviors and may be used with elementary, middle school, and high school students. Here is one example of a behavior contract.

Behavior Contract

Effective dates: March 1, 2004, to March 15, 2004

I, _____Doug_____, agree to do the following:

- Begin assignments when they are given to me.
- Ask for help by raising my hand if I am stuck.
- Put completed assignments in the "Completed Work" tray.

I, _____Ms. Coble_____, agree to do the following:

- Check with Doug to be sure he understands the assignment.
- Alert Doug when the time for completing an assignment is nearly up.
- Give Doug two points for beginning his work, one point each time he asks for help by raising his hand, and one point for putting work in the "Complete Work" tray. Doug may accumulate up to six points per class period.

Reward

- Each time Doug accumulates ten points, he may spend them on ten minutes of computer time.

Bonus

- If Doug accumulates twenty-five points for two weeks in a row, he may assist Mr. Ames in the computer lab for one class period.

Penalty

- If Doug does not attempt an assignment, he will be asked to complete it at home that evening.
- If Doug calls out instead of raising his hand for help more than two times in a class period, this information will be shared with his mother.

Signatures

_____   _____
Doug Shoales   Ms. Coble

_____
Mrs. Shoales

One cooperative learning method, called Numbered Heads Together, combines the skills and learning efforts of students with a bit of luck. Numbered Heads Together is described in the Specialized Instruction.

Students with Emotional and Behavior Disorders

Most students today are savvy about technology—sometimes more so than their teachers. What students with emotional and behavior disorders may lack, though, are key skills related to responsible technology use. Here are some topics that teachers can address to assist students in this area and strategies for teaching them:

- Etiquette (standards of conduct or procedures)
  - *Problem:* Cell phones and PDAs are used to text message during class.
  - *Strategy:* Use case studies to foster discussions on topics such as cheating through text messaging.

- Communication (electronic exchange of information)
  - *Problem:* Students exclude others in their use of cell phones or PDAs, forming, in essence, electronic cliques.
  - *Problem:* Students use text message strategies (no capital letters, shorthand) in formal written assignments.
  - *Strategy:* If electronic communication is used in a class, be sure all students are included.
  - *Strategy:* Address directly formal and informal writing. Permit informal writing as appropriate and assist students to grow in their use of formal writing skills.

- Access
  - *Problem:* Some students should use assistive technology (e.g., larger fonts, word prediction software, alternative keyboards, voice recognition software) but do not.
  - *Strategy:* Ensure that classroom computers and those in the school media lab are appropriately equipped with simple

technology. Help students learn to self-advocate for assistive technology that would facilitate their learning.

- Responsibility (electronic accountability for actions and deeds)
  - *Problem:* Students illegally download music and other materials.
  - *Problem:* Students copy materials from the Internet for their own projects, plagiarizing.
  - *Strategy:* Have students explore fair use and copyright law using electronic resources.
  - *Strategy:* Open a dialogue with students about how they feel when someone steals from them. Relate this dialogue to electronic theft.

- Security (electronic precautions to guarantee safety)
  - *Problem:* Students do not protect their identities when online.
  - *Problem:* Students do not keep virus protection on home computers up to date.
  - *Strategy:* Teach students to back up data (you should do this, too!).
  - *Strategy:* Teach students how to check for viruses and how to obtain and run virus protection software.
  - *Strategy:* Have students research school and district policies designed to protect electronic equipment from security threats.

Source: Based on Ribble, M. S., Bailey, G. D., & Ros, T. W. (2004). Digital citizenship: Addressing appropriate technology behavior. *Learning and Leading with Technology, 39*(1), 6–11.

For peer tutoring and cooperative learning to be effective with these students, it must be implemented carefully, following methods that have been demonstrated through research to be effective. In addition, students should receive instruction in appropriate leadership, communication, decision-making, and trust-building skills (Sutherland, Wehby, & Gunter, 2000). Finally, teachers or others implementing peer tutoring and cooperative learning should assess its impact on student achievement and monitor student behavior in these instructional arrangements.

Teacher-Led Instruction

One final area of intervention should be mentioned. Students with emotional and behavior disorders clearly struggle with academic achievement, and evidence increasingly points to the importance of using specific programs and procedures to help them learn (e.g., Barton-Arwood, Wehby, & Falk, 2005; Carroll et al., 2006; Nelson, Benner, & Gonzalez, 2005). In addition, many of the strategies that make instruction effective for all students are particularly important for these students, including the following (Quinn et al., 2000):

- Keep lesson objectives clear.
- Deliver lessons in a lively manner, and make sure that students are engaged.

Students with Emotional and Behavior Disorders

Numbered Heads Together

For some students with emotional and behavior disorders, peer-mediated instruction, including a variety of peer tutoring and cooperative learning approaches, holds promise for fostering academic achievement and improving social interactions with classmates. One effective peer-mediated approach is called Numbered Heads Together. Here are the steps to follow to implement Numbered Heads Together:

1. Assign students to groups of three or four. These groups should be heterogeneous, including students at various achievement levels. Students should be seated near one another when the approach is used.

2. Have students assign themselves numbers from one to three or four.

3. Ask the class a question.

4. Have students "put their heads together" so that they determine the correct answer or several answers, depending on the type of question asked. Students are instructed to be sure that every member of their group knows the answer(s).

5. Call the groups back together. Call a number (one to three or one to four) and have the students in the class with that number stand.

6. Call on one of the standing students to answer the question. If there is more than one correct answer, continue to call on students.

7. Ask the rest of the class to agree or disagree with the stated answer.

8. Award points or rewards. This can be done in several ways. Some teachers use a positive approach: As long as each student called on gets an answer, all teams are rewarded. Other teachers give each team one "pass" so that if a member does not answer correctly the team still has an opportunity to be rewarded.

In a review of research on Numbered Heads Together, Maheady, Harper, and Mallette (2001) found that this peer-mediated strategy was more effective than whole-group questioning. They also reported that students performed better on daily quizzes when this approach was employed instead of traditional question–answer methods. Students also preferred this teaching strategy to traditional approaches. Keep in mind that while this strategy is presented as it applies to students with emotional and behavior disorders, it is also successful with many other groups of students, with or without disabilities. It can be a central part of any educator's implementation of principles of universal design for learning and is a clear example of how differentiation can be effectively accomplished without extraordinary effort.

Source: Based on Maheady, L., Harper, G. F., & Mallette, B. (2001). Peer-mediated instruction and interventions and students with mild disabilities. *Remedial and Special Education, 22*(1), 4–14. Copyright © 2001 by Pro-Ed, Inc. Reprinted with permission.

Research Notes

Students with emotional and behavior disorders who received general (as opposed to occupation-specific) vocational training and on-the-job training were less likely to drop out and had higher postschool earnings than students who did not receive these transition supports (Corbett et al., 2002).

- Use concrete vocabulary and clear, succinct sentences.

- Give all students immediate encouragement and specific feedback.

- Use meaningful materials and provide examples to which students can relate.

- Have students recite in unison.

- Prompt student answers after allowing an appropriate amount of wait time (i.e., to encourage participation, which may vary for each student).

- Break long presentations into shorter segments that include student responding.

- Break down a large assignment into smaller ones. As students finish each mini-assignment, build in reinforcement for task completion.

- When students make mistakes, help them to learn from those mistakes. Be careful not to overcorrect, and praise any progress toward the desired behavior change.

- Follow low-interest activities with high-interest activities so that students get occasional breaks from difficult or less-interesting activities.

- Build on student interests. Students often learn by relating material to real-life situations that they find interesting.

- Allow students to make choices. Let them decide between two tasks or select the order in which they complete assigned tasks.

- Employ appropriate technology applications that can engage student interest and increase motivation.
- Use hands-on, experiential learning activities to enable students to apply learning to the real world. This is one of a teacher's most powerful tools.

What Are the Perspectives of Parents and Families?

Have you considered what it might be like to be the parent of a child with an emotional or behavior disorder? What do you think might be the greatest challenges you would face? The greatest joys? One report summarized in its title the experiences of these students and their families: "blamed and ashamed" (U.S. Department of Health and Human Services, 2003).

The Impact of Having a Child with an Emotional or Behavior Disorder

The parents and family members of students with emotional and behavior disorders face several unique challenges in working with school professionals (Taylor-Richardson, Heflinger, & Brown, 2006). First, these families are more likely than families of other students to have a low income and to be headed by a single parent with a less-than-average amount of education (Mundschenk & Foley, 2000). These demographic characteristics by themselves form a barrier to partnership because many school programs assume the existence of a nuclear family.

A second barrier for these families is the often negative set of interactions that occur regarding their children. Teachers frequently are frustrated with students with emotional and behavior disorders; this emotion may lead teachers to have an overall negative perception of the student and the family. Teachers may then contact the family in order to enlist their help in addressing school problems, too often asking the parents to punish the student for behavior problems at school and too seldom involving the parents in reward systems. The parents may not be able to carry out the requests made by the teachers, or the parents' efforts may not be successful. The result may be additional frustration on the parts of teachers and parents alike (Fox, Vaughn, Wyatte, & Dunlap, 2002).

The negative interactions between school professionals and family members sometimes are highlighted during meetings. Parents may be anxious about working with school personnel, worried about the behaviors of their child, and concerned that any meeting will be an opportunity to learn about yet another issue related to their child (Jones et al., 2004). Parents' behaviors at meetings may be viewed as combative or disruptive. Unless school professionals recognize the reasons for these behaviors, they may form even more negative opinions about the student and family.

PROFESSIONAL MONITORING TOOL

Council for Exceptional Children

Standard 10 Collaboration
. . . concerns of families

One other challenge faced by families of students with emotional and behavior disorders concerns advocacy (Mundschenk & Foley, 2003; Murray, 2005). Many disability groups are represented in the schools and the community by advocacy groups that are led by parents. These groups often can collectively ensure that their children's rights are upheld and foster positive perceptions of their children's special needs by educating professionals, other parents, and students and by seeking positive publicity concerning individuals with disabilities. Such advocacy generally does not exist among parents of students with emotional and behavior disorders (U.S. Department of Health and Human Services, 2003).

Building Positive Relationships

More than anything else, families need professionals to genuinely care about their children (Fox et al., 2002). And so for educators working with families of students with emotional and behavior disorders, it is essential to diligently strive to form strong partnerships using a collaborative focus such as that outlined earlier in this chapter and to be flexible in terms of expectations for family involvement. Efforts also may involve the following components.

Parent Education

In some cases schools can offer assistance to parents by teaching them strategies that might help them to address their children's behavior at home. Parent education also can address topics such as how to help their children with homework, how school services for their children are structured, how to access community resources, and how to advocate for their children (Anderson & Matthews, 2001).

Support Groups

For some families one of the most helpful options is a support group that includes the parents of other students with emotional and behavior disabilities. In support groups parents share information about local resources and services, trade ideas for addressing specific problems, and obtain the reassurance of knowing that they are not alone in dealing with day-to-day challenges. Although school professionals might arrange to start a support group, parents take the lead and give the group its identity and direction.

What Trends and Issues Are Affecting the Field of Emotional and Behavior Disorders?

CHECK Your Learning

Early in this chapter you learned about the functional, organic, and behavioral approaches to thinking about emotional and behavior disorders. What examples have you found in the chapter of how these approaches still influence the field today?

Many trends and issues related to the field of emotional and behavior disorders have been introduced elsewhere in this chapter. For example, you have learned about the controversy that exists about the definition of this disability and concerns about inclusive practices. However, if you asked experienced professionals to name the most important issue, they probably would respond by discussing the difficulty that students and their families face in obtaining essential mental health services.

The Problem of Access

Professionals generally agree that the number of students with emotional and behavior disorders in the United States has risen during the past decade and that the nature and severity of these students' disorders have become more serious (Walker, Zeller, Close, Webber, & Gresham, 1999; Walker et al., 2005). However, the first problem related to access concerns *identification:* Whether considering schools or community services, far fewer students are identified as needing services than those who receive them. In fact, it has been estimated that less than 20 percent of the approximately fourteen million youth who have mental illness receive treatment and that 90 percent of those who commit suicide have an emotional or behavior disorder (Zionts & Villiers, 2003). This situation has been referred to by advocates as a "hidden conspiracy" (Sachs, 1999).

For some families, access requires unthinkable sacrifices. In order to access Medicaid services that can provide mental health interventions, families who make enough money to survive but too much to be eligible must relinquish custody of their children. In one study 23 percent of parents reported that they had been told by public officials that they should give up custody so that their children could get the care they needed (Collins, 2003; Friesen, Giliberti, Katz-Leavy, Osher, & Pullmann, 2003).

Creating a Promising Future

To address the problem of access, professionals, parents, and community agency personnel are lobbying politicians to pass legislation to expand and strengthen services for students with emotional and behavior disorders and their families (Zionts & Villiers, 2003). These efforts address the need for better health care coverage for children, coverage that includes mental health services. These efforts also include strategies to make funding available to families that cannot otherwise afford services and to encourage more professionals to enter this field.

For school professionals, the emphasis is on access related to using best practices (Scheuermann & Johns, 2002). Instead of punishing students for misbehaviors, educators need to identify and implement programs and interventions that have been demonstrated to help students learn appropriate behaviors. Administrators, teachers, other school professionals, and even school board members should understand and observe the results that can be obtained using positive behavior supports. They also need to emphasize the prevention of these disorders by using schoolwide systems as outlined earlier in this chapter.

No one would say that addressing the needs of students with emotional and behavior disorders is easily accomplished. However, the current status of research about these students and the approaches that can help them succeed lets professionals know that there is promise. And if you think about the future for these students, the costs of helping them now are far less, and the benefits far greater, than the price of waiting.

SUMMARY

The study of children with emotional and behavior disorders began at the beginning of the twentieth century in the fields of medicine and psychology, and it was not until the 1960s that schools assumed responsibility for this group of students. Today, the definition of emotional and behavior disorders—called *emotional disturbance* in IDEA—and their prevalence continue to be debated, but professionals agree that both biological and psychosocial factors are contributing causes of these disabilities. Students with emotional and behavior disorders display internalizing and externalizing behaviors, and their emotional difficulties often lead to problems in social relationships. Typically, these students have low-average to average ability, but their achievement is below expected levels. Formal and informal assessment instruments and procedures used to identify whether students have emotional and behavior disorders include behavior checklists; interviews with professionals, parents, and

students; observations; ability and achievement testing; and medical information. Most students with emotional disabilities spend a significant amount of time in special education settings, a fact supported by the widely acknowledged difficulty of implementing inclusive practices for these students. Best practices for students with emotional and behavior disorders include prevention, particularly with early intervention; collaborative efforts on the part of school and community personnel; functional behavior assessments and behavior intervention plans; and classroom instruction designed to provide structure and engagement.

The parents and families of students with emotional and behavior disorders often feel isolated from others and struggle to find appropriate services to help their children. In fact, one of the most serious issues facing the field of emotional and behavior disorders today is the lack of mental health services for children and youth.

BACK TO THE CASES

Kayla

You are spending another sleepless night thinking about Kayla and what you can do to help her. Finally, you get out a pad of paper and begin to outline what you do and do not know about the student. To begin you ask yourself:

■ In what ways does Kayla fit the definition of a child with an emotional disorder? (See CEC Standard 2 and INTASC Principle 2.05.)

■ Considering Kayla's age and the onset of her behavior problems, what are the possible nonschool factors that might be influencing her behavior? (See CEC Standard 3 and INTASC Principle 5.04.)

■ How can you investigate these potential influences? (See CEC Standard 10 and INTASC Principle 10.04.)

As you work though the answers to these questions, you determine how you want to help Kayla. At the special education team meeting tomorrow morning, you will need to explain your plan and provide a rationale. (See CEC Standards 3 and 10 and INTASC Principle 5.05.) Take some time now to write down your thoughts.

Garrett

As you review Garrett's story, note that no cause for Garrett's behavior was mentioned and no successful interventions, accommodations, or collaborations were discussed. Instead, we read about a list of Garrett's problems in school and were told that these behaviors are not evident at home or are not seen as problems at home. Now the principal has asked you to take action and has offered his full support to your efforts. Hypothesize about what might happen if the situation continues as is.

What do you think should be done? Who should be involved in helping Garrett? (See CEC Standards 2 and 3, and INTASC Principles 2.01, 5.04, and 5.05.)

Carlos

Carlos has dropped out of school. Since he is old enough to leave school legally and has done so, the school is no longer responsible for him. Or are they? As a special education teacher what is your ethical responsibility for Carlos? (See CEC Standard 9 and INTASC Principles 9.01 and 9.02.) How could the system of care approach have been helpful to Carlos and provided a safety net that may have prevented his early departure from school? (See CEC Standard 3 and INTASC Principles 2.01, 5.04, and 5.05.)

KEY TERMS AND CONCEPTS

Behavior intervention plan (BIP)
Behaviorism
Conduct disorder
Correlated constraints
Day treatment program
Depression
Emotional and behavior disorder (EBD)
Emotional disturbance (ED)

Externalizing behaviors
Functional behavior assessment (FBA)
Internalizing behaviors
Mental disorder
Mood disorder
Oppositional defiant disorder (ODD)
Positive behavior supports (PBS)
Psychosocial factors

Resilience
Social maladjustment
Strengths-based assessment
System of care
Wraparound services

REVIEW, DISCUSS, APPLY

1. What are the most important similarities and differences between the IDEA and the National Mental Health and Special Education Coalition definitions of emotional disturbance? What might the impact be for school professionals if IDEA one day used the coalition definition? (Learning Objective 1)

2. What is the value for educators of understanding that both biological and psychosocial factors may contribute to the development of emotional and behavior disorders? Explain your response using specific examples. (Learning Objective 1)

3. What does it mean to say that a student has internalizing or externalizing behaviors? What is the relationship between these types of behaviors and the emotional and social characteristics of students with emotional and behavior disorders? (Learning Objective 2)

4. What is a strengths-based assessment? Why is it gaining importance in the assessment of students with emotional and behavior disorders? How does a strengths-based assessment help professionals in working with these students? (Learning Objective 3)

5. What are the arguments for and against inclusion of students with emotional and behavior disorders? What can

educators do to increase the success of inclusive practices for these students? (Learning Objective 4)

6. Why do some professionals consider collaboration more important in designing programs for students with emotional and behavior disorders than for any other group of students with disabilities? (Learning Objective 5)

7. Think about a student you have known or observed (or use a case study from another source). What function might this student's behavior be serving? Given the function of the behavior, what interventions in a behavior intervention plan (BIP) might help to address it? (Learning Objective 5)

8. What are the greatest barriers that parents of students with emotional and behavior disorders perceive in their interactions with school and other professionals? What should you as a professional do to reduce these barriers as much as you can? (Learning Objective 6)

9. In this chapter you learned that one of the most critical issues facing professionals and families of children and youth with emotional and behavior disorders is the lack of mental health services. What could be the impact of this dilemma for you as an educator? If you have the opportunity, ask a professional who works in this field to discuss this issue with you and your classmates. (Learning Objective 7)

Go to Allyn & Bacon's MyLabSchool (www.mylabschool.com) and enter Assignment ID SPV10 into the Assignment Finder. Watch the video *Behavior Disorder,* which shows how intervention strategies have helped Nick, a student who has had difficulty controlling his negative behavior both at home and at school.

Question: How would you compare the experiences described by Nick's teachers to those of first-year teacher Ashley Moran in this chapter's Firsthand Account? You may also answer the questions at the end of the clip and e-mail your responses to your instructor.

3

Students with Autism Spectrum Disorders

Students with Autism Spectrum Disorders

Chuck Crow/AP Images

learning objectives

- Outline how the study of autism spectrum disorders developed, define these disorders, and identify their prevalence and causes.

- Describe the characteristics of individuals with autism spectrum disorders.

- Explain how autism spectrum disorders are identified.

- Discuss how students with autism spectrum disorders receive their education.

- Outline recommended educational practices for students with autism spectrum disorders.

- Summarize the perspectives and concerns of parents and families of students with autism spectrum disorders.

- Identify issues and trends affecting the field of autism spectrum disorders.

Written by Brenda Smith Myles, University of Kansas; Taku Hagiwara, Hokkaido University of Education; Melissa Trautman and Elisa Gagnon, both of Blue Valley Public Schools, Overland Park, Kansas; and Marilyn Friend

Claudia

Claudia is a third-grade student who has autism. Although she has made great strides and usually manages the demands of the general education classroom fairly well, sometimes she still displays puzzling behaviors. For example, whenever Claudia is frustrated or angry, she loudly asks, "Do you want your Play-Doh doll?" At first, Claudia's teacher had no clue what Claudia was talking about, and the special education teacher could not provide any insight either. However, having a conversation with Claudia's mother helped: She explained that one night when Claudia was becoming agitated, she had asked this question of Claudia in an angry tone. This expression then became Claudia's own hallmark for signaling her frustration. Knowing this information has assisted the professionals in developing a plan for teaching Claudia to ask for a break in a more appropriate way, thus decreasing her frustration. They taped a small reminder card with a drawing of the Play-Doh doll and the words "I need a break" to the corner of Claudia's desk. Now when Claudia begins to grow frustrated, she is prompted to read the words on the card. She is then given a break to briefly play with her Play-Doh doll. Her teachers comment that this example is very typical of their work with Claudia. When a new challenge arises, they become investigators, observing Claudia, communicating with her family, and trying various options until they discover how to address the issue.

Geneva

Geneva is a seventh-grade student who has faced many challenges in her life. She was identified as having an intellectual disability and autism when she was only a year old. Her parents describe how difficult it was to get her to sleep as a young child and how worried they were about her future. In elementary school, Geneva spent most of her time in a separate classroom for students with significant disabilities.

This decision was made because of her high need for structure and order and her tendency to hit others or bite them when she was frustrated. With intensive intervention and the guidance of a paraprofessional, she gradually began to spend small amounts of time in general education classrooms with peers. Now in middle school, Geneva participates in general education science and art classes, but she still requires a small-group, structured learning setting for much of the school day. Her general education teachers have learned to follow a clear schedule in their classrooms, and if a change is planned, they remind Geneva often. Geneva is learning from a modified curriculum; that is, she is not expected to complete the high-stakes testing that her peers must take, and so her teachers work on her IEP goals and objectives in both general education and special education settings. One goal for Geneva this year is to walk unaccompanied from class to class.

Casey

Casey is a fifteen-year-old boy with autism from a large suburban high school. He is enrolled in a drama course, and some of the students in the course have befriended him, including Matt. On entering the classroom one day, Matt walked up to Casey and said, "What's up, dog?," a common greeting among the popular group at the high school. However, Casey did not understand and proceeded to become quite upset, repeatedly yelling "Don't call me *dog!*" Even though Matt tried to explain that it was a greeting, Casey did not understand. The special education teacher wrote a social story (explained later in this chapter) to help Casey understand that "What's up, dog?" is a greeting and does not mean that Matt is calling him a *dog*. It is just a funny way to be friendly and say "Hi." The social story was done with words and icons because Casey enjoys picture books. After the special educator introduced the story to him he understood and even began using the expression himself.

If you watch for information about individuals with autism in the media, you might wonder whether some professionals are making mistakes: In newspaper stories, magazine articles, movies, and novels, individuals with autism sometimes are portrayed as brilliant but eccentric, sometimes as significantly impaired, and sometimes as turned almost completely inward, as though incapable of dealing with the realities of day-to-day living. In fact, all of these descriptions could be based in truth. Autism, today usually referred to as **autism spectrum disorders (ASD),** has been described as an enigma because individuals identified as having this disability may have widely different characteristics that set them apart from typical peers and from peers with other disabilities (Simpson & Myles, 1998).

What Are Autism Spectrum Disorders?

The study of autism spectrum disorders is relatively new in the field of special education. However, you will see that the evolution of understanding about these disabilities has been rapid and that today's practices for students with these disabilities are informed by considerable research about their characteristics and needs.

Development of the Field

In 1943, psychologist Leo Kanner described a unique group of eleven children whose very unusual behaviors made them qualitatively different from children with other disabilities. According to Kanner (1943), these children's special needs were apparent even in early childhood and included the following:

- An inability to relate typically to other people and situations
- Delayed speech and language development, failure to use developed language for communication purposes, and other speech and language abnormalities, such as extreme literalness
- Typical physical growth and development
- An obsessive insistence on environmental sameness
- An extreme fascination and preoccupation with objects
- Stereotypic or repetitive behavior and other forms of self-stimulation

The characteristics of autism as first described by Kanner more than half a century ago have been revised, refined, and broadened in recent years. Nonetheless, today's definitions and conceptualizations of autism continue to reflect many of Kanner's original observations.

At approximately the same time that Kanner was writing about autism, Hans Asperger, a Viennese physician, was working with a group of children who exhibited a significant and chronic neurodevelopmental social disorder. Asperger described a group of children who today are diagnostically known by his name (Asperger, 1944). Specifically, Asperger's work accentuated the social peculiarities, social isolation, and average to above-average cognitive abilities of the children he studied. He believed that even though these children were in some ways similar to the children that Kanner studied, they formed a distinctly different group.

Early Beliefs

Throughout the 1950s and 1960s, medical professionals generally believed that autism was caused by detached, uncaring mothers—sometimes called "refrigerator mothers," a reference to their coldness—who failed to appropriately nurture their infants (Janzan, 2003). As a result of this belief, many mothers were unfairly accused of making their children autistic by failing to provide the warmth and love that enable young children to thrive. Researchers soon began to question this contention, but it was not until the 1970s that published studies of twins demonstrated a genetic basis for autism. Over the next ten years, these studies were

PROFESSIONAL MONITORING TOOL

Council for Exceptional Children

Standard 2 Development and Characteristics
. . . typical and atypical growth and development

fyi

Eugen Blueler, a Swiss psychiatrist, was the first person to use the word *autism*. He coined the term in 1911. It comes from the Greek word *autos,* meaning "self."

extended and revised, completely debunking the myth of deficient mothering as a cause of autism (Rutter, 2000).

Formalizing Understanding

In 1981, the distinction between autism and Asperger syndrome was forever drawn when Lorna Wing wrote about thirty-five children and adults with the latter disorder, sparking a wave of interest in its study and treatment. Since that time, professionals have learned a great deal about these two related but distinct disorders. For example, they have determined that individuals with these disorders may have mild symptoms or may be significantly affected (Wing, 1991). Autism was identified as a separate category of disability in the Individuals with Disabilities Education Act (IDEA) beginning in 1990, and in 1994 it was added as a specific disorder in the American Psychiatric Association's (APA) widely used *Diagnostic and Statistical Manual of Mental Disorders,* 4th edition (American Psychiatric Association, 1994).

Definitions of Autism Spectrum Disorders

As is true for other disability types, the language related to autism requires a brief explanation. The traditional term used for this group of students is *autism,* and that is the term used in IDEA and many state special education laws. The term *autism spectrum disorders (ASD)* is used in this discussion because it clarifies that these disorders occur in many forms and cannot be described in any one way; ASD is rapidly becoming the term of choice among professionals in the field. Finally, as you will learn later, in medical circles both autism and Asperger syndrome are considered part of a disability called *pervasive developmental disorder (PDD).*

Federal Definition

When autism was added to IDEA in 1990, it was defined as follows:

> (i) Autism means a developmental disability significantly affecting verbal and nonverbal communication and social interaction, generally evident before age three, that adversely affects a child's educational performance. Other characteristics often associated with autism are engagement in repetitive activities and stereotyped movements, resistance to environmental change or change in daily routines, and unusual responses to sensory experiences.

> (ii) Autism does not apply if a child's educational performance is adversely affected primarily because the child has an emotional disturbance. . . .

> (iii) A child who manifests the characteristics of autism after age three could be diagnosed as having autism if the criteria in paragraph (c)(1)(i) of this section are satisfied. (IDEA 20 U.S.C. §1401 [2004], 20 C.F.R. §300.8[c][1][i–iii])

This definition follows the pattern of IDEA, specifying some essential characteristics of students with the disorders, excluding other disabilities, and identifying the necessity of impact on educational performance. However, it does not provide much detail in terms of understanding the many types of students who might have these disorders.

Definitions of the American Psychiatric Association

Because autism spectrum disorders generally are diagnosed by the medical community using criteria set forth in the *Diagnostic and Statistical Manual of Mental Disorders,* Fourth Edition, Text Revision (*DSM-IV-TR;* American Psychiatric Association, 2000), it is important that you understand these definitions as well as the one provided in IDEA. As noted earlier, the *DSM-IV-TR* classifies autism as a type of **pervasive developmental disorder (PDD),** a term in which children and youth "are characterized by severe and pervasive impairment in several areas of development: reciprocal social interaction skills, communication skills, or the presence of stereotyped behavior, interests, and activities" (p. 69). Subcategories of pervasive

PROFESSIONAL MONITORING TOOL

Council for Exceptional Children

Standard 1 Foundations
. . . historical points of view
. . . issues in definition and identification

Why is it important to know both the IDEA definition and the APA definition of *autism*?

developmental disorders include autistic disorder, Asperger syndrome, and pervasive developmental disorder not otherwise specified (PDD–NOS).

The diagnosis of **autistic disorder** is reserved for individuals who display social interaction and communication impairments, as well as repetitive, stereotypic, and restricted interests and activities prior to thirty-six months of age. This disorder often is accompanied by moderate or severe mental retardation. The specific diagnostic criteria for this disorder are outlined in Figure 12.1.

Another disorder included in autism spectrum disorders is **Asperger syndrome.** The essential feature of Asperger syndrome is an impairment in social interaction. Children with this disorder usually speak fluently by age five, but their language may be unusual (e.g., mixing up the pronouns *I* and *you*) (Frith, 1991). They also are able to demonstrate interest in other people but often are challenged to act appropriately in social situations. The specific

Figure 12.1

DSM-IV-TR Criteria for Autism Disorder

A. A total of six (or more) items from (1), (2), and (3), with at least two from (1), and one each from (2) and (3):
   (1) qualitative impairment in social interaction, as manifested by at least two of the following:
      (a) marked impairment in the use of multiple nonverbal behaviors such as eye-to-eye gaze, facial expression, body postures, and gestures to regulate social interaction
      (b) failure to develop peer relationships appropriate to developmental level
      (c) a lack of spontaneous seeking to share enjoyment, interests, or achievements with other people (e.g., by a lack of showing, bringing, or pointing out objects of interest)
      (d) lack of social or emotional reciprocity
   (2) qualitative impairments in communication as manifested by at least one of the following:
      (a) delay in, or total lack of, the development of spoken language (not accompanied by an attempt to compensate through alternative modes of communication such as gesture or mime)
      (b) in individuals with adequate speech, marked impairment in the ability to initiate or sustain a conversation with others
      (c) stereotyped and repetitive use of language or idiosyncratic language
      (d) lack of varied, spontaneous make-believe play or social imitative play appropriate to developmental level
   (3) restricted, repetitive, and stereotyped patterns of behavior, interests, and activities, as manifested by at least one of the following:
      (a) encompassing preoccupation with one or more stereotyped and restricted patterns of interest that is abnormal either in intensity or focus
      (b) apparently inflexible adherence to specific, nonfunctional routines or rituals
      (c) stereotyped and repetitive motor mannerisms (e.g., hand or finger flapping or twisting, or complex whole-body movements)
      (d) persistent preoccupation with parts of objects
B. Delays or abnormal functioning in at least one of the following areas, with onset prior to age three years: (1) social interaction, (2) language as used in social communication, or (3) symbolic or imaginative play.
C. The disturbance is not better accounted for by Rett's disorder or childhood disintegrative disorder.

Source: Adapted from American Psychiatric Association. (2000). *Diagnostic and statistical manual of mental disorders* (4th ed., Text revision). Washington, DC: Author. Copyright © 2000 American Psychiatric Association. Reprinted with permission.

Figure 12.2

DSM-IV-TR Criteria for Asperger Disorder

A. Qualitative impairment in social interaction, as manifested by at least two of the following:
   (1) marked impairment in the use of multiple nonverbal behaviors such as eye-to-eye gaze, facial expression, body postures, and gestures to regulate social interaction
   (2) failure to develop peer relationships appropriate to developmental level
   (3) a lack of spontaneous seeking to share enjoyment, interests, or achievements with other people (e.g., by a lack of showing, bringing, or pointing out objects of interest to other people)
   (4) lack of social or emotional reciprocity
B. Restricted, repetitive, and stereotyped patterns of behavior, interests, and activities, as manifested by at least one of the following:
   (1) encompassing preoccupation with one or more stereotyped and restricted patterns of interest that is abnormal either in intensity or focus
   (2) apparently inflexible adherence to specific, nonfunctional routines or rituals
   (3) stereotyped and repetitive motor mannerisms (e.g., hand or finger flapping or twisting, or complex whole-body movements)
   (4) persistent preoccupation with parts of objects
C. The disturbance causes clinically significant impairment in social, occupational, or other important areas of functioning.
D. There is no clinically significant general delay in language (e.g., single words used by age two years, communicative phrases used by age three years).
E. There is no clinically significant delay in cognitive development or in the development of age-appropriate self-help skills, adaptive behavior (other than in social interaction), and curiosity about the environment in childhood.
F. Criteria are not met for another specific pervasive development disorder or schizophrenia.

Source: Adapted from American Psychiatric Association. (2000). *Diagnostic and statistical manual of mental disorders* (4th ed., Text revision). Washington, DC: Author. Copyright © 2000 American Psychiatric Association. Reprinted with permission.

DSM-IV-TR criteria for Asperger syndrome are outlined in Figure 12.2. To learn more about ASD, read about Temple Grandin in the Firsthand Account on the next page.

The third category of exceptionality included as part of pervasive developmental disorders, **pervasive developmental disorder not otherwise specified (PDD–NOS),** including atypical autism, is described as follows in the *DSM-IV-TR:*

> This category should be used when there is a severe and pervasive impairment in the development or reciprocal social interaction association with impairment in either verbal or nonverbal communication skills or with the presence of stereotyped behavior, interests, and activities, but the criteria are not met for a specific Pervasive Developmental Disorder. (p. 84)

For example, a child who seems to meet the criteria for autistic disorder but who did not display those characteristics until school age might receive a PDD–NOS classification.

Making Sense of the Definitions

The number of terms associated with autism spectrum disorders can be confusing; their relationship to one another is outlined in Figure 12.3. Keep in mind that IDEA definitions are the ones generally used in public schools. However, the added detail of the *DSM-IV-TR* definitions provides a deeper understanding of these students. Taken together, the definitions should lead you to conclude that if you learn you will be working with a student with autism,

INTERNET RESOURCES
www.asperger.org
The Asperger Syndrome Coalition of the United States is a national nonprofit organization focusing on Asperger syndrome. The site includes links to books, articles, and other resources.

CHECK
Your Learning

What are the similarities and differences among these terms: *autism, Asperger syndrome, pervasive developmental disorder?*

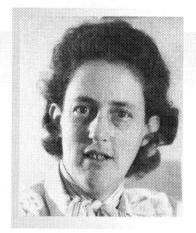

Meet Temple Grandin

Temple Grandin is one of the most famous individuals with autism. She is the author of two books about autism and has also written an autobiography. Now at Colorado State University, she is an associate professor who designs livestock facilities.

I was 2-and-a-half years old when I began to show symptoms of autism: not talking, repetitive behavior and tantrums. Not being able to communicate in words was a great frustration, so I screamed. Loud, high-pitched noises hurt my ears like a dentist's drill hitting a nerve. I would shut out the hurtful stimuli by rocking or staring at sand dribbling through my fingers.

As a child, I was like an animal with no instincts to guide me. I was always observing, trying to work out the best ways to behave, yet I never fit in. When other students swooned over the Beatles, I called their reaction ISP—interesting sociological phenomenon. I wanted to participate but did not know how. I had a few friends who were interested in the same things I was, such as skiing and riding horses. But friendship always revolved around what I did rather than who I was.

Early education and speech therapy pulled me out of the autistic world. Like many autistics, I think in pictures. My artistic abilities became evident when I was in first and second grade, and they were encouraged. I had a good eye for color and painted watercolors of the beach.

But words are like a foreign language to me. I translate them into full-color movies, complete with sound, which run like a videotape in my head. When I was a child, I believed that everybody thought in pictures. Not until I went to college did I realize that some people are completely verbal and think only in words. On one of my earliest jobs, I thought the other engineer was stupid because he could not "see" his mistakes on his drawings. Now I understand his problem was a lack of visual thinking and not stupidity.

Autistics have trouble learning things that cannot be thought about in pictures. The easiest words for an autistic child to learn are nouns because they relate directly to pictures. Spatial words such as *over* and *under* had no meaning for me until I had a visual

> *"Early education and speech therapy pulled me out of my autistic world."*

image to fix them in my memory. Even now, when I hear the word *under* by itself, I automatically picture myself getting under the cafeteria tables at school during an air-raid drill, a common occurrence on the East Coast in the early 1950s.

Teachers who work with autistic children need to understand associative thought patterns. But visual thinking is more than just associations. Concepts can also be formed visually. When I was little, I had to figure out that small dogs were not cats. After looking at both large and small dogs, I realized that they all had the same nose. This was a common visual feature of all the dogs but none of the cats.

I credit my visualization abilities with helping me understand the animals I work with. One of my early livestock design projects was to create a dip-vat and cattle-handling facility for a feedyard in Arizona. A dip vat is a long, narrow, 7-ft.-deep swimming pool through which cattle move in single file. It is filled with pesticide to rid the animals of ticks, lice and other external parasites. In 1978 dip-vat designs were very poor. The animals often panicked because they were forced into the vat down a steep, slick decline. They would refuse to jump into the vat and would sometimes flip over backward and drown.

The first thing I did when I arrived at the feedlot was put myself inside a cow's head and see with its eyes. Because their eyes are on the sides of their head, cattle have wide-angle vision. Those cattle must have felt as if they were being forced to jump down an airplane escape slide into the ocean.

One of my first steps was to convert the ramp from steel to concrete. If I had a calf's body and hooves, I would be very scared to step on a slippery metal ramp. The final design had a concrete ramp at a 25° downward angle. Deep grooves in the concrete provided secure footing. The ramp appeared to enter the water gradually, but in reality it abruptly dropped away below the water's surface. The animals could not see the dropoff because the dip chemicals colored the water. When they stepped out over the water, they quietly fell in because their center of gravity had passed the point of no return.

Owners and managers of feedlots sometimes have a hard time comprehending that if devices such as dip vats and restraint chutes are properly designed, cattle will voluntarily enter them. Because I think in pictures, I assume cattle do too. I can imagine the sensations the animals feel. Today half the cattle in the U.S. are handled in equipment I have designed.

Source: Grandin, T. (2002, May 6). Myself. *Time.* Copyright 2002 Time Inc. Reprinted with permission.

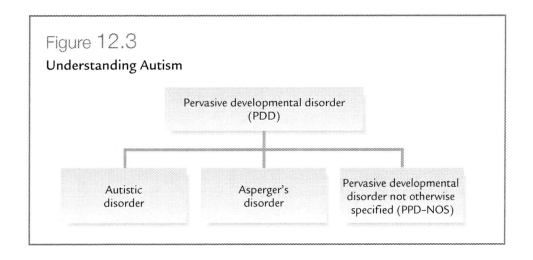

Figure 12.3

Understanding Autism

Pervasive developmental disorder (PDD)
- Autistic disorder
- Asperger's disorder
- Pervasive developmental disorder not otherwise specified (PPD–NOS)

you need to ask many questions before you can begin to understand the strengths and needs of that student.

Prevalence of Autism Spectrum Disorders

The prevalence of autism spectrum disorders is hotly debated. IDEA provides an estimate of the prevalence of autism as 0.18 percent of all students ages six to twenty-one (U.S. Department of Education, 2004), or about 118,000 students. However, that estimate is based on school data which are usually incomplete. The *DSM-IV-TR* reports a prevalence rate of autism of 5 per 10,000, but these data do not address Asperger syndrome or PDD–NOS. Upon studying the children in one town, Scott, Baron-Cohen, Bolton, and Brayne (2002) found that 57 in 10,000 had what they termed *autistic spectrum condition,* which included autism, atypical autism, PDD–NOS, and Asperger syndrome. As you can see from these estimates, no consensus exists on the prevalence of this disability.

Other Prevalence Considerations

Autism exists at approximately the same level in all racial and ethnic groups and among individuals at all income levels. In terms of gender, the rate of autism is four to five times higher in males than in females and the rate of Asperger syndrome is more than five times higher in males (*DSM-IV-TR*). Scott and his colleagues (2002) reported a 4:1 ratio. Agreement seems to exist that autism spectrum disorders are more common in boys than girls, but no single, clear conclusion has been reached to date on the extent of the difference.

Causes of Autism Spectrum Disorders

As with many disabilities, the specific causes of autism spectrum disorders are not truly understood. Professionals generally agree that symptoms of these disabilities are triggered by malfunctions in the brain (Szatmari, Jones, Zwaigenbaum, & MacLean, 1998) and that trauma related to abuse or neglect by caregivers is not a cause (Gillberg & Coleman, 2000). Research on the causes of ASD is leading to rapid changes in the field. To learn about how to find the most current information, access the resources explained in the Professional Edge.

Biological Factors

Researchers currently are focusing on genetic factors related to autism spectrum disorders, speculating that DNA might be responsible for causing developmental dysfunction in the brains of individuals with these disabilities. Simple logic based on this hypothesis is that parents with autism spectrum disorders are likely to have a child with ASD. However, such cases are very rare. Extensive genetic research has shown that genes that might cause autism spectrum disorders are inherited, but the degree of exhibited symptoms varies across family

The Centers for Disease Control and Prevention reported in 2001 that autism and its associated behaviors have been estimated to occur in as many as 1 in 166 individuals.

As you read this chapter, you probably are noticing that many topics related autism spectrum disorders are changing rapidly. More students are being identified with ASD; medical studies are increasing knowledge about the causes of this disability; and studies are under way to identify treatments and interventions that would be most beneficial to students. If you are interested in keeping up with research related to autism, here are resources to use:

■ The Collaborative Programs of Excellence in Autism (CPEA) network is supported by the National Institutes of Health. Its purpose is to conduct research on the causes of autism, and studies underway address genetics, environmental contributions, and immunological factors. The CPEA network also is charged with examining the diagnosis of autism, including early detection, the characteristics of individuals

with autism with an emphasis on behavior and communication, and treatments. You can learn more about this project, visit websites of the participating universities, and learn about recent research results at this website: www.autismresearchnetwork.org/AN/wfCPEA.aspx.

■ The Studies to Advance Autism Research and Treatment (STAART) network also is supported by the National Institutes of Health as part of the Children's Health Act of 2000. This project includes eight centers, and each one is conducting at least three research projects. Like the CPEA network, STAART is exploring the causes, diagnosis, and treatment of autism. However, this network also is researching prevention. You can read about the university members of this network and their recent research results at www.autismresearchnetwork.org/AN/wfSTAART.aspx.

structure (Gillberg & Coleman, 2000). For example, the father of a child identified with an autism spectrum disorder might have subtle characteristics (e.g., as relatively intense concentration) compared with others or odd social skills but function in an acceptable manner in his social life. Evidence also suggests a high frequency of autism spectrum disorders among siblings when compared to other disabilities (Yirmiya, Shaked, & Erel, 2001). Research to date, though, suggests that no single genetic factor is responsible for causing autism spectrum disorders. Rather, multiple genetic factors seem to intricately connect to form a wide range of developmental malfunctions (Gillberg & Coleman, 2000).

Autism Spectrum Disorders and the Brain

If genes are the cause of autism spectrum disorders, what symptoms are found in the brain? Recent technology, such as magnetic resonance imaging (MRI), enables researchers to obtain accurate information about the brain, and a number of brain functions that may trigger autistic symptoms have been observed. For example, individuals with autism spectrum disorders have been found to have abnormalities in the cerebellum, the part of the brain that controls motor coordination, balance, and cognition (Courchesne et al., 2001; Ryu et al., 1999). Similarly, research has surveyed the frontal and temporal lobes; the frontal lobe manages social and cognitive functions (Carper & Courchesne, 2000; Klin, Jones, Schultz, & Volkmar, 2003; Pierce & Courchesne, 2001), while the temporal lobe is involved in understanding facial expressions and in social cues and memory (Hubl et al., 2003; Itier & Taylor, 2004; Passarotti et al., 2003). Researchers generally have found that in these parts of the brain, individuals with autism spectrum disorders have fewer cells, higher cell density, or less volume than in typical individuals (e.g., Sowell, Thompson, Welcome, Henkenius, Toga, & Peterson, 2003).

Environmental Factors

Although the early belief that autism spectrum disorders were caused almost exclusively by environmental factors such as maternal neglect has long been proven untrue, most professionals agree that these factors can influence the number and intensity of symptoms (London & Etzel, 2000). For example, the quality of care by family members and professionals plays an important role in the development of children with autism spectrum disorders (Simpson & Zionts, 2000). A positive, structured environment can significantly improve behavior problems often displayed by these children and youth. In many cases, positive supports, unconditional family love, and similar factors probably have a positive effect on how the symptoms of autism spectrum disorders occur.

Autism and Immunizations

One of the most controversial causal issues related to autism spectrum disorders is immunization, especially that given for measles, mumps, and rubella (MMR) (Wakefield et al., 1998). However, findings to date on the causal relationship between MMR shots and autism spectrum disorders do not warrant stopping these immunizations. For example, most of the authors of a key study on this topic have retracted their original conclusions, now indicating that no causal link was established (Centers for Disease Control and Prevention, 2004), a position that is also supported by experts from the Institute of Medicine and the American Academy of Pediatrics. Further, several studies have completely refuted the autism–MMR vaccination link (Dales, Hammer, & Smith, 2001; Stratton, Gable, Shetty, & McCormick, 2001).

What Are the Characteristics of Individuals with Autism Spectrum Disorders?

Beginning at an early age and typically continuing throughout the life span, individuals with autism spectrum disorders have difficulty relating appropriately to others. They usually have a wide range of language and communication disorders. Many have an obsessive insistence on environmental sameness and are well known for their atypical and often difficult-to-understand behavior, including stereotypic, repetitive, and self-stimulatory responses (American Psychiatric Association, 2000). However, each student with these disabilities may have a unique combination of strengths and needs.

PROFESSIONAL MONITORING TOOL

Council for Exceptional Children

Standard 2 Development and Characteristics
. . . similarities and differences of individuals

Michael Newman/PhotoEdit

Children with autism spectrum disorders often are identified before they begin school. With early intervention and ongoing support, they often can successfully learn with their peers.

Students with Autism Spectrum Disorders

PROFESSIONAL MONITORING TOOL

Council for Exceptional Children

Standard 2 Development and Characteristics
. . . educational implications of exceptionalities

Bernard Rimland founded the National Society for Children and Adults with Autism in 1968. In 1992, he reported a 400 percent increase in the diagnosis of autism over the previous twelve years.

Cognitive and Academic Characteristics

Children and youth with ASD often have irregular patterns of cognitive and educational strengths and deficits, with the majority of individuals with autism disorder having some level of intellectual disability and those with Asperger syndrome having average to above-average ability (Barnhill, Hagiwara, Myles, & Simpson, 2000; Jordan, 1999). Although children and youth with autism share some characteristics with students with other disabilities, their unique features set them apart and sometimes create significant challenges for those who serve them. These distinguishing characteristics include overreliance on rote memory, problems with theory of mind, and problem solving challenges.

Rote Memory

Rote memory is the ability to easily remember things without necessarily knowing what they mean. Have you ever memorized a phrase in a different language or a mathematical formula so that you could say it or write it when you needed to—even if you did not understand what it meant? Those are examples of rote memory. Although rote memory usually would be considered an asset, it can be a great liability for students with autism spectrum disorders. Because they have well-developed rote memory skills, students with these disabilities can give the impression that they understand certain concepts when in fact they do not. For example, a student with autism may hear certain words or phrases in conversation and then use them in a rote manner that mimics comprehension. This parroting gives the inaccurate impression that the student has well-developed higher-level comprehension skills.

Rote memory may be a disadvantage for students with autism spectrum disorders in another way as well. Adults often assume that having strong rote memory skills means that students can remember, at any time, pieces of information or events. But this is not true for many individuals with autism spectrum disorders. Although chunks of information are stored in memory, students with this exceptionality may have trouble retrieving them. Often, a question worded in a specific manner must be used to prompt retrieval from memory. For example, Devon, a twelve-year-old boy with autism, has memorized all of the items at a fast-food restaurant. However, unless the server asks "May I take your order?" Devon cannot recall what he wants to order and may repeat all the items on the menu. The server's words need to be precise in order for Devon to access the information he has memorized.

Theory of Mind

One of the core cognitive deficits of autism spectrum disorders concerns **theory of mind.** This relatively new explanation of autism is based on the belief that people with these disorders do not truly understand that others have their own thoughts and points of view and that people with autism face challenges in understanding others' beliefs and emotions (Baron-Cohen et al., 1999; Begeer, Rieffe, & Terwogt, 2003; Travis, Sigman, & Ruskin, 2001). Difficulties with theory of mind can be seen when individuals with autism spectrum disorders have difficulty explaining their own behaviors, predicting others' emotions or behaviors, comprehending others' perspectives, understanding how behavior affects others' thoughts and feelings, participating in conversations, and distinguishing fact from fiction (Myles & Southwick, 2005).

"Some professionals contend that it is theory-of-mind deficit that sets individuals with autism spectrum disorders apart from those with other disabilities."

Some professionals contend that it is theory-of-mind deficit that sets individuals with autism spectrum disorders apart from those with other disabilities. For example, Robert, a high school sophomore with Asperger syndrome, could not understand why he was in trouble for loudly announcing that his history teacher had bad breath. In his mind, he was only telling the truth.

Problem Solving

Many students with autism spectrum disorders have access to only one problem solving strategy for a particular situation and use it consistently even if the situation changes and regardless of whether it is successful. Difficulty retrieving information or strategies may make problem solving even more challenging (Scheuermann & Webber, 2002). For example, when Alex could not find his toothbrush, he discontinued brushing his teeth. It did not occur to him to ask his mother to purchase a new toothbrush or to help him to find the old one. Although learners with autism spectrum disorders may be able to recite several problem-solving strategies and verbally report that they can be generalized, often they are not able to recall any of these strategies when needed. That is, even though Connor has learned that if he is not sure how to find his classroom he can ask another student, ask an adult, or look to see if he is near the office and ask someone there, when he suddenly becomes disoriented, he cannot remember what to do and begins screaming.

Problem solving becomes even more difficult if abstract concepts are involved. Making the situation more complex, the problem solving deficits of some students, particularly those with Asperger syndrome, may not be recognized easily. Their pedantic style, advanced vocabulary, and grammatically perfect responses often mask their skill levels. For these reasons, by the time they realize that a problem exists, they often are so confused or angry that their reactions are inappropriate, often involving tantrums or withdrawal.

Motivation

In addition to the other cognitive and academic difficulties that students with autism spectrum disorders face, motivation can be a serious issue. Students with these disabilities generally are interested only in a small number of activities or rewards. Sometimes professionals and parents struggle to figure out what these interests are, but without warning, these students also may completely change their preferences. Taken together, these factors make motivating students with autism spectrum disorders an ongoing challenge (Baker, Horner, & Sappington, 2000; Gagnon, 2001). In the Firsthand Account on the next page, Kelly Prestia, an occupational therapist, talks about the complexities of working with students with autism spectrum disorders and her determination to find strategies effective for addressing her students' needs.

Social and Emotional Characteristics

The social and emotional challenges that students with autism spectrum disorders encounter are directly related to their other special needs. In particular, language disorders, unconventional language use, and immaturity often characterize these students.

Language Disorders

Many students with autism spectrum disorders have extraordinary difficulties in language development. This, in turn, has a significant negative impact on their abilities to interact successfully with others. For example, they may experience delays in developing language. In addition, they may fail to use language to communicate, or they may lack the desire to interact with others.

Several examples of language disorders can clarify how important this area is for students with autism spectrum disorders. Students may have problems with **proxemics**—that is, knowing the socially acceptable distance to maintain between people during conversation. These students may stand closer to or farther away from another person than is customary. They also may stare intensely at another person while interacting, making that person very uncomfortable. In contrast, some students may fail to make any eye contact at all, looking to the side or up or down during conversation. This makes it difficult for the other person to judge whether the student is engaged in the topic being discussed. In addition, students may fail to understand or respond to others' gestures and facial expressions during communication. As a result, they may not notice that the other person is bored or that the person wants to ask a question.

FIRSTHAND ACCOUNT

The Joys and Challenges of Working with Children with Autism Spectrum Disorders

Students with autism benefit from the services of many different school professionals. Kelly, an occupational therapist, shares her experiences in working with these learners.

When I entered the school system as an occupational therapist, I was surprised by the number of students on my caseload with a diagnosis of autism. Approximately 25 percent of my caseload consisted of students with autism. That percentage continued to increase over the next several years. The continuous increase of students with autism both intrigued and challenged me personally and professionally.

The intense needs of my students with autism were overwhelming at first. I wanted to tackle every problem and every need of these students but was unsure which approach was best. Was it a sensory need? Was it a physical difficulty? Was it a behavioral problem? How many minutes per day or per week of therapy would resolve this problem? I quickly realized that the only approach I could use was to understand that each child, each behavior, and each need might have a different foundation. This made me not only an

> *"I wanted to tell the world about autism and the potential that these students have."*

occupational therapist but also a detective, negotiator, and advocate.

After seeing success with several of my students, I wanted to tell the world about autism and the potential that these students have, but everyone else seemed content to focus on the challenges the students faced, rather than their potential. I turned my frustration into determination, and I developed presentations, handouts, and resources for anyone who would listen. I had a wonderful team of special educators who supported my vision of bringing positive attention to students with autism in the educational environment.

Experience, exposure, and education have molded my approach to providing therapy and intervention to students with autism in the school setting. I learn something new each day and believe that I will never have all the answers. My passion for these students only strengthens with every challenge I encounter.

Communicative Intent

One characteristic that is somewhat unique to individuals with autism spectrum disorders concerns problems with **communicative intent.** That is, these students often do not communicate in order to obtain the attention of others, and they may not communicate for social purposes (Scheuermann & Webber, 2002). Approximately 50 percent of individuals with autism are nonverbal; that is, they have few or no verbal language skills.

Those who do have verbal skills often engage in **echolalia,** repeating words and phrases that have been uttered by someone else with little or no understanding of their conventional meanings. Students also may have problems with pronoun reversals, using *you* for *I* and vice versa. They also may lack voice tone or inflection. Known as **prosody** problems, individuals with autism may use a monotone or sing-song tone of voice, regardless of the intended message (Shriberg et al., 2001).

Other Language Problems

Students at the higher end of the autism spectrum—those with Asperger syndrome—often have unusual traits in their language skills (Barnhill, 2001; Frith, 1991; Janzen, 2003; Wing, 1981). For example, Louise, a six-year-old with Asperger syndrome, told her mother that she "waved" her clothes on the bathroom floor. She was using the word *waved* instead of *left.* Her reason was that you "wave when you leave."

Many students cannot comprehend language related to abstract ideas such as democracy and justice. They also may struggle with understanding and correctly using figures of speech such as metaphors, idioms, parables, and allegories and grasping the meaning and intent

Andy Levin/Photo Researchers

An area of challenge for most students with autism spectrum disorders is understanding how to interact in social situations.

of rhetorical questions. For example, when Rick was told, "Put your best foot forward," he looked down and asked which foot was his best foot!

Students with Asperger syndrome also may have good structural language skills, such as clear pronunciation and correct syntax, but poor pragmatic communication abilities. For example, some students may repeat the same phrase over and over, talk with exaggerated inflections or in a monotone and droning style, discuss at length a single topic that is of little interest to others, or experience difficulty in sustaining a conversation unless it focuses exclusively on a particular narrowly defined topic. These communication problems are not surprising, given that effective communication requires that individuals have mutually shared topics to communicate about and are willing to listen as well as to talk.

Immaturity

When you think of an individual whom you consider mature, what characteristics come to mind? Maturity is often assessed by actions in social situations. To be socially adept, people must be able to perceive and understand social cues such as frowns, smiles, boredom, and other expressions of emotion. They must be able to think clearly about their own behaviors and the behaviors of others. Because of the many language disorders and communication challenges experienced by students with autism (including those with Asperger syndrome), they often make statements that do not make sense or give inappropriate responses to the questions of others. They also experience frustration when their communication does not accomplish its purpose. As a result, these students often seem extraordinarily naïve or immature.

Behavior Characteristics

A final domain to consider in characterizing students with autism spectrum disorders is behavior. Some of the challenges these students may have include self-stimulatory behaviors, difficulty with generalizations, and sensory responses.

Self-Stimulatory Behaviors

Self-stimulatory behaviors may involve rocking, hand flapping, and any other repetitive, stereotyped behavior patterns that appear to have no apparent function. These behaviors, common for students with autism, tend to stigmatize them, interfering not only with social acceptance and integration but also with learning. Other similar behavioral challenges, such as self-injurious behaviors (e.g., biting, head banging), also can be serious issues; however, such behaviors are relatively uncommon.

Research Notes

Robertson, Chamberlain, and Kasari (2003) studied the relationship between general education teachers and elementary students with autism. An inverse relationship was found—that is, teachers' perceptions were more positive when students exhibited lower levels of behavior problems.

Council for
Exceptional
Children

Standard 4 Instructional
Strategies
. . . maintenance and generalization of skills
Standard 2 Development and
Characteristics
. . . educational implications of
exceptionalities

Generalization Difficulties

A major challenge facing educators and others who work with students with autism spectrum disorders relates to their difficulty in transferring information to new settings, individuals, and conditions. As a result, a child who is able to perform a written task in one classroom cannot be assumed to be able to perform the same task correctly in another classroom. To address generalization, professionals must spend considerable time developing strategies for enabling students to use information and skills flexibly. These strategies may include practicing skills in community and regular classroom settings (Simpson & Myles, 1998).

Sensory Issues

Students with autism spectrum disorders experience a myriad of sensory processing issues. That is, they have difficulty with the (1) tactile, (2) vestibular, (3) proprioception, (4) visual, (5) auditory, (6) gustatory, and (7) olfactory senses. Figure 12.4 provides an overview of each of the sensory systems, including its location and function. The figure also provides examples of how students with autism may experience difficulties related to the senses. For example, you may know a person with autism who can hear sounds that are not discernible to those without autism or who finds the feeling of a tag inside a shirt very painful. Because the visual perception area tends to be a strength for students with autism spectrum disorders, visual supports often are used to assist in learning (Myles & Savner, 2000).

Sensory difficulties affect all areas of learning. Many students with autism spectrum disorders require occupational therapy to address these issues and to receive the maximum benefit from instruction (Cook & Dunn, 1998). All professionals who work with students with autism spectrum disorders should be aware of the impact of sensory issues on behavior and achievement (Myles, Cook, Miller, Rinner, & Robbins, 2000).

How Are Autism Spectrum Disorders Identified?

The definition of *autism* in IDEA is very general, and so it is common for this disorder to be diagnosed using the criteria in *DSM-IV-TR*. However, identifying these students is rather complex because the symptoms occur in so many different ways. As for all students, a team, including the parents, must participate in the assessment and eligibility process.

Assessment Practices and Procedures

Many students are identified as having an autism spectrum disorder before they enter school. Assessing for this disability usually includes checking whether a student displays the characteristics known to be associated with autism spectrum disorders. In addition, information is gathered concerning the child's cognitive, academic, and adaptive behavior skills. Finally, the child's developmental history is reviewed and observations of behavior are assessed.

Assessment Related to Characteristics of Autism

Deciding whether a student has the characteristics of an autism spectrum disorder involves both formal and informal assessment. Psychologists and psychiatrists may use standardized instruments that are designed just for this purpose. One example is the Autism Diagnostic Interview–Revised (ADI–R) (Lord, Rutter, & Le Couteur, 1994). However, teachers and other professionals also may be asked to complete rating scales designed to screen students for the disability. Two examples of these rating scales are the Modified Checklist for Autism in Toddlers (M-CHAT) (Robbins, Fein, Barton, & Green, 2001) and the Asperger Syndrome Diagnostic Scale (ASDS) (Myles, Bock, & Simpson, 2001).

Figure 12.4

Understanding Sensory Systems and Autism

Students with autism often experience difficulties related to sensory processing. This figure explains each of the sensory systems, its location, and its functions. It also provides examples of the sensory problems that may affect individuals with autism.

System	Location	Function	Example of Sensory Problems
Tactile (touch)	Skin—density of cell distribution varies throughout the body. Areas of greatest density include mouth, hands, and genitals.	Provides information about the environment and object qualities (e.g., touch, pressure, texture, hard, soft, sharp, dull, heat, cold, pain).	Feel of fabric texture on skin may be painful; student may not feel heat or cold and so is more at risk for injuries.
Vestibular (balance)	Inner ear—stimulated by head movements and input from other senses, especially vision.	Provides information about where our body is in space and whether we or our surroundings are moving. Tells about speed and direction of movement.	Student may lose balance more easily than classmates or experience difficulty in some games or activities (e.g., jumping rope, playing basketball).
Proprioception (body awareness)	Muscles and joints—activated by muscle contractions and movement.	Provides information about where a certain body part is and how it is moving.	Student may seem clumsy, bumping into desks in narrow aisles or knocking crayons off a table.
Visual (sight)	Retina of the eye—stimulated by light.	Provides information about objects and persons. Helps us define boundaries as we move through time and space.	Student may be very sensitive to bright lights such as those found in classrooms.
Auditory (hearing)	Inner ear—stimulated by air or sound waves.	Provides information about sounds in the environment (loud, soft, high, low, near, far).	Certain sounds (e.g., fire alarm) may be too loud for the student; student may focus on sounds others do not attend to (e.g., electrical hum from classroom equipment).
Gustatory (taste)	Chemical receptors in the tongue—closely associated with the olfactory (smell) system.	Provides information about different types of taste (e.g., sweet, sour, bitter, salty, spicy).	Student may refuse to eat anything except certain preferred foods.
Olfactory (smell)	Chemical receptors in the nasal structure—closely associated with the gustatory system.	Provides information about different types of smell (e.g., musty, acrid, putrid, flowery, pungent).	Student may have a strong reaction to certain scents (e.g., perfume, materials used in a science experiment).

Source: Myles, B. S., Cook, K. T., Miller, N. E., Rinner, L., & Robbins, L. A. (2001). *Asperger syndrome and sensory issues: Practical solutions for making sense of the world* (p. 5). Shawnee Mission, KS: Autism Asperger Publishing. Reprinted with permission from Autism Asperger Publishing Co.

One additional evaluation informs professionals about whether a student has an autism spectrum disorder: sensory assessment. Usually administered by a trained professional, an instrument such as the Sensory Profile (Dunn, 1999) can be used to pinpoint specific sensory problems such as the ones about which you have already read.

Cognitive Ability, Academic Achievement, and Adaptive Skills

Part of the assessment for autism spectrum disorders is similar to the assessments completed for students who may have other disabilities. That is, individual intelligence tests are administered, as are both formal and informal assessments of academic achievement using standardized achievement tests and curriculum-based measures. Language assessment often is part of this process because most students with autism spectrum disorders have language-related delays or problems. In addition, students' adaptive behaviors are measured, including tasks related to self-help (e.g., dressing, brushing teeth) and functioning in the community (e.g., ordering in a fast-food restaurant, riding a bus).

Developmental Measures

Because autism spectrum disorders are considered developmental disabilities, comprehensive assessment also must explore developmental characteristics. Using an instrument such as the Psychoeducational Profile 3 (PEP 3) (Schopler, Lansing, Reichler, & Marcus, 2005), a professional can ask parents about their child's fine- and gross-motor skill development, language development, and related areas. For older students, questions may be asked concerning vocational skills, independent functioning, leisure activities, functional communication, and interpersonal behavior.

Behavior Assessment

Students with autism spectrum disorders nearly always have behavior problems. These behaviors usually are assessed by asking parents, teachers, and others who interact with the student to complete a behavior checklist, a procedure that is also used for students with emotional disabilities.

In addition, a functional behavior analysis also may be helpful for determining the relationships between behavior and the environment for students with autism. As you may recall, the functional behavior analysis usually involves investigating antecedent events and their consequences based on a previously developed hypothesis about what is causing a behavior. Through this process, environmental, social, and communicative factors that might trigger problem behaviors are revealed and interventions can then be planned (Aspy & Grossman, 2006).

Eligibility

After assessment data are gathered, the team of educators, medical professionals, parents, and related services personnel address the questions that guide special education decision making:

- Does a disability exist?
- Does it have a negative impact on educational performance?
- Is the student eligible for special education services?
- Will the student benefit from those services?

As for all students with disabilities, the most important part of the identification process is not what label is assigned but what services are provided to meet the student's needs. Continuous data collection, monitoring, and analysis through assessments and flexible interventions are essential to effectively educate such a student.

INTERNET RESOURCES
www.teacch.com/ teacch.htm
TEACCH (Treatment and Education of Autistic and related Communication-handicapped CHildren) is an organization at the University of North Carolina–Chapel Hill. Its mission is to ensure that individuals receive high-quality interventions. It provides extensive training to professionals and support to parents.

PROFESSIONAL MONITORING TOOL

Council for Exceptional Children

Standard 8 Assessment . . . administer formal and informal assessments
Standard 1 Foundations . . . issues, assurances, and due process rights

How Do Learners with Autism Spectrum Disorders Receive Their Education?

Because children and youth with autism spectrum disorders differ greatly in their skill levels, their educational options vary as well. Generally, however, early and intensive education provides the best outcome.

Early Childhood

The National Research Council (2001) studied educational programs that provide early intervention services to young children with autism. It found many instructional approaches and many variations regarding the setting in which the program was offered. For example, one program used the home as the instructional setting, and one used a school-only model. The programs shared the following features:

- Intervention prior to age three
- Twenty to forty-five hours of intervention per week
- Active family involvement
- Highly trained staff providing services to children with autism and their families
- Ongoing assessment of children's progress
- A systematically implemented curriculum
- A highly supportive teaching and learning environment
- A focus on communication goals and other developmental areas
- Plans to help students apply skills they learn in a variety of settings and to maintain their skills over time
- Individualized interventions for each student
- Plans to assist the young child and family transition from early childhood services to school-age programs

dimensions of
DIVERSITY

At least one study (Mandell, Listerud, Levy, & Pinto-Martin, 2002) has found that African American children receiving Medicaid benefits tend to be diagnosed with autism approximately two years later than comparable white children.

In 2001, the Council for Exceptional Children's Division for Developmental Disabilities adopted ASD as an area of emphasis.

Robin Sachs/PhotoEdit

Success for students with autism spectrum disorders is accomplished through the collaborative efforts of professionals and parents.

Figure 12.5

Educational Placements of Students Ages Six to Twenty-One Who Have Autism Spectrum Disorders (in percentages)

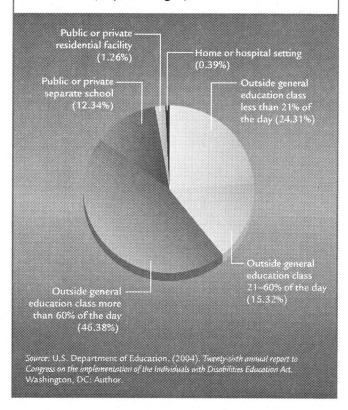

Public or private residential facility (1.26%)

Home or hospital setting (0.39%)

Public or private separate school (12.34%)

Outside general education class less than 21% of the day (24.31%)

Outside general education class 21–60% of the day (15.32%)

Outside general education class more than 60% of the day (46.38%)

Source: U.S. Department of Education. (2004). *Twenty-sixth annual report to Congress on the implementation of the Individuals with Disabilities Education Act.* Washington, DC: Author.

As you review this list, how unique do you think it is for young children who have autism spectrum disorders? Which of the items would apply to high-quality services for all young children with disabilities?

Elementary and Secondary School Services

According to current statistics, nearly half of the students with autism are educated primarily in a setting away from the general education classroom (U.S. Department of Education, 2004). Figure 12.5 illustrates the range of settings in which these students are located.

You should be aware that comparable data for students identified as having Asperger syndrome are not available because this group of students is not treated as a distinct category in the reporting provisions of IDEA. If they are determined to have a disability according to IDEA criteria, they are often counted in the general category of autism. In general, these students are served in general education classrooms with or without paraprofessional support as well as in resource rooms and self-contained settings that serve children and youth with learning disabilities or emotional and behavior disorders.

Inclusive Practices

Although no single approach is always correct when deciding how students with disabilities should receive an education, a trend is emerging to support students with autism spectrum disorders in the general education setting more often than was common in the past. One of the few models available to guide professionals implementing inclusive practices for these students is the autism inclusion collaboration model.

Exploring the Autism Inclusion Collaboration Model

The *autism inclusion collaboration model* is designed to support general educators in their work with students with autism through collaboration with special educators and ancillary staff. The model has the following four components (Simpson & Myles, 1998):

■ *Environmental and curricular modifications and general education classroom support.* For children and youth with autism, a variety of modifications and supports are particularly important because of these students' unique needs. The supports may include availability of appropriately trained support personnel, reduced class size, access to collaborative problem solving relationships, adequate teacher planning time, professional development, and availability of paraprofessionals.

■ *Attitudinal and social support.* Administrators, general and special education teachers, students with autism spectrum disorders, and their nondisabled peers must all understand and support each other in the educational system. Success depends on many types of collaboration.

■ *Coordinated team commitment.* This component includes opportunities for planning and carrying out programs across all environments. It also recognizes that educational professionals need support to ensure that students' needs are met in all environments. For example, if a student needs a visual schedule (explained later in this chapter), a special educator might be responsible for making that schedule available on small cards that can be carried from the classroom to the lunchroom to the gym.

■ *Home–school collaboration.* For successful inclusion, educators and parents must work together in a strong partnership to ensure that a comprehensive program is implemented for the student with an autism spectrum disorder and that the skills learned at school are generalized at home and in the community (Myles & Simpson, 1998).

Adequate supports can make inclusive practices a real possibility for some students with autism spectrum disorders. When educated in general education classrooms, these students can learn from their peers and readily access the general curriculum. Jean Paul Bovee, an adult with autism who describes his experiences in the Inclusion Matters on the next page, supports an inclusive model for students with autism spectrum disorders. He received his education in the general education classroom and attributes much of his life success to having been a full participant in that setting.

Transition and Adulthood

Individuals with autism spectrum disorders often have difficulty learning skills that their nondisabled peers learn with little or no formal instruction (Scheuermann & Webber, 2002). For example, students with autism may not know how to approach another student to ask him to play. Adults with autism may not know how to talk to a supervisor with respect. They may not realize the need for both formal and informal communication techniques, depending on the situation (Gutstein & Whitney, 2002). Thus, careful planning for the transition to adulthood is necessary for these students. That is, although teaching work skills is important, all areas of adulthood need to be addressed in a transition plan. Generally identified areas of importance include self-help skills such as eating, dressing, personal hygiene, and grooming; play, leisure, and recreation skills; social skills; sexuality; home management skills such as bill paying, grocery shopping, and cleaning; and vocational skills (Scheuermann & Webber, 2002). Stewart (2001) calls these topics *community membership skills,* and she emphasizes that they should be taught long before the student's formal transition steps begin at age sixteen. One model of life span issues for community membership is included in Figure 12.6.

Figure 12.6
Essential Components of Community Living

Making the transition from childhood to adulthood can be challenging. For students with autism, Stewart (2001) recommends that families and professionals consider all the following areas which can lead to successful transition:

- Family and individual goals and preferences
- Residential preferences or plans
- Communication needs support plan
- Health and medical needs and services
- Community supports specific to purpose and place
- Community access and participation plans
- Environmental and physical supports (setting specific)
- Family and individual social supports (formal, informal, natural)
- Transportation plan (linked to purposes)
- Education plan
- Recreation and leisure plans
- Transition plan
- Employment plan
- Funding sources
- Person or agency coordinating
- Team members' roles and responsibilities

Source: Adapted from Stewart, R. (2001). Essential components of community living: A life span approach. *Indiana Resource Center for Autism Reporter, 5*(1), 18–27.

Inclusion Matters

The Perspectives of Jean Paul Bovee

Professionals have the responsibility of ensuring that their students are educated in the least restrictive environment. Sometimes it helps to remember that students grow up to be adults who remember their experiences well. Here is a perspective on inclusive practices from Jean Paul Bovee, an adult with autism.

When I started kindergarten in the fall of 1973, I was in a school and a classroom of typical children. When I graduated in 1986 from Seymour High School, I was still in classes with typical peers. The point is that I was in typical classrooms all the way through school. This did not happen naturally; decisions had to be made and there was never a guarantee that I would stay there.

I started school before P.L. 94-142 was passed, and so there was not a federal mandate at that time that required schools to teach children like me. At the time, my family lived in northern Minnesota, and I attended a small school. We were fortunate that Minnesota was and is a leader in public education. My mother volunteered as a teaching assistant to work in my classroom while I was in kindergarten, first, and second grade. That made it possible for the teachers to spend more time working with me. I had an educational diagnosis of learning disabilities—autism was not an educational diagnosis in those days, and I also received speech therapy. I had this kind of help through fifth grade.

Between my second- and third-grade years, my family moved to Winona, Missouri. It took a little while to get used to a new school. I was not comfortable in my class, so I went back to the back of the room and started reading the encyclopedias. My teacher had never taught a child like me, and she did not know what to do. I would stay in the back and read those encyclopedias except when it was time for lunch or time to go home. This went on for three days and part of a fourth. On the third day of this, my teacher and the principal decided that I would be placed in the classroom for students with mental retardation because they had no other place to put me. They sent a note home with me to my mom. She came to school the next day and told me to get up, get back to my seat, and pay attention to the teacher. She also made it very clear that putting me in the special education classroom for reading encyclopedias was not an option. After that, there was never any more talk about taking me out of the general education classroom (other than to get LD help and speech therapy for an hour a day for each).

In sixth grade, my teacher, Mrs. Ince, told Mom that she could handle me in the classroom full time. She kept my attention by slamming a paddle on my desk and putting my desk up in front of hers. I would not daydream or doze off because she would definitely keep my attention. She had faith in me and thought that I could do well.

In junior high and high school, I took college-prep courses because I was sure that I would go on to college. I did take typing which was a big help for me, but the class was modified so the focus was on learning rather than speed typing. In most other classes, I did well—other than math, that is, which was the bane of my existence.

Having been included in general education classrooms my whole educational experience, I believe, was the best thing for me. Once I was more aware of what I was supposed to do as far as homework and tests were concerned, I did much better. Socially, I was different from my peers, but I learned from them. Inclusion was a good thing for me, and it helped me as far as being able to do things in the world. Just as importantly, it also helped my peers to realize that there are people like me in this world.

Autism-Europe prepared a Charter of Rights for People with Autism, and in 1996, a written declaration of their rights was approved by the European Parliament. This document states that people with autism have the same rights enjoyed by all European Union citizens.

Schelvan, Swanson, and Smith (2005) discuss incorporating skills in transition planning for adulthood in areas such as postsecondary education, integrated employment, independent living, and community participation.

Gerhardt's (2001) perspective on transition is particularly relevant for students with autism spectrum disorders. He notes that transition should go beyond basic needs and involve such quality-of-life skills as personal control, exposure to opportunities in all transition areas, and access to choices. It is essential that individuals with autism spectrum disorders be provided with these options.

What Are Recommended Educational Practices for Students with Autism Spectrum Disorders?

Surprisingly little research has been conducted to identify best-practice interventions for students with autism spectrum disorders (National Research Council, 2001). Generally, though, recommended practices include early intervention, intensive instruction, planned but brief instructional periods, and sufficient one-to-one or small-group instruction to meet students' goals (National Research Council, 2001). All of these practices are designed to address the social, behavior, and sensory challenges of these students, and many of the practices benefit other students with disabilities as well. Similarly, many of the academic interventions introduced for students with learning disabilities, emotional disabilities, intellectual disabilities, and communication disorders also enhance learning for students with autism spectrum disorders.

Environmental Supports

Environmental supports are changes in a student's surroundings that are considered key to effective programming. Some of the most common environmental supports include visual supports, a home base, and assistive technology.

Visual Supports

Students with autism spectrum disorders benefit from visually presented information because it is more concrete than auditory information and allows for greater processing time. One example for younger students involves labeling items (e.g., *desk, door, table*) in the general or special education classroom in order to help expand these students' vocabularies. Another example is a *visual schedule,* which presents a list of activities using a combination of icons, photographs, words, or clock faces to help students anticipate upcoming events and activities, develop an understanding of time, and predict change.

Task cards are similar. They help students with Asperger syndrome recall academic content, routines, or social skills. Typically presented on business-card-size paper, the task card lists the steps the student must follow in a series of directive statements, expressed in concise language. For adolescents, task cards can provide an overview of the routines and teacher expectations in each class. For younger children, a task card may outline four conversation starters that can be used with peers during lunch. Examples of visual schedules and task cards that special education teachers or general education teachers might use are included in the Specialized Instruction on the next page.

The *travel card* is yet another type of visual support for students with autism spectrum disorders in middle or high school settings (Carpenter, 2001; Jones & Jones, 1995). This type of card provides an efficient and effective means for dealing with the complex scheduling and shortage of time for personalized communication that characterizes secondary schools. As you read about travel cards in the Specialized Instruction, think about how they would be helpful to parents, teachers, and students.

Home Base

Home base is a place students can go when they are beginning to feel anxious or upset and need to calm themselves (Myles & Adreon, 2001; Myles & Southwick, 2005). For example, students with autism spectrum disorders can go to a home base to (1) plan or review the day's events; (2) escape the stress of the classroom; (3) prevent a "meltdown"; or (4) regain control if a tantrum, rage, or meltdown has occurred. A resource room or counselor's office commonly is used as the home base. When a student feels the need to leave the classroom, whether general education or special education, she can take assignments to the home base and work in that less stressful environment.

School personnel frequently schedule the school day of students with autism spectrum disorders so that they begin at the home base and have frequent stops there throughout the day. This creates a consistent student–teacher relationship and specifies a place to go when the need arises. It also can help students participate in general education by providing them with breaks from the social stress of the classroom.

Assistive Technology

You have learned about the importance of assistive technology for many students with disabilities, and you probably can surmise that students with autism spectrum disorders access

PROFESSIONAL MONITORING TOOL

Council for Exceptional Children

Standard 9 Professional and Ethical Practice
. . . demonstrate commitment to developing highest quality of life
Standard 5 Learning Environments and Social Interactions
. . . supports needed for integration
Standard 4 Instructional Strategies
. . . use instructional strategies and materials according to characteristics

fyi

Ivor Lovaas and colleagues introduced intensive behavioral programs for children with autism spectrum disorders in 1966. Today, you may still hear people refer to *Lovaas treatment.*

PROFESSIONAL MONITORING TOOL

Council for Exceptional Children

Standard 7 Instructional Planning
. . . incorporate instructional and assistive technology

Visual Supports

Students with autism spectrum disorders often benefit by having tasks, schedules, and activities clearly explained to them ahead of time. Using words, pictures, or a combination of both, professionals can prepare students for the school day, help them know what happens next, clarify expectations, and foster independence. Two examples of visual supports are given here. What is the purpose of each? Try making a simple visual support for a student with autism. You might think about one of the students described at the beginning of the chapter or another student with whom you are familiar.

Get Ready for Lunch	
1. Put books in desk	_____
2. Put math papers in blue folder	_____
3. Put pencils in pencil case	_____
4. Get lunch from backpack	_____
5. Sit at desk	_____
6. Look at teacher and wait	_____
7. When the teacher calls my name, give her this paper and get in line	_____

Source: S. T. Moore. (2002). *Asperger syndrome and the elementary school experience: Practical solutions for academic and social difficulties.* Shawnee Mission, KS: Autism Asperger Publishing. Reprinted by permission of Autism Asperger Publishing Co.

Today Is Monday, April 16, 2000	
Attendance	8:15
Math	8:20–9:00
Reading and Centers	9:00–10:00
Spelling	10:00–10:15
Writing	10:15–10:45
Assembly	10:45–11:30
Lunch and Recess	11:30–12:15
Music	12:30–1:15
Science	1:15–1:50
Read Aloud	1:50–2:20
Journal	2:20–2:25
Get Ready to Go	2:25
Bell Rings	2:30

Sometimes the schedule changes

INTERNET RESOURCES
http://autism researchinstitute.com
The Autism Research Institute provides a comprehensive and well-organized bank of research-based information for professionals and parents. The links to information on a variety of hot topics are particularly useful.

technology, too. These students may use items that other students with disabilities use such as adapted eating utensils, talking calculators, pencil grips, voice output devices, audible word-scanning devices, and talking word processors with text.

In a novel use of technology, Hagiwara (1998) created a multimedia program that successfully taught students self-help and on-task skills. Specifically, the program contained videotaped segments that showed students engaging in appropriate target behaviors as well as a story-type format that told the students the steps and outcomes for completing their individually targeted skills (Hagiwara & Myles, 1999). You can read more about this innovative assistive technology in the Technology Notes.

Instructional Practices

Many instructional strategies have been demonstrated to be effective with students with autism spectrum disorders. Three examples that illustrate successful strategies are priming, discrete trial training, and prompting.

Priming

Priming was devised by Wilde, Koegel, and Koegel (1992) to familiarize students with academic material prior to its use in school, reduce stress and anxiety by bringing predictability

Travel Card

As students move from elementary school to middle and then high school, ensuring clear communication becomes more difficult. More teachers work with the students; the schools are larger; and maintaining close communication with parents can become more challenging. A travel card is designed to support students with autism spectrum disorders who are in middle schools or high schools. It is designed to

- Increase appropriate student behavior across environments
- Facilitate collaboration among teachers
- Increase awareness among teachers of the academic, behavior, and social goals on which the student is working

- Improve home-school communication (Carpenter, 2001; Jones & Jones, 1995)

As you can see by looking at the accompanying figure, the travel card lists four or five of a student's target behaviors across the top and the classes the student attends along the left side. Classes include reading, science, social studies, and others. At the end of each period, the teacher indicates whether the student performed the desired behaviors by marking a + (yes), 0 (no), or NA (not applicable) on the card. At the end of the day, the positive notations are tallied and graphed. Points are accumulated toward a menu of rewards that have been negotiated by the student and the professionals responsible for the travel card.

Travel Card
Rocky

Date _____

Key   + = Yes   0 = No   NA = Not applicable

	Did student follow class rules?	Did student participate in class?	Did student complete assignments?	Did student turn in homework?	Teacher's initials
Reading					
Science					
Social Studies					
Study Skills					
English					
Spanish					
Bonus Points	Went to nurse after getting off bus?			Has assignment book?	
Total	+	0			

Teacher Comments/Suggestions/Announcements:

Source: Travel card from Myles, Brenda S., & Adreon, D. (2001). *Asperger syndrome and adolescence: Practical solutions for school success.* Shawnee Mission, KS: Autism Asperger Publishing. Reprinted by permission of Autism Asperger Publishing Co.

to new tasks, and increase student success. **Priming** occurs when a parent, paraprofessional, teacher, or trusted peer previews with a student the day, the evening, or the morning before a lesson or activity occurs the actual materials that will be used in that lesson or activity. In

Using Personal Digital Assistants (PDAs)

Personal digital assistants (PDAs) as well as other handheld electronic devices are becoming more frequently used by the general public. This same type of handheld device has also proven to be effective in encouraging organization and independence among children with special needs. Though not much research has been documented on the use of such devices by children with special needs, a few studies do exist (Davies, Stock, & Wehmeyer, 2002; Ferguson, Myles, & Hagiwara, 2005; Norris & Soloway, 2003).

One such study gathered data on the use of a PDA by an adolescent with Asperger syndrome (Ferguson et al., 2005). The goal of the research was to increase the individual's independence with morning, school, and evening routines and to evaluate time management and the rate of task completion. Within each of these target time periods, four tasks were highlighted on which to collect data. Each of the tasks was familiar to the individual and part of a previously expected routine. On the individual's PDA,

he was able to set an alarm to ring and flash to indicate for him to check his visual reminder on the screen. This individual became more independent, recording his own appointments and personal information and setting alarms for reminders. He also became more aware of tracking time and reminding others to transition—a previously difficult and typically prompted task.

Though more study is still needed in this area, research such as this is promising. Personal digital assistants are increasing in popularity and use in the general public, are discreet in size, and are easily portable, making them a viable tool for students with autism spectrum disorders.

Source: Based on Ferguson, H., Myles, B., & Hagiwara, T. (2005). Using personal digital assistants to enhance the independence of an adolescent with Asperger syndrome. *Education and Training in Developmental Disabilities, 40,* 60–67.

---

some instances, priming occurs just prior to an activity. Priming is most effective when it is built into the student's routine. It should occur in a relaxed environment and be facilitated by a primer who is both patient and encouraging. Finally, priming sessions should be short, providing a brief overview of the day's tasks in ten or fifteen minutes (Myles & Adreon, 2001).

Discrete Trial Training

Unlike most of the practices outlined so far that might be implemented by general education teachers, special education teachers, or others working with students with autism spectrum disorders, **discrete trial training (DTT)** is a highly specialized approach that requires a significant time commitment and often is supervised by a special educator or sometimes a parent (Leaf & McEachin, 1999; Maurice, Green, & Luce, 1996). Most commonly implemented with preschool children, this practice follows a basic pattern in which the teacher gives a prompt (i.e., cue) to which the student attends, a command for the student to perform, and finally a reward to the student for the desired behavior (Lovaas, 1987).

For example, the student could be given a prompt such as "Look at me" or a nonverbal cue such as pointing to the teacher's eyes. Once this command is given, the teacher waits for the student to focus attention as directed. In some instances, the teacher may need to guide the child physically through the desired behavior, such as lifting the child's chin so her eyes focus on the teacher when the command "Look at me" is given. In addition, the teacher may decide to reward behavior that is similar to or leading toward the desired behavior, a technique referred to as *shaping the behavior.* For example, when the command "Look at me" is given, a reward would be given if the student lifted her head briefly, even if she did not maintain eye contact. Of course, the goal is for students to be able to use the skills they learn in the discrete trial training across settings and situations.

Prompting

As you just learned, a **prompt** is a cue designed to get a student to perform a specific behavior, and it is effective in promoting student achievement. Prompts frequently are used by professionals working with students with autism spectrum disorders, and prompts vary based on their intrusiveness. For example, a physical prompt is very intrusive, with the teacher

physically engaging the student (e.g., moving the student's hand to the pencil or turning the student's head toward the task). Somewhat less intrusive are gestures, such as pointing or signing, guiding the student where to look or move. Verbal questions or statements are even less intrusive prompts, involving no physical prompting at all. Finally, a written prompt, such as a cue card or keyword taped to the student's desk, is the least intrusive prompt. Prompts help students to learn without repeatedly making mistakes. How might you use prompts if you were working with students like Claudia, Geneva, or Jeremy, the students introduced at the beginning of the chapter?

Social Skills Supports

Perhaps the most important area of intervention for students with autism spectrum disorders is social skills. Social skills interventions generally are positive behavior supports designed to enhance opportunities for social interaction, reduce problem behaviors, and build new competencies that have a positive impact on quality of life (Dunlap & Koegel, 1999; Gutstein & Whitney, 2002; Myles et al., 2000). Specific issues that can be addressed include understanding the thoughts and feelings of others, following social rules, and learning self-monitoring (Barnhill, Cook, Tebbenkamp, & Myles, 2002; Myles & Simpson, 2002).

Ellen B. Senisi

*M*any students with autism spectrum disorders understand expectations when they are communicated using visual prompts as well as words.

Instruction

Unlike many typical learners, students with autism spectrum disorders must be directly taught the social skills they need to be successful. One example of an intervention for this purpose is the *power card strategy,* a visually based technique that uses a student's special interests to facilitate understanding of social situations, routines, and the meaning of language (Gagnon, 2001). This intervention contains two components: a script and a power card. A teacher, therapist, or parent develops a brief script, written at the child's comprehension level, detailing the problem situation or target behavior. It includes a description of the behavior and describes how the child's special interest has addressed that social challenge. The power card, which is the size of a business card or trading card, contains a picture of the special interest and a summary of the solution. The power card can be carried; attached to the inside of a book, notebook, or locker; or placed on the corner of a child's desk (Gagnon, 2001). The Positive Behavior Supports on the next page provides an example of this technique.

Social Stories

A **social story** is an individualized text or story that describes a specific social situation from the student's perspective. The description may include where and why the situation occurs, how others feel or react, or what prompts their feelings and reactions (Gray, 2000; Gray & Garand, 1993; Kuttler, Myles, & Carlson, 1998). Social stories may be written documents, or they can be paired with pictures, audiotapes, or videotapes (Swaggart et al., 1995). They may be created by any professional or the parent, often with student input. You reviewed examples of social stories earlier in this chapter.

SOCCSS

The *situation, options, consequences, choices, strategies, simulation (SOCCSS)* strategy helps students with social disabilities understand social situations and develop problem solving skills by putting social and behavioral issues into a sequential form (Roosa, 1995). Specifically, this teacher-directed strategy helps students understand cause and effect and realize that they can influence the outcomes of many situations with the decisions they make. The strategy can be used with an individual student or as a group activity, depending on the situation and students' needs. Although this strategy is designed to be interpretive, it also can be used as an instructional strategy. That is, teachers can identify problems students are likely

Research Notes

Starr, Szatmari, Bryson, and Zwaigenbaum (2003) compared students with autism and Asperger syndrome. They found that the latter group displayed fewer and less severe symptoms of the disorder and that these results were stable across time.

Research Notes

In a small-scale study, carefully constructed social stories were found to be effective in decreasing the disruptive behavior of school-age children (Scattone, Wilczynski, Edwards, & Rabian, 2002).

Power Card: Teaching Appropriate Behavior Using Special Interests

Professionals sometimes use the special interests of students with autism to help them learn appropriate ways to behave in particular situations. For example, for Cheyenne, a student who was fascinated with Elvis Presley, the following story was written. Then it was summarized, incorporating an appropriate picture, onto a power card that Cheyenne could keep on her desk or carry in her backpack.

1. Think before you say anything. Say it in your head first before saying it out loud.

2. If you can't think of anything nice to say, don't say anything.

3. You do not have to say every thought out loud that you think.

When kids who love Elvis remember these three things, Elvis says, "Thank you, thank you very much!"

Elvis and His Fans

Elvis Presley loves being the king of rock-and-roll, but sometimes it is difficult for him to be nice to everyone. At the end of a long day in the recording studio or after a concert, he is often tired, and it is difficult for him to be nice to fans and friends. Elvis has learned, however, that is important to smile at people he meets and say nice things to everyone, even when he is tired. He has learned that if he can't say something nice, it is better to just smile and say nothing at all. He stops and thinks about comments he makes before he says anything.

Just like Elvis, it is important for young people to think before they talk. It would make Elvis proud when preteens and teenagers remember to do the following:

1. Think before you say anything. Say it in your head first before saying it out loud.

2. If you can't think of anything nice to say, don't say anything.

3. You do not have to say every thought out loud that you think.

When kids who love Elvis remember these three things, Elvis says, "Thank you, thank you very much!"

---

to encounter and address them using SOCCSS so that students have a plan prior to a situation occurring. More detail on this strategy can be found in the Positive Behavior Supports on the next page.

What Are the Perspectives of Parents and Families?

Parents of children with autism spectrum disorders usually are the first to recognize that their youngsters are responding differently to the world than typically developing children. Some parents have reported that as an infant, their child was perfectly content to lie quietly in the crib staring at toys. The infant appeared to be a "good baby." One mother was convinced that her toddler was gifted because before the age of two, he recognized all of the letters of the alphabet and could read several sight words. However, the child seldom initiated interactions with those in his environment.

Many parents of children with autism spectrum disorders begin to suspect that something is different in their child's development sometime after the child's first birthday. For example, the child may become attached to an object such as a stuffed animal and tantrum

Helping Students Learn Appropriate Behavior

One strategy for helping students with autism spectrum disorders to understand cause and effect and to plan how to respond in certain situations is called SOCCSS (situation, options, consequences, choices, strategies, simulation). These are the six steps special educators, general educators, and other professionals use to implement it:

1. *Situation.* The teacher and student identify what happened or what could happen using questions such as these: What was the problem? What is the goal to prevent a problem?

2. *Options.* Brainstorming is the next step: What are things to do to reach the goal? Note that at this step the teacher accepts all the student's responses.

3. *Consequences.* For each option, possible consequences are identified. The purpose of this step is to help the student understand cause and effect.

4. *Choices.* With teacher guidance, the student prioritizes the choices, selecting the one with the most positive consequences.

5. *Strategies.* The teacher and student develop a plan of action for the choice selected. The goal is for the student to feel a sense of ownership of the plan.

6. *Simulation.* The student role plays the situation, incorporating the selected choice, or writes out the plan in order to be prepared to respond to the situation.

The accompanying SOCCSS worksheet illustrates how the steps are implemented. What are the advantages of implementing the SOCCSS strategy with students with autism spectrum disorders? For what types of classroom situations might it be valuable? What challenges might arise when using it?

SOCCSS Worksheet		
Situation		
Who	What	
When	Why	

Options	Consequences	Choices

Strategies

Simulation Type	Simulation Outcomes

Follow-Up

Source: Adapted from Myles, B. S., & Simpson, R. L. (2001). Understanding the hidden curriculum: An essential social skill for children and youth with Asperger syndrome [Electronic version]. *Intervention in School and Clinic, 36,* 279–286. Copyright © 2001 by Pro-Ed, Inc. Reprinted with permission.

uncontrollably when the object is not in sight, or the child may show no interest in play, preferring to watch videos for hours on end. Initially, the pediatrician may assure worried parents that there is nothing to be concerned about, but usually nagging doubts persist.

Jan Sonnenmai/Aurora & Quanta Productions

Family Needs for Information and Support

Following diagnosis, parents may become frustrated because even though they have a name for their child's unique differences, they have little idea what to do about them. Many families of children with autism have found that early intervention, often with an intensive one-to-one home program, enables their children to make progress in the areas of behavior, communication, socialization, and self-help. This type of program, although beneficial to many children with autism spectrum disorders, requires a time commitment of thirty or forty hours per week and can be emotionally and financially taxing for families.

Parents of children with autism spectrum disorders may find themselves forced to play demanding roles in the lives of their children. In order to provide appropriate education, parents need to be familiar with the latest research on autism, understand special education law, and know how to be effective advocates for their children. Many parents have learned how to collaborate effectively with the professionals who provide services to their children and are valuable members of the school's educational team. These parents understand the value of knowing the characteristics of autism and effective educational practices. Parents of children with these disorders also need skills related to resolving differences within a constructive atmosphere and providing support for the professionals who work with their children.

Like parents of children with other disabilities, parents of children with autism spectrum disorders often feel concern about their children's welfare in the years ahead, their children's ability to function independently at some point, and the community's acceptance of their children (Koegel et al., 1992). Mothers of children with autism also report more stress in their lives than do mothers of children with other disabilities (Rodrigue, Morgan, & Geffken, 1990).

Parents of children with autism spectrum disorders benefit from the availability of both formal and informal social support, but such support must be individualized to meet the needs of each family. Potential sources of support include classroom teachers, IEP team members, pediatricians and other health professionals, and other families of children with autism. Families often find that attending a local support group provides much-needed information and support.

The Roles of Siblings

Siblings often play important yet demanding roles in the lives of their brothers or sisters with autism spectrum disorders, often believing that they need to assume parental roles in the lives of their brothers or sisters with autism (Bleach, 2001; Harris, 1994). For example, they may be required to take on additional responsibilities in the home and serve as care providers in the absence of a parent. Despite having demands placed on them, siblings' knowledge of the disability may be limited. They should have access to resources appropriate to their developmental levels and be as well educated as their parents in the area of autism (Glasberg,

2000). Many nondiagnosed siblings feel that they frequently are ignored in day-to-day family life. They may exhibit more difficulties in emotional, behavioral, and social adjustments and with peer interactions (Hastings, 2003). It is vital that parents help siblings pursue their own interests and spend time with them away from the sibling with autism.

What Trends and Issues Are Affecting the Field of Autism Spectrum Disorders?

The field of autism spectrum disorders is still relatively young, yet it is faced with several significant issues. Among those issues identified by the National Research Council (2001) are those related to more accurate information on assessment, diagnosis, and prevalence; the need for research to identify effective interventions; and the lack of adequate professional preparation programs.

Assessment, Diagnosis, and Prevalence

One dilemma for the field of autism is the difficulty of early identification. Many parents of young children who eventually are diagnosed as having autism spectrum disorders initially are told that nothing is amiss. Given that the most positive outcomes tend to accrue to children who begin interventions at the earliest ages, it is imperative that better assessment procedures be identified for use with young children, that pediatricians become more sensitive to the possibility of autism being present, and that efforts be made to more accurately identify the prevalence of these disorders.

PROFESSIONAL MONITORING TOOL

Council for Exceptional Children

Standard 1 Foundations
. . . issues in definition and identification

In addition, a research agenda is needed that will lead to a greater understanding of the neurological, behavioral, and developmental characteristics of autism spectrum disorders. This, in turn, might help professionals identify key indicators of autism much earlier in a child's life.

As you learned earlier in this chapter, the prevalence estimates for autism spectrum disorders vary significantly. Does this matter? Yes. Resources often are allocated to study a disorder and to provide innovative treatments based on its prevalence, and so more accurate prevalence estimates of autism might lead to more resource allocation. For example, the National Institutes of Health could play a role in collecting and disseminating better prevalence data.

Evidence-Based Interventions

Many professionals who work with individuals with autism spectrum disorders advocate for particular intervention approaches. They are well intentioned, but often their preferences are based on personal experience and not on research. In fact, many debates about the effectiveness of interventions for students with autism spectrum disorders rely more on emotion than on data. For example, these are some of the interventions that have been recommended for which researchers have not been able to independently replicate the claims of those advocating the treatments (Kallen, 2003): auditory integration training, facilitated communication, use of steroids, use of secretin (i.e., a hormone aiding digestion that sometimes is given therapeutically to children), use of vitamin B6 and magnesium, and dietary interventions (e.g., eliminating gluten and casein). A web search would yield many sites related to these unproven approaches.

PROFESSIONAL MONITORING TOOL

Council for Exceptional Children

Standard 9 Professional and Ethical Practice
. . . methods to remain current regarding research-validated practice

To address treatments such as these, studies that compare their impact on students need to be undertaken and the results shared with practitioners and parents. In the meantime, you may find that parents insist on the effectiveness of particular treatments or interventions, and you should be prepared to seek out accurate information about them. You also may need to consider the complex ethical issues that may be raised: You should not advocate such treatments, and although you can discuss your concerns with parents, you may not be able to convince them of your views.

PROFESSIONAL MONITORING TOOL

Council for
Exceptional
Children

Standard 9 Professional and
Ethical Practice
. . . uphold high standards
of competence

Training and Support

Before autism was included as a separate disability category in IDEA in 1990, students with these disorders often received services from professionals prepared to work with students with severe and multiple disabilities or intellectual disabilities. Since 1990, the number of students identified with ASD has grown quickly, but far too few university programs provide coursework to prepare professionals to work with these students. Further, regional resource and training centers and local agencies still are unable to adequately support the needs of local schools and families for information and skills. For example, teachers have to become familiar with rapidly changing theories and approaches, they need to clearly understand behavioral techniques, they have to know how to select and use appropriate assistive technology, and they must have considerable knowledge of language acquisition and use and how to foster language development in their students. In addition, they have to be adept at creating needed adaptations in the environment, gathering data, and working collaboratively with parents, paraprofessionals, and colleagues (National Research Council, 2001). The need for school personnel and families to receive accurate and up-to-date information remains a challenge for this field.

SUMMARY

The study of autism spectrum disorders is relatively young, having begun with Kanner's work published in 1944. Since that time, researchers have clarified that the disorders probably have biological, not environmental, bases, and they have identified at least two distinct groups of students with these disabilities: those with autism and those with Asperger syndrome. Although the term *autism spectrum disorders (ASD)* is not used in federal or American Psychiatric Association definitions, it now is used to convey the heterogeneity of individuals with these disabilities. Students with autism spectrum disorders may experience difficulties in cognitive and academic functioning, social and emotional abilities, and appropriate behavior. They also may experience a variety of sensory challenges. These students usually are identified at a young age, and they are entitled to the same special education services and supports as other children with disabilities, although they are less likely than many other students to participate in inclusive education. Interventions for students with these disabilities can be grouped into these categories: environmental supports, assistive technology, instructional supports, and social skills supports.

Parents of children with autism spectrum disorders often need information about how to work with their children and support for themselves. Siblings, too, may need assistance. Issues facing the field of autism include the need for better assessment and identification procedures, more accurate prevalence estimates, more and better quality research on the effectiveness of interventions, and additional resources for preparing professionals to work with these students.

BACK TO THE CASES

Claudia

Although Claudia has been identified as having autism and placed in a special education setting, she may need to have other assessments to provide adequate information to her teachers and caregivers. As noted in the case study, she sometimes has puzzling behaviors. After a new behavior occurs, teachers search for reasons and try options until one or the other works. Additional assessment might provide an answer for a proactive approach.

■ Why would additional assessment be useful in this situation? (See CEC Standard 8 and INTASC Principle 8.10.)

■ Which assessments should be administered? (See CEC Standard 8 and INTASC Principle 8.02.) Discuss both formal and informal assessments that might add useful information to Claudia's profile.

■ How might Claudia's family be involved or contribute to this assessment process? (See CEC Standard 8 and INTASC Principle 8.07.)

Geneva

Geneva's parents have expressed concern about her future. She is at the age when discussions about her postsecondary adult life should begin. Regardless of which work or educational setting is selected or the circumstances of her living situation, Geneva will need skills for adult living.

■ Select two skills that may present problems or concerns for Geneva. (See CEC Standard 2 and INTASC Principle 2.05.) Explain your rationale for selecting them.

■ Besides walking independently to class, what other activities can be planned that will help Geneva work toward a more independent life? (See CEC Standard 7 and INTASC Principle 7.01.) Your answer should reflect a collaborative effort, including general and special education teachers, paraprofessionals, Geneva's family members, and same-age peers. (See CEC Standard 10 and INTASC Principle 10.04.).

Casey

In this chapter you learned about methods and strategies to help learners with autism learn, practice, and generalize socially appropriate behaviors across school settings. Now you are faced with helping Casey's teachers decide how to teach him expectations for each of their classes.

▓ Review the strategies and methods provided in your text, and then select two that you believe are appropriate for a student like Casey. (See CEC Standard 2 and INTASC Principle 2.04.) How is the strategy implemented with learners who have autism. Provide an example of how you might implement each with Casey and discuss their pros and cons.

▓ Which strategy seems to have the most potential for success? Why?

KEY TERMS AND CONCEPTS

Asperger syndrome
Autism spectrum disorders (ASDs)
Autistic disorder
Communicative intent
Discrete trial training (DTT)
Echolalia
Environmental supports

Pervasive developmental disorder (PDD)
Pervasive developmental disorder not otherwise specified (PDD–NOS)
Priming
Prompt
Prosody
Proxemics

Rote memory
Self-stimulatory behavior
Social story
Theory of mind

REVIEW, DISCUSS, APPLY

1. How have beliefs about the causes of autism changed from its discovery in Kanner's work in 1944 to contemporary times? (Learning Objective 1)

2. Create a Venn diagram or another type of visual aid that explains how the IDEA and American Psychiatric Association definitions of *autism* and related disorders relate to each other. How are the concepts similar and different? (Learning Objective 1)

3. What are at least four examples of sensory issues that students with autism spectrum disorders may experience? How might each of these affect students' educational experiences? (Learning Objective 2)

4. You already have learned that deafness and hearing loss often are most accurately described in terms of communication challenges. You also have learned that speech and language disorders can significantly affect many students. In this chapter, considerable attention was focused on the communication needs of students with autism. How are these three groups of students similar? Different? Why do you think that so many challenges related to disabilities turn out to be about communication? (Learning Objective 2)

5. How is assessment for students with autism similar to and different from assessment for other students who might have a disability? (Learning Objective 3)

6. Why are so many students with autism spectrum disorders educated in settings that do not include typical peers? What are the benefits and drawbacks of these service options? (Learning Objective 4)

7. Identify a common challenge faced by students at the level you are interested in (elementary, middle school, high school). It could concern teasing, forgetting assignments, or being respectful of others. Create a social story to help students successfully face the challenge. What did you learn by completing this exercise? (Learning Objective 5)

8. Parents of children with autism often need assistance in learning how to respond to their children's behaviors and how to advocate for their children at school. How can professionals help ensure that collaboration occurs with these parents? (Learning Objective 6)

9. Why is it so important in twenty-first century schools to emphasize finding research-based interventions for students with autism spectrum disorders? Look at articles in professional journals. What is one example of an intervention for these students that appears to have a strong research base? (Learning Objective 7)

(mylabschool
Where the classroom comes to life!

Go to Allyn & Bacon's MyLabSchool (www.mylabschool.com) and enter Assignment ID SIM02 into the Assignment Finder. Work through the MLS simulations, *Accessing the General Education Curriculum: Inclusion for Students with Disabilities, Parts I & II*, which address issues related to the inclusion of all students with disabilities.

Question: How do the issues raised in these simulations relate to students with autism spectrum disorders? You may also complete the activities included in the simulations and e-mail your work to your instructor.

4

Students with Speech and Language Disorders

Students with Speech and Language Disorders

Robin Sachs/PhotoEdit

learning objectives

- Outline the development of the study of speech and language disorders, define speech and language disorders, and explain their prevalence and causes.

- Describe characteristics of individuals with speech and language disorders.

- Explain how speech and language disorders are identified.

- Outline how learners with speech and language disorders receive their education.

- Describe recommended educational practices for students with speech and language disorders.

- Explain the perspectives and concerns that parents and families of students with speech and language disorders may have.

- Identify trends and issues influencing the field of speech and language disorders.

Andrew

Andrew's second-grade teacher describes him as a very quiet child who rarely speaks unless asked to do so—a student she worries about overlooking. His academic performance in math is nearly average, but he seems to be struggling more and more with reading. When he is observed on the playground, he is by himself most of the time. Andrew's mother explains that he always has had difficulty pronouncing certain words and that she and her husband did not worry too much about what they thought were minor developmental problems, thinking that he would "grow out of it" as many children do. However, Andrew still is substituting the sound /t/ for /k/ and the sound /f/ for /th/. Andrew might say "tite" when he means "kite," "tountry" when he means "country," and "fink" when he means "think." Andrew began receiving assistance from a speech/language pathologist soon after he enrolled in kindergarten, and he now works with this professional twice each week for thirty minutes. In addition, his teacher helps him in the classroom setting to practice the sounds he is learning.

Jade

Jade appears to be an average middle school student, a girl who seems most interested in boys, music, and the current pop icons. She is a below-average student but attends school regularly and sincerely tries to complete her work. However, Jade has rather complicated special needs. After she received a gunshot wound to her head as an innocent bystander in a gang incident, she was diagnosed with traumatic brain injury and also has a learning disability. The physical effects of her injury have long since healed, but Jade now receives special education services both in her English and math classes as well as in a resource room. Jade also receives services twice each week from Ms. Ochoa, a speech/language therapist. Ms. Ochoa is working with Jade in several areas. For example, it sometimes is clear that Jade knows what she wants to say but cannot seem to get her brain to instruct her throat, jaws, mouth, and tongue to form the words she needs. Ms. Ochoa is helping Jade to relearn these skills, working closely with her special education teacher and meeting regularly with her general education teachers. Ms. Ochoa also assists Jade in areas that might traditionally be considered language arts—that is, developing vocabulary and writing. A key component of Jade's services is restoring her confidence in her communication skills.

Mason

Mason is about to graduate from high school, and he is grappling with the many decisions about further schooling and careers that all young adults face. He told the guidance counselor that he would like to go to college, but he is worried about taking that step. Mason has stuttered for as long as he can remember, and he is anxious about leaving his long-time circle of friends who do not seem to notice his speech difficulties anymore. Mason relates that he used to hate himself because of his disability, and he remembers that he would speak as little as possible to avoid the teasing of his classmates. He now explains, "I don't need to feel sorry for myself. There are worse problems to have. I'm fortunate to have a strong and supportive family, to have great friends, and to have had the benefit of participating in varsity sports—I learned many important lessons by being on the basketball team." Mason received speech services throughout his school years, and he is far more fluent than he was when younger. However, in stressful situations he knows he will likely have difficulty speaking. When he discusses possible careers, Mason mentions those in the computer field. He thinks that he would be most successful in an environment with only a few employees in which his colleagues could get to know him well.

At some point in your life, you may have experienced a speech or language problem. Perhaps your parents have a recording of your preschool rendition of a favorite song in which you say "wabbit" for "rabbit" or "tate" for "cake." Everyone who hears the tape now chuckles at the mispronunciations that you have long since outgrown. More recently, you may have encountered a momentary problem in recalling a particular word you wished to write on your exam answer, probably because of fatigue or stress. You knew you knew the word, but you simply could not bring it to mind when you needed it. If you are uncomfortable speaking to groups, you might have found that giving presentations to classmates made you feel as though you could not coherently string words together into sentences or smoothly transition from one topic to another. The fifteen minutes you spoke felt like fifteen hours.

The speech and language challenges that you have faced are brief episodes, unsettling but temporary. As such, they provide no more than a glimpse of what it is really like to have a speech or language disorder. Imagine sitting in an elementary classroom and not being able to pronounce common words. Imagine being in high school and having difficulty grasping verbal directions and expressing your thoughts aloud. What might be the impact of these chronic problems on academic achievement? Interactions with peers and adults? Behavior? These are some of the topics considered in this chapter.

What Are Speech and Language Disorders?

Today's practices in the field of speech and language disorders are based on work that began nearly two centuries ago. This discipline has been influenced by research in medicine, psychology, and education, and it has progressed from simple approaches to complex understandings.

Development of the Study of Speech and Language Disorders

Some of the earliest work related to speech and language disorders was undertaken in Europe at the beginning of the nineteenth century on behalf of individuals who were deaf (Duchan, 2006). It focused on how these individuals should communicate, using either voice (oral method) or sign language (manual method). Soon professionals expanded their interests to the need for speech correction for individuals who were not deaf, particularly for those who stuttered. In the United States, the first textbook on speech disorders was published in 1802 by S. C. L. Potter. Shortly after that an individual known to history only as Mrs. Leigh wrote about her method for curing stuttering by placing rolls of linen under the tongue each evening so that the tongue was in the correct position for speech. Mrs. Leigh's method characterizes much of the remainder of the nineteenth century: Individuals working to cure speech problems developed unusual treatments or surgeries that seldom had any basis in research, that were closely guarded secrets usually not recorded so as to avoid theft, and that had dubious value.

Emergence of a Profession

Although much of this early work was completed by medical specialists, by the end of the nineteenth century it was clear that a new group of professionals called *speech clinicians* was emerging to address speech and language disorders. Some of these first clinicians were from well-known occupations such as education and medicine. Others trained for their work by studying under experienced clinicians, developing their own approaches to speech correction, or successfully overcoming their own speech problems (Duchan, 2001). The first formal training programs for speech/language pathologists were not established until the

"The first formal training programs for speech/language pathologists were not established until the 1930s, but by then the profession was already flourishing."

1930s, but by then the profession was already flourishing (Duchan, 2006). The American Academy of Speech Correction was founded in 1925, and it included physicians, scholars, and administrators. This group eventually became the American Speech-Language-Hearing Association (ASHA), the professional organization that today credentials speech/language professionals and sets the standards for their professional practice.

Beginning in the early twentieth century, most interventions for children with speech or language disorders took place in public schools (Duchan, 2001). From 1900 until the end of World War II in 1945, instruction emphasized the correct production of specific speech sounds and included repeating sounds, words, and sentences. Also recommended were relaxation exercises based on the belief that some speech disorders were the result of anxiety. After World War II, the study of speech and language disorders was influenced by many of the same forces that shaped the field of learning disabilities. Gradually, the focus of intervention moved from the mechanics of speech production to children's overall ability to use language to communicate.

E. Dygas/Photodisc/Getty Images

The most critical period for learning language is during the first few years of life.

Contemporary Practices

Like other fields related to serving students with disabilities, speech and language services were greatly influenced by the passage of Public Law (P.L.) 94-142 in 1975 and the subsequent refinements of that law. In the 1960s speech/language pathologists sometimes worked with 150 or more students at a time, but the requirement to deliver specific services to students with disabilities led to a significant reduction in such caseloads (Whitmire, 2002). Further, as the concept of least restrictive environment was introduced and refined, the places where speech and language services were offered expanded from separate classrooms or offices and schools to include the general education classroom.

In the past two decades, conceptualizations of speech and language disorders have expanded yet again to stress the role of communication. That is, professionals now acknowledge that not only is it important to recognize whether students can produce complete sentences using the correct tense, but it is also essential to think about what students are trying to express and to whom (Duchan, 2001). This most recent thinking is particularly significant for students with disabilities because it places speech and language in a social context and highlights the importance of successful day-to-day interactions with peers and adults as the ultimate goal of any intervention. Read the Firsthand Account on the next page to learn more about a speech/language therapist's view of the field and the work of these professionals.

Definitions of Speech and Language Disorders

The number of terms and concepts associated with the field of speech and language disorders reflects the wide range of conditions it encompasses. In this chapter the term **speech and language disorders** is used to refer to all the disorders that can occur within this disability category. However, you also may come across the term **communication disorders**. It, too, is a global term for all the conditions that comprise this disability, but it sometimes is used to include difficulties with communication that arise from hearing loss whereas the other term sometimes excludes those individuals.

INTERNET RESOURCES
www.asha.org
The American Speech-Language-Hearing Association is the professional organization for audiologists, speech/language pathologists, and other professionals concerned with speech and language disorders in children and adults. Its website includes articles on many topics and information about specific disorders.

PROFESSIONAL MONITORING TOOL

Council for Exceptional Children

Standard 1 Foundations . . . issues in definition and identification

Understanding the Many Roles and Responsibilities of a Speech/Language Therapist

Jennifer Santangelo is a speech/language therapist who works in a small district about seventy-five miles from New York City. She has a total of eight years of experience. Her description of the many dimensions of her job can help you to understand the valuable role such professionals play in meeting the needs of students with speech, language, and communication disorders.

I always knew I wanted to do *something* with children. As I was growing up I had the opportunity to observe a master speech/language therapist at the preschool where my mother worked. She got the kids so engaged and it was amazing what she got them to do; that's how I chose being a speech/language therapist as *exactly* what I wanted to do with children.

What I do as a therapist varies all the time—and includes augmentative communication, communication boards, social skills—along with therapy. My first year, I had five elementary schools that I traveled to. And then another year I worked in only one school. One year I was doing an intervention program for kindergarten. I went into nine different kindergarten classes to teach the children listening skills, comprehension skills, language development, and vocabulary—depending on their needs.

Right now, I also go into self-contained special education classrooms in order to do language lessons. What I'm saying is that I don't just stay in my therapy room. I like to be in classrooms a lot. Of course, I also pull students out. I go to a smaller building (which means I'm there for a very limited amount of time), and don't have the option to schedule going into classrooms, even though that is where I'd rather be. When I do pull students out, I try to connect what we're doing with the classroom. For example, a fourth-grade teacher gives me review materials for tests. When I work with the students I'll use those materials to also teach them strategies to be successful.

That way they see that what I'm doing with them is really related to what they are doing in fourth grade.

Another part of my job is working with teachers. For example, with a student getting articulation therapy I'll go

> *"What I do as a therapist varies all the time."*

into the classroom to observe. Sometimes I'll remind the teacher to say to the student, "I know you can say the sound the way Ms. XXX taught you . . ." instead of saying "Say the sound the 'right' way. . . ." I don't want kids to feel like they are doing something "wrong" and I have to count on the teacher to help on that.

Working with parents is important, too. Sometimes parents don't really want their children to get speech therapy or to leave the classroom to go to the therapy room. You have to convince them. Or, sometimes we have to get them what they need in other ways. The reading teacher came to me and asked me to teach her how to help a student make certain sounds. The parent wouldn't let the child receive speech therapy but would agree to reading instruction. Now I'm teaching the reading teacher strategies to help the child, and the parents are fine with it because it is taught as part of reading.

Other parents are completely the opposite. The other day I had a parent call me concerned that her son could not say the /r/ sound. I explained that we had been working on it in therapy

and that I could send some information home so that the parent could practice with him correctly (how to move his lips, what to do with his tongue) at home for about five minutes each night. She was so grateful to know what to do to help him. She asked about other concerns, but I told her just to work on one sound at a time, that we would eventually address all the areas of need.

My job involves both articulation therapy and language therapy, and they intertwine all the time. I usually don't focus just on articulation because you can do it through language activities like reading stories. You can go through a story and identify the sounds that students need to work on and stress those sounds as you go. Another type of therapy I sometimes do is called *oral-motor*. This year, for example, there is a student who has feeding goals. During lunch time, you teach the student how to take a fork, put it in his mouth, take the food off the fork, and then chew it. Sometimes I also help students learn how to swallow because that could affect their articulation.

When I think about advice I would give to professionals new to the field, I know that I was lucky to have had a wonderful mentor. If you can form a relationship with another therapist or a classroom teacher, you can learn so many strategies that you never would learn in school. I think it's also important to stay flexible when you work in schools because your job probably is going to change—from year to year, but also from session to session.

In IDEA, the term **speech or language impairment** is used, and it is defined as

a communication disorder such as stuttering, impaired articulation, language impairment, or a voice impairment that adversely affects a child's educational performance (IDEA 20 U.S.C. §1401 [2004], 20 C.F.R. §300.8[c][11])

This definition is far less detailed than the definitions of most of the other disabilities covered by IDEA, but it is deceptively simple. Combining speech and language problems into a single definition allows considerable variation to exist among states in terms of which students receive services and how they receive services. In all states, students whose primary disability is a language disorder are served within this category. However, because IDEA includes speech services both within this category and as a related service, states vary in their regulations. In some states, students can have IEPs that are "speech only"; that is, the primary disability is considered the speech disorder, and special education services are offered for it even if those are the only services needed. In other states, students only can receive services for speech disorders as a related service—that is, only if the students have been identified as having other disabilities under IDEA. If speech therapy is the only special need, students are not eligible for special education.

Approximately 7.5 million Americans have difficulty using their voice, between 6 and 8 million have some type of language disorder, and 3 million stutter.

Concepts to Describe Speech and Language Disorders

To appreciate the scope of special needs addressed in this disability category, more explanation is needed than is offered in the IDEA definition. A beginning point for exploring speech and language disorders is an overview of human communication.

Communication is the exchange of information and knowledge among participants (Lue, 2001), and it is a basic human need (Romski, Sevcik, Adamson, & Bakeman, 2005). Communication requires a *message* (the information or knowledge), a *sender* (the person who transmits the message), and a *receiver* (the person who grasps the message). It also involves a *channel*, or a route through which the message travels. Finally, communication involves a sort of volleyball game, in which the sender and receiver send messages back and forth. For example, when a friend says to you "Are you ready to go?" while looking at his watch, standing in the doorway with his coat on, and fidgeting, the friend is the sender, you are the receiver, and the message concerns being late. The channel is both *verbal*—the words he spoke—and *nonverbal*—the glance at his watch and the posture of fidgeting while standing in the doorway. The volleyball game would continue when you responded to your friend.

> *"Communication is the exchange of information and knowledge among participants, and it is a basic human need."*

Elements of Language

Language is the system of symbols, governed by complex rules, that individuals use for communication, and it is based on their culture (Newman, 2006). More than 6,800 languages are spoken across the world (National Virtual Translation Center, 2006), but not all languages rely on speaking. The clearest example of a nonspoken language is American Sign Language (ASL), the language used by some individuals who are deaf. Language also must be thought of in terms of its application.

Expressive language refers to the ability to produce language. **Receptive language** refers to the ability to comprehend language. If you have studied Spanish, French, Mandarin, or any language that you did not speak as you were growing up, you are very familiar with the difference between these two concepts. You probably gained skill in comprehending the language when it was spoken to you or when you read it (receptive language) faster than you acquired the skills necessary to accurately speak the language or write it (expressive language).

When language is spoken, it has five components, any of which can be the source of problems for a student with a disability. The first three components—phonology, morphology, and syntax—give language its form; the next component, semantics, refers to a language's content; and pragmatics, the last component, refers to the function or use of the language.

■ *Phonology.* Every spoken language includes a set of sounds, called **phonemes,** on which the language is based. Further, rules govern which sounds may be combined and where they may be used in words. For example, in English it is acceptable to blend the letters /n/ and /d/ to form /nd/, as in the words *sand* and *window,* but that combination of letters never appears at the beginning of a word. **Phonology** is the ability to hear the sounds used in a language and to use them correctly in words. Perhaps you have heard that one effective strategy for helping struggling readers is by improving their **phonemic awareness.** As you might guess, this refers to assisting them to make the fine discriminations among the sounds that make up the English language as is illustrated in the words *pan, pen, pin,* and *pun.* **Phonological awareness** is the ability to identify those sounds and to manipulate them, for example, by rhyming.

■ *Morphology.* **Morphemes** are the smallest units of a language that have meaning, and they are composed of phonemes. English has two types of morphemes. The first is called a *free morpheme,* meaning that it can exist without being attached to any other morpheme. Examples of free morphemes include many basic words such as *child, pretty, to,* and *run.* The second type is a *bound morpheme.* This type of morpheme has meaning, but it must be attached to another word according to the rules of the language. For example, when you see the suffix /-ed/, you know that generally it means past tense. You also know that this set of letters must be attached to another word. Other examples of bound morphemes include /-s/ and /pre-/. What are other examples? **Morphology,** then, is the ability to form words using one or more morphemes within the rules of the language.

■ *Syntax.* Every language has a set of rules that determine the order in which words are used. The ability to recognize and follow these rules is what is meant by **syntax.** For example, in English adjectives generally precede the nouns they describe, and so *The clear blue sky* is correct but *The sky blue clear* is not. Young children learning to speak often experience difficulty with syntax. They might say something such as *I car go* instead of *I'm going in the car* and *Cookie me* instead of *I want a cookie.*

■ *Semantics.* As mentioned at the beginning of this section, **semantics** pertains to the content of one's language, or to the meaning and precision of the words selected. Think about the differences in these two sentences: *It was bad outside* and *The temperature was below zero, the heavy, wet snow was accumulating quickly, and the wind was howling.* Which presents a more accurate description that clearly communicates what was meant? Another example is common in day-to-day interactions: Have you ever known a person who peppers conversation with words such as *things* or *stuff?* The absence of better word selections relates to semantics.

■ *Pragmatics.* The fifth and final component of language concerns **pragmatics,** the function or use of language within a social context. Each language has a unique set of rules that govern pragmatics. In English, for example, the rules include these: Only one person speaks at a time; everyone contributes to the conversation; interruptions usually are to be avoided; and topics generally are introduced, explored, and then completed (Owens, Metz, & Haas, 2003). Pragmatics is important because the primary purpose of language is to communicate with others. Even if individuals have mastered all the other components of language, if they cannot put the language to effective use in interactions with others, they are at a disadvantage.

> "Even if individuals have mastered all the other components of language, if they cannot put the language to effective use in interactions with others, they are at a disadvantage."

When children do not have speech and language disorders, their ability to use language develops rapidly during the first few years of life. Figure 9.1 illustrates the milestones in this development.

INTERNET RESOURCES
www.nidcd.nih.gov/index.asp
The National Institute on Deafness and Other Communication Disorders (NIDCD) is part of the National Institutes of Health, and its mission is to improve the lives of individuals with communication disorders. The website includes clear, concise descriptions of many disorders as well as information about causes and interventions.

Figure 9.1

Milestones in the Development of Children's Speech and Language

The most critical time for speech and language development is early childhood. These are a few of the milestones and the ages when they are reached for normally developing children.

Age	Milestone
1	■ Recognizes name
	■ Says two to three words in addition to *Mama* and *Dada*
	■ Understands simple instructions
	■ Recognizes words as symbols for objects (e.g., saying "meow" when prompted with the word *cat*)
1–2	■ Understands *no*
	■ Uses ten to twenty words, including names
	■ Combines two words, such as "Car. Go."
	■ Makes the sounds of familiar animals
	■ Waves good-bye and plays Pat-a-Cake
2–3	■ Identifies body parts
	■ Uses two-word negative phrases such as "No want."
	■ Understands simple time concepts such as *last night.*
	■ Solves problems by talking instead of hitting or crying
	■ Matches three or four colors; knows *big* and *little*
3–4	■ Can tell a story
	■ Has a vocabulary of nearly 1,000 words
	■ Understands *yesterday, summertime, lunchtime*
	■ Begins to obey requests such as "Put the block under the chair."
	■ Knows last name and home street name
4–5	■ Uses past tense correctly
	■ Has a vocabulary of nearly 1,500 words
	■ Identifies triangles, circles, and squares
	■ Can speak of imaginary conditions such as "I hope"
	■ Asks many questions, including "Why . . . ?"
5–6	■ Has a vocabulary of about 2,000 words
	■ Knows spatial relations such as *on top* and *behind*
	■ Knows address
	■ Knows common opposites such as *big–little*
	■ Distinguishes left and right hands without assistance
	■ Uses all types of sentences

Sources: Adapted from Learning Disabilities Association of America. (2003). Speech and language milestone chart. Retrieved November 11, 2003, from www.ldonline.org/ld_indepth/speech-language/lda_milestones.html.

Language Disorders

Students with language disorders may have significant and chronic problems related to any one of the discrete components of language outlined, or they may have disabilities that encompass several of these components. When students have language disorders that cannot be explained by physical disabilities, intellectual disabilities, hearing loss, or other disabilities, they are

Many school professionals wonder if a student's apparent difficulties in the classroom, lunchroom, gym, or playground are symptoms of a language disorder. Here are some behaviors that might signal the need to seek input from a speech/language pathologist.

Receptive Language Problem Behaviors

- Responds inconsistently to sounds or speech
- Has a short attention span for things he/she likes to do
- Sometimes looks "blank" when spoken to
- Seems to have difficulty understanding abstract concepts
- Seems to be distracted by extraneous sounds when spoken to
- Has problems with multiple word meanings
- Has difficulty recognizing relationship of words to ideas
- Has difficulty using phonics as a method of recognizing words
- Often gives inappropriate answers
- Has difficulty learning meanings for new words
- Has difficulty sequencing events (days of the week, numbers, etc.)
- Generally repeats a question rather than responding to it
- Tends to shadow questions (subvocalizes or repeats them)

Expressive Language Problems

- Seems unusually quiet
- Does not contribute to class discussions
- Often uses words incorrectly
- Sometimes uses words in incorrect order in sentences
- Seems lethargic and unanimated when talking
- Uses more physical behavior rather than verbal expression
- Cannot find descriptive words in conversation and writing
- Uses short sentences most of the time
- Rambles when telling a story or responding to questions
- Uses an excessive number of "ums," pauses, and repetitions
- Overuses words that define concrete ideas
- Talks excessively without making him/herself understood
- Fails to recognize cues indicating that he/she should stop talking
- An excessive inability to remember

Source: Glazer, S. M. (2001). Communication disorders: How to identify when students are having difficulty connecting [electronic version]. *Teaching K–8, 31*(5), 86–87. From the February 2001 issue of *Teaching K–8* magazine, Norwalk, CT 06854. Reprinted with permission of the publisher, Early Years, Inc.

referred to as having **specific language impairments (SLI)** (Pratt, Dotting, & Conti-Ramsden, 2006). For example, some students are not able to clearly distinguish among the words being spoken because they cannot discriminate among similar sounds. When a teacher, referring to a page in the social studies text, says "Let's look at the map," the student may focus her attention on the picture of a famous explorer (man) on the opposite page because she did not correctly hear the ending sound /p/. This is a language disorder related to phonology. Some students make errors in forming words, perhaps saying "I getted three book at the library," a disorder related to morphology. Yet others experience challenges in forming sentences, saying "I overslept because I was late" instead of "I was late because I overslept," a syntactical error.

Students who have difficulty finding correct words or understanding the nuances of language (e.g., not understanding the expression *It's raining cats and dogs* or *You're trying to butter me up*) have problems with semantics. Finally, some students experience difficulty participating in the social aspect of communication. They might monopolize a conversation, unaware that others would like to speak as well. Or they might start talking about a topic unrelated to the one currently being discussed, causing peers or adults to look at them questioningly. These are issues related to pragmatics.

The Professional Edge on this page includes many additional examples of student behavior that might signal the presence of language disorders. As you look at this list, which behaviors might you expect to see in Jade, the middle school student introduced at the beginning of the chapter?

PROFESSIONAL MONITORING TOOL

Council for Exceptional Children

Standard 2 Development and Characteristics of Learners . . . typical and atypical development

Students with Speech and Language Disorders

Many language disorders cannot be characterized based on a single dimension. These are some examples of language disorders that have several components:

■ Some students acquire language at a rate slower than is typical. This is referred to as a **language delay.** Some of these students eventually will catch up, and their language skills will be comparable to those of their peers. Others may always lag behind, but they may continue to make progress. For a few students, the delay can be significant, and the students do not progress. Early intervention, a topic introduced later in this chapter, is particularly helpful for students with language delays.

■ **Aphasia** refers to loss of language after it has developed. Although this term is most commonly applied to adults, children can become aphasic as a result of a traumatic brain injury (TBI), as might occur after an accident or an injury such as the one experienced by Jade, whom you met in the chapter opening. Aphasia includes difficulty in using language, receptively or expressively, and it can range from mild to severe. Examples include difficulty in recalling the words that describe common objects (e.g., *chair, glass*), forming sentences, and listening and reading with understanding (Shames & Anderson, 2002).

■ In order to use speech and language, the ears and their related structures and the brain must take in and interpret auditory information. Students who have **central auditory processing disorders (CAPD)** do not have hearing loss, but for some reason their brains do not effectively interpret the auditory information that comes from their ears (Nittrouer, 2002). They may have difficulty in several related areas, including listening and speaking using the rules of the language. It should be noted, though, that professionals disagree about whether CAPD is a unique disorder (MacFarland & Cacace, 2006); some view it instead as related to attention deficit–hyperactivity disorder(ADHD), learning disabilities, or specific language impairment (Bailey & Snowling, 2002).

Elements of Speech

Speech is the use of the oral channel for exchanging information and knowledge. Hundreds of muscles and structures can be involved in speech (Shames & Anderson, 2002), and some of these are highlighted in Figure 9.2. First, breath has to be expelled from the lungs using the muscles of the rib cage and the diaphragm. This air has to be forced through the larynx (also called the *voice box*), which includes structures and muscles in the neck. Here the muscles control the amount of air flowing out at one time, causing the vocal folds (also called the *vocal chords*) to vibrate and produce sound. Professional singers provide an example of how important this part of speech production can be. The y have learned to precisely control these muscles so that they can make exactly the correct pitch at exactly the correct loudness. Finally, the structures and muscles in the head, including the lips, jaws, tongue, teeth, and soft palate, provide for the fine-tuning of speech. Think about what you do to form the highlighted sounds in these words: *bond, pond*. You rely mostly on your lips to form the sounds correctly. Here is another example. Say these words: *this, think*. These sounds require touching the tip of the tongue to the upper teeth. If you have ever been to the dentist for work that involved numbing your mouth, you know exactly how much clear speech relies on controlling your lips, teeth, and tongue.

Speech has these dimensions (Lue, 2001): voice, resonance, articulation, and fluency.

■ **Voice** includes three components: (1) *Pitch* is the highness or lowness of the sound; (2) *intensity*, or loudness, is the perceived volume of speech; and (3) *quality* concerns the extent to which speech would be characterized as smooth or hoarse. Spoken language requires voice, but voice also is used for laughter, singing, and crying. The air exhaled from the lungs may be voiced by the vibration of the vocal folds within the larynx. In contrast, whispered sounds are not voiced, nor are a few speech sounds such as /p/, /t/, and /k/.

■ The nasal or oral aspect of spoken sound is called **resonance,** and it sometimes is considered part of voice. It is the component of speech that is determined by the balance of sound vibration in the mouth, nose, and throat. Resonance can be affected by the physical make-up

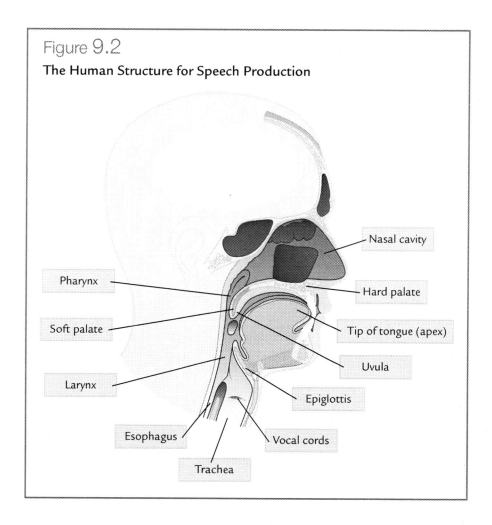

Figure 9.2

The Human Structure for Speech Production

of these structures or by problems in using them (Kummer, 2006). You can think of resonance in terms of people's voices: Some people have rich and full voices, but others have voices that might be considered weak or reedy.

■ Of all the dimensions of speech, school professionals often are most familiar with articulation. **Articulation** involves the movement of the tongue, teeth, lips, and palate to produce the sounds of a language. In the examples given previously (*bond, pond; this, think*), it is articulation skills that enable a person to say each word correctly.

■ It is not enough to be able to voice the sounds of our language. **Fluency** refers to the ability to speak without hesitations that interfere with clear communication. Children are considered fluent when they can produce speech smoothly, making words, sentences, and paragraphs that follow the cadence of English, with pauses for taking breaths.

> "Children are considered fluent when they can produce speech smoothly, making words, sentences, and paragraphs that follow the cadence of English."

Speech Disorders

Tiger Woods, Bruce Willis, James Earl Jones, and Carly Simon are all famous people who overcame stuttering difficulties.

Just as with language disorders, students who have **speech disorders** may have problems in any of the four components (voice, resonance, articulation, or fluency) of speech or in a combination of them. **Voice disorders** occur when students have difficulty with pitch, intensity, vocal quality, or resonance. For example, Evelyn is a student with a voice disorder. When she speaks, she breathes very shallowly and her voice seldom reaches above a whisper. Brittany also has a voice disorder; if you heard her speak, you would describe her voice as having a harsh, rough quality. Judd's voice is muffled. He sounds as though he has a cold even when he does not. Some voice disorders are caused by physical disabilities such as cleft lip and palate, discussed later in the chapter.

Many young children experience **articulation disorders,** including **omissions** (*bo* for *boat*), **substitutions** (*wan* for *ran*), or **additions** (*ammaminal* for *animal*). **Distortions** are yet another articulation disorder. They occur when a sound not found in the child's language is used for another sound. For example, if *soup* was said with air escaping from the side of the mouth, a distortion would have occurred. These errors are considered disorders only when they persist beyond the typical developmental period as illustrated in Figure 9.3. Andrew, the student introduced at the beginning of this chapter, has an articulation disorder.

The most common of **fluency disorders** is stuttering (Olsen, Steelman, Buffalo, & Montague, 1999). **Stuttering** occurs when a person's speech is broken by sound repetitions (e.g., *w-w-want*), prolonged sounds (e.g., *wwwant*), or unanticipated stoppages of sound (Venkatagiri, 2005). Some individuals who stutter also make unusual facial expressions or body movements as they struggle to speak. Mason, introduced in the chapter opening, is a student who has received speech/language services for stuttering. Interventions such as those outlined in the Specialized Instruction on the next page can have a strong positive impact when you work with students who have this disorder (e.g., Blomgren, Roy, Callister, & Merrill, 2005; Pellowski & Conture, 2002; Weiss, 2004).

Another fluency disorder is called cluttering. **Cluttering** occurs when an individual speaks in bursts or pauses in unexpected places during speech. The rhythm of speech may be described as jerky when a person clutters, and that person may not be aware that this is a problem.

An example of a particularly complex speech disorder is called *apraxia of speech* (American Speech-Language-Hearing Association, 2004). This disorder exists when an individual has extraordinary difficulty in producing speech that other people manage easily. When a child has this disorder, it is called **childhood apraxia of speech.** No matter how hard the child may try, she cannot put together the movements and patterns required to speak. Her lips, tongue, and other speech mechanisms seem to be unable to do what her brain is telling them to do. Students with apraxia usually understand language very well; the disorder is one of expression. As a result of apraxia of speech, some students' words are unintelligible. Many students with this disorder speak as little as possible, and so they often are perceived as being very shy or quiet. Some peers and adults may perceive them as lazy or unmotivated; others sometimes mistakenly assume that they lack the ability to achieve (Lewis, Freebairn, Hansen, Iyengar, & Taylor, 2004).

INTERNET RESOURCES
www.mankato.msus.edu/dept/comdis/kuster/stutter.html
The Stuttering Homepage was developed by a specialist at Minnesota State University. The site contains a wide variety of resources for children and adolescents, parents, teachers, and other professionals.

INTERNET RESOURCES
www.apraxia-kids.org/index.html
Apraxia-Kids is the website of the Childhood Apraxia of Speech Association. The website includes information about this disorder, links to many other resources, FAQs, and stories about children with this disorder and their families.

Figure 9.3

Mastery of English Speech Sounds

Although most children master vowel sounds by two to three years of age, it takes several additional years to learn consonant sounds and blends and to use them in the beginning, middle, and end of words.

Student Age	Sounds Typically Mastered
2	p, h, n, b, k
3	m, w, g, f, d
4	t, ʃ ("sh"), j ("y")
5	s, v, ŋ ("ng"), r, l, ʧ ("ch"), z, ʤ ("j")
6	θ ("th" in "<u>th</u>in"), ð ("th" in "<u>th</u>e"), ʒ ("zh" in "mea<u>s</u>ure")
8	Consonant blends and clusters

Source: Adapted from Owens, R. E., Metz, D. E., & Haas, A. (2003). *Introduction to communication disorders: A life span perspective* (2nd ed., p. 107). Boston: Allyn & Bacon.

Interacting with Students Who Stutter

More than anything, students who stutter need a communication environment that is supportive. Professionals can help by following these guidelines:

- Try to find a quiet time to share language with the student.

- Avoid the temptation to fill in words or finish sentences for the student.

- Do not react emotionally when the student has fluency difficulties.

- Do not interrupt the student.

- Maintain eye contact and wait patiently until the student finishes speaking. Give the student your full attention.

- Talk in a relaxed but slower than normal manner. Model relaxed, unhurried speech for all students in the class.

- Avoid giving advice that is not helpful such as "Slow down," "Relax," and "Take a deep breath."

- Practice all the skills that you have learned for being an effective listener.

- Teach speaking manners to all students; do not allow students to interrupt, speak for others, or finish their words for them.

- If reading aloud is necessary, have students read in unison in small groups. Gradually reduce the group size until the student is reading one to one with a naturally slow reader. Eventually, the other reader should begin to remain silent for every other word and then for more words.

- Do not force the student to talk or to perform tasks orally (e.g., reading in front of a group).

- Provide successful group speaking experiences for all students. In addition to choral responding, many students who stutter are far more fluent when they sing.

- Stay in touch with the speech/language pathologist, and ask for additional ideas for day-to-day communication and for situations in which problems have occurred.

Source: Adapted from Lue, M. S. (2001). Problems of voice and fluency: Identification and remediation. In M. S. Lue, *A survey of communication disorders for the classroom teacher* (pp. 137–157). Boston: Allyn & Bacon.

Prevalence of Speech and Language Disorders

According to recent figures from the U.S. Department of Education (2004), approximately 1.1 million students received services for a speech or language disorder as their primary area of disability. This group constitutes nearly 19 percent of students ages six to twenty-one receiving special education and approximately 1.7 percent of all school-age students. However, these data do not provide a complete picture of the number of students who receive speech and language services because, as noted earlier, they do not include students whose needs are addressed by related services.

Distinguishing between Speech and Language Prevalence Data

An additional dilemma exists in considering the prevalence of speech and language disorders. IDEA reports data only for the combined prevalence for these disorders, not for each separately. However, several studies have examined prevalence of speech and language disorders individually. Overall, researchers estimate that 5 percent of all children in first grade have a speech disorder and that nearly 6 percent of children in the primary grades have a language disorder not caused by a physical or sensory disability (National Institute on Deafness and Other Communication Disorders, 2002). Recognize, though, that even this information does not necessarily provide a clear picture of

CHECK
Your Learning
What factors might be responsible for the underestimating of the actual number of students who receive special education services for speech or language impairments?

"Researchers estimate that 5 percent of all children in first grade have a speech disorder and that nearly 6 percent of children in the primary grades have a language disorder not caused by a physical or sensory disability."

prevalence. As you learned in the section outlining the numerous types of speech and language disorders, some students have disorders that affect more than one area of speech or language, and many students have combinations of both speech and language disorders (Nippold, 2001, 2002; Spooner, 2002).

Other Prevalence Considerations

Several studies have examined whether speech and language disorders occur among boys and girls at approximately the same rate. Generally, boys are more likely than girls to be identified as having speech disorders in a ratio of approximately 2:1 (National Institute on Deafness and Other Communication Disorders, 2002). Boys are more likely than girls to be identified as having language disorders in a ratio of approximately 1.75:1. Prevalence related to race or ethnicity is difficult to estimate because of the many complicating factors that can arise in evaluating these students' speech and language skills, a topic addressed later in this chapter.

Causes of Speech and Language Disorders

Speech and language disorders are caused by many different factors. The following section highlights some of the most common.

Elena Rooraid/PhotoEdit

Many students with disabilities have speech and language disorders, including those with autism, intellectual disabilities, learning disabilities, and hearing loss.

Biological Causes

Some speech and language disorders are the result of problems related to the central nervous system or to the structure and functioning of other systems within the body. For example, many individuals who have intellectual disabilities also have speech and language disorders, and so intellectual disability is considered a biological cause of the related speech or language disorder. Other disabilities or special needs that involve the central nervous system, including the brain, also are part of this category—for example, autism and attention deficit–hyperactivity disorder. Likewise, hearing loss or deafness and vision loss or blindness can be causes of speech and language disorders. When students have physical disabilities that include muscle weaknesses as occurs in the disorder cerebral palsy, they may not be capable of producing the sounds needed for speech and language. Emotional disabilities also can cause speech and language disorders. Think about a young child with an internalizing disorder, who is focused inward and who largely ignores other children and adults. The child's inattention to the speech and language occurring in the environment can lead to delays or disorders.

Many other types of biological causes of speech and language disorders also can be identified. For example, some of these disabilities may be the result of a specific brain injury, as is the case with aphasia, a disorder described earlier. Other biological causes may be related to heredity (Bishop, 2002; Felsenfeld, 2002; Starkweather, 2002).

PROFESSIONAL MONITORING TOOL

Council for Exceptional Children

Standard 1 Foundations
. . . issues in definition and identification

Yet another cause of speech and language disorders is referred to as *congenital,* meaning the disorder is present at birth as a result of a known or unknown cause. One example of a congenital disorder is **cleft lip and/or palate**, the most common birth defect in the United States, affecting one out of every six hundred newborns (Cleft Palate Foundation, 2005). A child born with a *cleft lip* has a separation between the two sides of the lip that often also involves the upper jaw. In a *cleft palate,* an opening exists in the roof of the mouth. Some children have cleft lips, some have cleft palates, and some have both conditions.

As is occurring in several other disciplines, professionals who study individuals with speech and language disorders are exploring whether and how their brains may be different from those of other individuals (e.g., Ingham, 2001; Plante, 2001), and this research may in the future provide insights and new approaches to interventions. For now, though, this work generally is considered preliminary, and the results should be treated with caution.

Environmental Causes

A second group of causes of speech and language disorders relates to a child's environment. For example, some disorders occur because of repeated ear infections that interfere with hearing and eventually affect speech and language development (National Institute on Deafness and Other Communication Disorders, 2006). Another example of an environmental cause is neglect or abuse. Perhaps a young child is left alone much of the time without peer or adult language models. Alternatively, perhaps the child is punished for being noisy—for experimenting with speech sounds as all babies do, or for talking as a toddler. In either case, a negative impact on speech and language development is likely.

The activities in which students engage comprise another environmental cause of speech and language disorders. Some students abuse their voices. They scream or yell too frequently, causing problems that may lead to hoarseness or an inability to speak loudly enough. Others damage their speech structures by speaking in a way that stresses the muscles involved in producing speech. In addition, some students have significant allergies that when aggravated may affect their speech.

An additional environmental factor that can lead to speech and language disorders is one that you have read about in other chapters—poverty (Justice & Ezell, 2001; Nancollis, Lawrie, & Dodd, 2005). Children who live in poverty are more likely to be malnourished, possibly leading to brain damage and a variety of disabilities, including speech and language disorders. These children also are less likely than others to receive adequate medical care, and so illnesses such as ear infections and allergies are more likely to go untreated. Once again, speech and language disorders can be the outcome.

Making Sense of the Factors Contributing to Speech and Language Disorders

This discussion of causes of speech and language disorders could leave you with the impression that each cause is distinct and that identifying a cause is essential to intervention. This is not the case. As you learned in the discussions about learning disabilities, emotional and behavior disorders, and intellectual disabilities, in many cases the cause of a disability is unknown; the same is true for speech and language disorders. For example, a child's mother might have been a substance abuser, and during the birth process a brief period of anoxia may have occurred. The child may have a slight hearing loss, a fact that goes undetected until the student reaches kindergarten. Although the child then receives services at school, the family is not able to provide reinforcement at home and so progress is slow. Often no single cause is identified, and in many cases, identifying a cause is not particularly helpful for planning the child's instruction.

PROFESSIONAL MONITORING TOOL

Council for Exceptional Children

Standard 2 Development and Characteristics of Learners ...effects of environmental milieu

In 1996 the American Speech-Language-Hearing Association published its conclusion that CAPD is a real disorder and that specific interventions are needed to address it—interventions distinct from those used for related disorders and disabilities.

What Are the Characteristics of Individuals with Speech and Language Disorders?

Students who have speech and language disorders are a diverse group, and any discussion of what they are like cannot completely describe them. However, in the following sections, some of the most common cognitive and academic, social and emotional, and behavior characteristics of these students are outlined.

Cognitive and Academic Characteristics

No generalizations can be made concerning the cognitive characteristics of students with speech and language disorders. These students may be academically gifted, they may be average in their cognitive ability, or they may struggle to learn and understand. In addition, many students who have intellectual disabilities also have speech and language disorders.

Academic Characteristics

Although the academic achievement of some students with speech and language disorders is comparable to that of their peers, these disorders often have a profound impact on students' ability to learn (Watson et al., 2003). From the day that children begin to comprehend language, it is an essential means through which they explore their world and come to understand it. When they enter school, the importance of language is magnified. Early school learning relies largely on the sharing of information using oral language. At the same time, students begin to learn how to use language for reading and writing. As students progress through school, they are expected to have an increasingly sophisticated vocabulary, spoken and written, to compose stories and essays and to comprehend complex written materials such as those found in textbooks. No matter what age, students also need speech and language skills for communication and learning in all their other subject areas. Can you think of examples related to math? Science? Art or music? School activities such as lunch, assemblies, or after-school programs?

Speech and Language Disorders and Reading

Most of the research on the influence of speech and language disorders on student learning focuses on reading, and the available information is sobering (Al Otaiba & Smartt, 2003). Children who have significant speech or language delays are at high risk for reading difficulties (e.g., Catts, Hogan, & Fey, 2003; Smith, Pennington, Boada, & Shriberg, 2005). In fact, approximately 83 percent of kindergarteners with these disorders eventually qualify for remedial reading or special education services. Further, children with speech and language disorders often are unable to benefit from the early literacy experiences that are common in kindergarten, and so they are at an academic disadvantage almost from the time they begin school.

The types of reading difficulties students experience are directly related to their speech and language problems (Catts, Gillispie, Leonard, Kail, & Miller, 2002). Some students have

> *"Children who have significant speech or language delays are at high risk for reading difficulties."*

difficulty learning to sound out words they read because they cannot distinguish among similar sounds. Others do not understand how to add prefixes or suffixes to words or to recognize compound words. Some students do not hear the rhythm of language in their heads as they read, and this interferes with comprehension. Review all the elements of speech and language that have already been presented in this chapter and try to list reading problems that are likely to be related to each.

PROFESSIONAL MONITORING TOOL

Council for Exceptional Children

Standard 2 Development and Characteristics of Learners
. . . similarities and differences among individuals
. . . educational implications of exceptionalities

Research Notes

In a ten-state study of students in elementary, middle, and high school, Arndt and Healey (2001) found that among students with fluency disorders (i.e., students who stutter), 44 percent had an additional speech or language disorder (e.g., difficulty making certain sounds or delayed language development).

PROFESSIONAL MONITORING TOOL

Council for
Exceptional
Children

Standard 3 Individual Learning
Differences
... effects on an individual's life

Social and Emotional Characteristics

Many students with speech and language disorders struggle socially and emotionally (Law & Garrett, 2004). First, they must deal with their own self-concepts and their perceptions of how others interact with them. Students with fluency disorders, for example, may be the targets of peer teasing as described by this student:

> I like participating in class, but when I'm answering questions (and stutter) I always hear whispers of people imitating my stuttering and giggling. Even when I'm not stuttering I can hear them imitate me in a stuttering voice. The other day this kid named Scott says, "It's funny when you stutter." When I tried to tell him to buzz off, he imitated me with every word, even though I hardly stuttered.

When students have negative experiences such as these, they may need assistance maintaining positive views of themselves.

In addition to teasing, students with speech or language impairments may experience difficulty in social situations in any number of ways. If they mispronounce words, others may have difficulty understanding them. If they cannot find the word they need during a conversation or if they do not use the conventions of grammar, they cannot fully participate in the interactions. In addition, some students face challenges because they do not understand how to participate in conversations, and so they may become socially isolated. The problem can be compounded by adults who form negative opinions about students with speech and language disorders and their ability to achieve (e.g., Wood & Valdez-Menchaca, 1996).

Behavior Characteristics

Young children who cannot express their needs in words sometimes resort to inappropriate behaviors, as in the example of a toddler who bites a playmate in order to get a desired toy. A similar pattern can be seen among school-age students who have speech and language disorders. A strong body of evidence is emerging to indicate that students with speech and language disabilities are at high risk for behavior problems and even for being identified as having emotional and behavior disorders (Nelson, Benner, & Cheney, 2005). This relationship is explored in more detail in the Positive Behavior Supports.

"A strong body of evidence is emerging to indicate that students with speech and language disabilities are at high risk for behavior problems and even for being identified as having emotional and behavior disorders."

Speech and Language Disorders and Other Disabilities

The term *comorbidity* refers to the simultaneous existence of two or more disabilities. As mentioned earlier in this chapter, students with many different disabilities often have a comorbid speech or language disorder. In addition to students you have already learned about (i.e., those with learning disabilities, emotional disabilities, or intellectual disabilities), students with hearing loss, autism, physical or health disabilities, as well as multiple disabilities also may have a speech or language impairment.

Think about the issue of comorbidity as it is related to speech and language disorders. What might be the implications for students who have these disorders as well as another disability in terms of learning and behavior? Think, too, about the professionals who work with these students—whether they are general education teachers, classroom teachers, or speech/language pathologists. How would the presence of two disabilities affect their work with students?

CHECK Your Learning

What are the social and behavior characteristics of students with speech or language disorders? How might this disability affect these areas of functioning?

Linking Speech and Language Disorders and Emotional and Behavior Disabilities

Have you ever observed a young child whose language skills are just developing try to get a toy from a shelf that is out of reach? First, the child may go to an adult and point at the shelf. Then he may make a noise that might be an approximation of the desired toy (/kee/ for *kitty*). If the adult does not get the message, the child may become frustrated, crying and possibly hitting the adult in an attempt to make her understand. When language fails, children use behaviors, often disruptive ones, in their efforts to communicate. Although this dilemma is common among young children, it usually resolves itself as children's language skills improve. However, for some school-age students, the problem may persist.

Researchers have clearly demonstrated that a link exists between emotional disabilities and speech and language disorders (Benner, Nelson, & Epstein, 2002). In a review of pertinent studies, nearly nine out of every ten students with emotional disabilities in public schools also had language disorders. Among more specific findings were these:

- Students with language deficits are at substantially higher risk for antisocial behavior than students with speech disorders.

- Students with receptive language problems often are undiagnosed, and these students have higher rates of behavior problems than other students.

- The coexistence of language problems in students with emotional disabilities is ten times higher than it is in the general population.

- Language disorders significantly and negatively affect interpersonal relationships, often leading to antisocial behavior.

It is not clear which problem comes first. That is, do the speech and language impairments cause the emotional problems, or do the emotional disabilities lead to the communication disorders? It really does not matter. Instead, this information suggests that educators should be alert for the simultaneous presence of both disabilities so that appropriate assessment, diagnosis, and intervention can be implemented as follows:

- Students with emotional and behavior disorders should be screened for the presence of language disorders. This type of screening often is skipped with this group of students because of the immediate need to address their behaviors.

- Appropriate language interventions should be designed with input from speech/language pathologists for students needing these services.

- Screening and intervention should occur as early as possible in the student's educational career. Students benefit from language instruction primarily when they are very young, and missing this opportunity is likely to lead to later emotional and behavior problems. A proactive approach emphasizing prevention is far superior to later attempts at remediation.

Source: Benner, G. J., Nelson, J. R., & Epstein, M. H. (2002). Language skills of children with EBD: A literature review. *Journal of Emotional and Behavioral Disorders, 10,* 43–59. Copyright © 2002 by Pro-Ed., Inc. Reprinted with permission.

How Are Speech and Language Disorders Identified?

The procedures used to evaluate students with possible speech or language disorders and determine they are eligible for special education services are similar to those for identifying other students with disabilities. Cognitive ability is assessed using formal testing instruments, and overall school achievement is considered. Screening is completed to determine whether a vision or hearing loss is present. In this section, emphasis is placed on the evaluation strategies that directly address the speech or language disorder. Keep in mind that speech/language pathologists play a key role in assessing students with possible speech and language needs. You can review the scope of their responsibilities in the Professional Edge on the next page.

Roles and Responsibilities of Speech/ Language Pathologists in Schools

Speech/language pathologists play a lead role in ensuring that students with speech and language disorders receive appropriate services. Here is a summary of their roles and responsibilities, although these may vary slightly from state to state because of regulations, policies, and preferred practices.

Role	Examples of Responsibilities
Prevention	Providing staff development for school personnel, consulting with teachers
Identification	Screening for hearing, speech, and language disorders; participating in the prereferral process
Assessment/eligibility/IEP	Collecting assessment data, interpreting data, contributing to the determination of whether a disability exists, developing appropriate sections of the IEP
Caseload management	Scheduling, creating service options for students, managing caseload
Intervention	Designing and implementing interventions, arranging for technology support as needed
Counseling	Setting goals, making referrals as needed
Reevaluation	Participating in annual, triannual, and ongoing assessment activities
Transition	Facilitating the move from preschool to school, elementary to middle school, middle school to high school, and high school to postschool; fostering less restrictive placements
Dismissal	Determining if a student no longer needs services based on federal and state regulations
Supervision	Supervising practicum students and volunteers
Documentation/accountability	Creating all required documentation of assessments and services, including progress reports, treatment outcome measures, and paperwork required by federal and state regulation

Source: Adapted from American Speech-Language-Hearing Association. (2000). *Guidelines for the roles and responsibilities of school-based speech-language pathologist* (pp. 258–259). Rockville, MD: Author. Copyright © 2000 by the American Speech-Language-Hearing Association. Reprinted with permission.

dimensions of DIVERSITY

The National Black Association for Speech–Language and Hearing (www.nbaslh.org/index.htm) was formed in 1978 to increase the number of African American speech/language and hearing professionals and to represent the needs of individuals of African heritage who have communication disorders.

PROFESSIONAL MONITORING TOOL

Council for Exceptional Children

Standard 8 Assessment . . . administer formal and informal assessments

Assessment

A hallmark of assessment for speech and language disorders is the importance of integrating information obtained from formal assessments, data gathered from students' spontaneous conversations, and the contributions made by teachers and parents.

Speech Assessments

Several types of assessments may be completed to help professionals decide whether a student has a speech disorder. For many students, the speech/language pathologist administers a standardized test to determine whether a problem with articulation is present. Common tests include the Goldman–Fristoe Test of Articulation 2 (Goldman & Fristoe, 2000) and the Fisher–Logemann Test of Articulation Competence (Fisher & Logemann, 1971). Although the tests used for this purpose vary, they all have the common goal of detecting errors in articulation that are not expected given the child's age. By asking a child to finish sentences or to name pictures that are part of the test, the speech/language pathologist can determine whether he is omitting certain sounds, substituting one sound for another, adding sounds, or distorting the way a sound is made.

However, formal tests are not enough because they do not capture the way a student speaks in day-to-day activities. Speech/language pathologists also gather a spontaneous language sample that can help them to assess whether a student has an articulation disorder, a problem with voice or fluency, or a combination of disorders. They may ask a young student to talk about a toy or a game. They may engage an older student in a conversation about school, friends, or any other topic that seems likely to encourage him to provide several paragraphs of conversation. In addition, the professional likely will ask parents to provide a history of the student's development related to speech and ask teachers to describe the student's strengths and problems.

Speech/language pathologists also examine the student's physical structures for producing speech. They may observe whether a student's teeth are aligned well enough for sounds to be correctly produced. They also may look for abnormalities in the student's hard palate (i.e., the roof of the mouth). Other items assessed include the student's ability to easily use the lips and tongue to produce speech sounds. Finally, the speech/language pathologist notes whether the student's breathing patterns are typical. How might each of these areas affect a student's ability to produce speech?

Language Assessments

Students with specific language impairments may experience difficulty in any of several areas, and the assessment must address each of these. Examples of language components that might be assessed include the following:

- Receptive and expressive vocabulary
- Ability to retrieve words as needed (sometimes called *word finding*)
- Comprehension and processing of sentences
- Correct use of the rules of grammar
- Comprehension of stories and other narratives
- Ability to produce language, whether to tell a story or to participate in a conversation

To gather information about these areas, the speech/language pathologist uses both formal and informal measures. Tests such as the Comprehensive Assessment of Spoken Language (CASL) (Carrow-Woolfolk, 1999), the Clinical Evaluation of Language Fundamentals 3 (CELF-3) (Semel, Wiig, & Secord, 1995), and the Test of Adolescent and Adult Language 3 (TOAL-3) (Hammill, Brown, Larsen, & Wiederholt, 1994) are used to systematically assess the student's language production. Additionally, samples of the student's written schoolwork are reviewed, the student is observed in the classroom setting as well as in less structured environments (e.g., the lunchroom or playground), and parents and teachers are interviewed.

Assessment for Students Whose First Language Is Not English or Whose Use of English Is Nonstandard

One common dilemma faced by speech/language professionals is evaluating a student whose native language is not English or who speaks a variation of English that is considered nonstandard. In such a case, many precautions must be taken so that the assessment is accurate and fair (Brice, 2001; Kohnert, Windsor, & Yim, 2006). For example, in the use of standardized tests, speech/language pathologists must ensure that the test was developed for use with the students to whom it is being administered (Shames & Anderson, 2002). They also must ensure that directions and other aspects of the test are not confusing to individuals who do not speak standard English; this may lead to incorrect responses, not because of language problems but because of the style in which the directions are given.

"One common dilemma faced by speech/language professionals is evaluating a student whose native language is not English or who speaks a variation of English that is considered nonstandard."

PROFESSIONAL MONITORING TOOL

Council for Exceptional Children

Standard 8 Assessment . . . administer nonbiased assessments

Other general factors also must be reviewed in this type of assessment. The testing situation itself may be particularly stressful for a student who is not a native English speaker. The

Purestock/Getty Images

Students who are not native speakers of English or who do not speak standard English are sometimes confused by test directions and procedures and thus may be assessed incorrectly.

dimensions of
DIVERSITY

When learning English as a second language in school, a student's progress in continuing to learn the first language may be slowed or stopped. The student will then be at risk for having a language disorder in either language: The first language is still at a basic level and the second language cannot yet be used for complex communication tasks (Bernstein & Tiegerman-Farber, 2002).

PROFESSIONAL MONITORING TOOL

Council for Exceptional Children

Standard 3 Individual Learning Differences
. . . variations in beliefs, traditions, and values

expectation for the student to participate in a conversation with the professional administering the assessment may violate some students' cultural norms (e.g., children should not speak at length to an adult who is an authority figure). Can you identify other dilemmas that might arise in assessing students whose native language is not English or whose language is not standard English?

Later in this chapter, additional information is provided on language differences or variations and speech/language services. For now, it is important to remember that the assessment of students from diverse backgrounds poses challenges to the speech/language pathologist as well as to the team making a decision about eligibility for special education.

Eligibility

Along with data regarding cognitive ability, achievement, and other domains, the information about a student's speech and language skills is considered by a team that includes the parents, the student if appropriate, general and special educators, an administrator, specialists such as the speech/language pathologist, and others as needed. They respond to these questions:

1. *Given the student's age, does the student have a significant delay or difference in speech or language that would be considered a speech or language impairment?* As noted in the preceding section, the professionals addressing this question must take into account whether the assessment data suggest a true disorder or a language difference because of native language or culture.

2. *Does the student's speech or language impairment adversely affect educational performance?* As you know, this question must be asked because IDEA stipulates that special education services can be offered only if the disability negatively affects educational performance.

3. *Can the student benefit from special education intervention?* Although the answer to this question generally would be yes, if that has been the case for the other questions, sometimes the issue is not completely clear. Particularly for a student who is older—perhaps in high school—whether services can still address certain speech disorders may be doubtful. Issues such as these must be considered.

Based on the answers to these questions, the multidisciplinary team determines whether the student needs special education. However, keep in mind the fact that in some states students are eligible for services because of their speech or language disorders alone, whereas in other states services in this area are provided only if students also have other disabilities. In the latter case, the student would have been evaluated for speech and language services to be provided as a related service, not as special education.

How Do Learners with Speech and Language Disorders Receive Their Education?

Students with speech and language disorders receive their education in the setting most appropriate for them based on their special needs. If the speech or language disorder is the primary disability, emphasis is placed on providing services in general education with peers. If other disabilities also exist, the team that makes the decision about placement will take these into account as well.

PROFESSIONAL MONITORING TOOL

Council for Exceptional Children

Standard 1 Foundations . . . issues, assurances, and due process rights

Early Childhood

Most young children are not given a specific disability designation because of the difficulty of completing an accurate assessment and the resulting risk of misidentification. However, the most critical time in life for speech and language development is early childhood, and much is known about typical speech and language development and problems that can occur for very young children (e.g., Paden & Yairi, 1999). In fact, of the approximately 638,000 children ages three to five who received special education services through IDEA in 2002–2003, more than 309,000 were identified as having speech or language impairments as the primary disability (U.S. Department of Education, 2004).

The Importance of Early Intervention

The rationale for providing intensive speech and language intervention for young children can be justified in several ways. First, research suggests that when a problem exists, the earlier an intervention is begun and the longer it is implemented, the more likely the problem will be addressed effectively. Second, when early intervention is undertaken, services can be intense; that is, they can involve a speech/language pathologist, a teacher, and the family. By involving all the important adults in the intervention process, more services can be delivered and more positive results can be expected. The final justification also is related to the notion of intensity. Specifically, the progress that young children make in overcoming speech and language disorders will more likely be maintained if support is provided during these critical years across settings and across time. In recognition of this, there has been an increase in the extent to which speech/language therapists work even with children between birth and age three.

Approaches for Early Speech and Language Intervention

Traditionally, speech/language services were offered in a *pullout model,* even for very young children. That is, the speech/language pathologist would come to the home or preschool classroom to get the child to receive services; take the child to a separate room, classroom, or office; provide intervention individually or in a small group; and then return the child to the parent or classroom. This approach had the benefit of eliminating distractions for the child, but it removed the child from the natural setting in which speech and language occur and had the potential for stigmatizing the child.

Although a traditional approach sometimes is still appropriate, other options can be implemented as well. Some young children receive their speech/language services in the context of the early childhood center, preschool setting, or kindergarten classroom. The advan-

dimensions of
DIVERSITY

Mendez-Perez (2000) found that Mexican American mothers believed their preschool children's language disorders were not disabilities and that they resulted from young age, teething, or ear infections. These mothers also believed that their children would learn English but at a later age than children who did not experience language difficulties.

tage of this approach is that the speech/language pathologist can observe the child's ability to function in the natural environment. However, the presence of an additional adult in the classroom can be distracting to a group of young children, and some youngsters with speech or language problems may dislike being singled out for intervention in the presence of their peers.

One additional option is an approach that combines separate service, in-class service, and indirect service. In some cases, the speech/language pathologist periodically may work directly with a child in a separate setting, often to check on progress, to address particularly complex problems, and to make decisions about subsequent steps in intervention. However, at least some of the services are offered within the classroom context. The final component of this approach is consultation. The speech/language pathologist meets with the early childhood specialist or special educator to problem solve about the child's needs and to discuss interventions. The goal is for classroom personnel to play significant roles in helping the child's skill development; this is an important factor because the speech/language pathologist may only be available for direct services on a limited basis.

Elementary and Secondary School Services

Nearly all students who have been identified as having speech or language disorders receive their education in a typical school setting. In fact, as you can see by reviewing Figure 9.4, approximately 87 percent of students with this disability are educated in general education classrooms; that is, they are in a special education setting for less than 21 percent of the school day (U.S. Department of Education, 2004).

The way in which speech/language services are implemented depends on the nature of the student's disability. For example, many elementary students receive speech/language therapy services once or twice each week, usually for thirty minutes per session. In this model the speech/language pathologist provides direct services in a separate setting. You may hear this service model referred to by children as "going to speech." When this approach is employed, the general education teacher and speech/language pathologist stay in touch so that the teacher knows which skills should be reinforced and the specialist knows what topics are the focus in the classroom language arts program as well as other areas of the curriculum. Keep in mind that in many school districts speech/language pathologists work in two or more schools, and so their time to meet with teachers and to attend critical team meetings sometimes is limited.

For students who have disabilities in addition to speech or language disorders, services are part of their overall education program. Some of these students receive services in a pullout model similar to that previously described. For other students, a speech/language pathologist may provide services in the special education classroom. For example, if a student has a significant hearing loss that is affecting the clarity of her speech and receives special education services in a separate setting for half of the school day, the speech/language pathologist may provide services in the special education classroom. A similar approach might be employed for

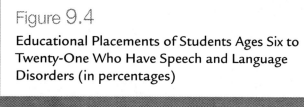

Figure 9.4

Educational Placements of Students Ages Six to Twenty-One Who Have Speech and Language Disorders (in percentages)

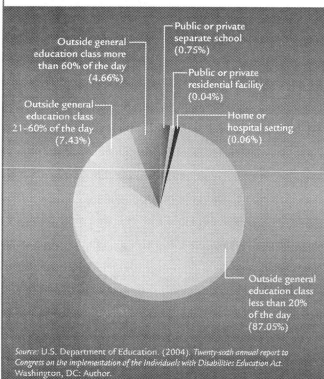

Public or private separate school (0.75%)

Public or private residential facility (0.04%)

Home or hospital setting (0.06%)

Outside general education class more than 60% of the day (4.66%)

Outside general education class 21–60% of the day (7.43%)

Outside general education class less than 20% of the day (87.05%)

Source: U.S. Department of Education. (2004). Twenty-sixth annual report to Congress on the implementation of the Individuals with Disabilities Education Act. Washington, DC: Author.

students with significant intellectual disabilities. Sometimes both in-class and pullout services are delivered.

Inclusive Practices

If you think about the nature of speech and language disorders and the impact they can have on all aspects of students' lives—their academic performance, their relationships with peers and teachers, and their interactions in the family and community—it really is not surprising that inclusive practices are readily supported for students with this disability. The most appropriate setting in which students can learn and practice speech and language skills is in general education. The Inclusion Matters on the next page highlights how the trend over the past decade to provide more and more support for students with speech and language disorders in general education settings has positively affected those services.

> *"One relatively new role for professionals working with students with speech and language disorders is co-teaching."*

One relatively new role for professionals working with students with speech and language disorders is co-teaching (Boswell, 2005). When this inclusive approach is used, speech/language pathologists and general education teachers design and deliver language-based interventions to all the students in a class. For example, students may be divided into three groups. One group works with the general education teacher on a comprehension activity related to the story being read. The second group works with the speech/language pathologist on vocabulary related to the story. The third group works independently to write a different ending for the story or to draw pictures to illustrate their favorite scenes. Each group eventually completes all three activities.

Transition and Adulthood

Some of the needs of students with speech and language disorders who are transitioning from childhood to adulthood are similar to those of other students with disabilities including the ability to self-advocate, the importance of making wise choices regarding higher education and careers, and the skills to function successfully in a job and the community. Some students also may need assistance in building self-esteem so they leave school with a true appreciation of their strengths and talents in addition to an understanding of their special needs (Bashir, Goldhammer, & Bigaj, 2000). Although fewer students receive speech/language services as they continue through school, some receive services until they graduate.

Language requirements become increasingly complex as students get older (National Dissemination Center for Children with Disabilities, 2003). Students need to read and comprehend textbooks that are content dense, participate in conversations both inside and outside the classroom with increasingly sophisticated skills (e.g., reading nonverbal cues), and learn the vocabulary of postsecondary education and specific occupations (Garcia, Laroche, & Barette, 2002). All of these demands can cause stress for students and their families (Patchell & Hand, 1993).

One indicator of the challenges faced by adolescents and young adults with speech and language disorders is found by looking at information about behavior. Experts estimate that the prevalence of language disorders among female juvenile delinquents is three times greater than in the rest of the population (Castrogiovanni, 2002). Most researchers agree that speech and language disorders are far more prevalent among juvenile offenders than among other young adults (Sanger, Moore-Brown, Montgomery, & Larson, 2002). As with young children, professionals clearly find that students who experience difficulty in communicating with words may turn to aggression or other inappropriate behavior as an alternative. This issue must be addressed or students will be unlikely to make a smooth transition from school to adulthood.

Research Notes

One recent study queried employees with communication disorders and their employers and found that noise, tasks that required speed, jobs that included speaking to groups, and co-worker attitudes all were barriers that had to be overcome (Garcia, Laroche, & Barette, 2002). Issues such as these should be considered in transition planning for students with speech and language disorders.

Research Notes

Catts, Adlof, and Weismer (2006) examined the language abilities of eighth-grade students who had poor comprehension as measured on standardized reading tests. Not surprisingly, they found that these students had problems in overall language comprehension. However, they did not have deficits in phonological processing.

Comparison of Traditional and Classroom-Based Service Delivery for Students with Speech and Language Disorders

In the past, speech/language pathologists provided services to students with speech and language disorders largely in separate settings—sometimes individually and sometimes in small groups. Although some situations still call for this approach, speech/language services increasingly are being delivered in close collaboration with special educators, classroom teachers, and parents. These are some of the most significant differences between the two approaches, although the precise roles of these professionals may vary somewhat state by state.

	Separate Pullout Services	Classroom-Based Services
Intervention contexts	Isolates students from authentic contexts; presents intervention in a separate room	Includes students in authentic social situations; presents intervention in functional contexts (classroom, playground, lunchroom)
Role of the SLP*	Serves as primary service provider; presents the intervention	Plans an intervention program (decides where, when, and who will facilitate language)
Relationship of the SLP to parents and teachers	Serves as the expert; engages teachers and parents as helpers	Collaborates with and values the expertise of parents and teachers; draws upon parents and teachers as change agents
Goals and objectives	Selects goals on the basis of test measures and language analyses; determines contents and tasks arbitrarily, without regard to curriculum	Bases goals on curricular content and tasks; individualizes expectations; determines need for adaptations or supports
Language focus	Addresses components of language removed from real discourse events	Focuses on language components as they relate to functioning in whole discourse events; integrates language parts
Assessment mechanisms	Relies on standardized measures; identifies students' weaknesses, what they can't do; compares students' performance to test norms	Assesses performance within curricular tasks; identifies abilities and influence of supports; determines functioning relative to curricular demands
Evaluation methods	Readministers tests periodically, charts attainments of specific targets	Monitors outcomes continually; assesses functioning in context; analyzes products
Student roles	Places students in structured one-on-one interactions; leads to limited, passive roles	Draws upon an array of communicative events; permits active social roles and varied types of participation
Communicative options, demands	Limits or structures response options and participation in types of communication events	Requires flexible use of communication skills; leads to participation in a variety of "whole" communicative events

*Speech/language pathologist

Source: Adapted from Culatta, B., & Wiig, E. H. (2002). Language disabilities in school-age children and youth. In G. H. Shames & N. B. Anderson (Eds.), *Human communication disorders: An introduction* (6th ed., pp. 218–257). Boston: Allyn & Bacon. Copyright © 2002 by Pearson Education. Adapted by permission of the publisher.

What Are Recommended Educational Practices for Students with Speech and Language Disorders?

Students with speech and language disorders may benefit from the academic and behavior interventions that are effective for students with learning and behavior problems, but specialized interventions are needed as well. Some students receive articulation therapy,

Working with Students with Speech and Language Disorders: Getting the Message Across

The severity of students' speech or language disorders can range from mild to extensive. These ideas can help school professionals communicate clearly with these students:

- Before giving the message, say the student's name and wait for the student to look at you.

- Speak slowly, clearly, and loud enough to be heard. If possible, use hand gestures, too.

- Keep instructions short. Give several short instructions rather than "laundry lists" when you speak.

- Emphasize important words. Do not use adverbs and adjectives unless the student knows the meaning of these words. That is, separate ongoing interaction from the need for instruction and teach words at another time.

- Keep the ideas in messages simple. Use one sentence for each idea. For example, say, "I like the way you finished your work." "Now go get your science book." This form is better than making the two messages into a single sentence.

- If you want to give a multistep instruction, use visual reminders with the instructions. For example, use pictures, symbols, or written words to depict each part of the instruction.

- If you want to give an if–then instruction, say, for example, "We will go to the store after you clean the blackboard." That is, give the instruction in "then–if" order with emphasis on what is required by the student.

- If a student does not respond, wait at least ten seconds, get his or her attention, give the message again using fewer words, and with emphasis on the important words.

- If the student responds incorrectly, get his or her attention and repeat the message using different words.

- If the student consistently responds incorrectly, teach the student by using modeling and feedback to follow the instruction.

- Most importantly, remember to keep your "cool." Sometimes the easiest message to convey is anger.

How could you apply each of these ideas to the professional role that you plan to have? How might these strategies vary depending on whether you work in an elementary, a middle, or a high school?

Source: Adapted from Saunders, M. D. (2001). Who's getting the message? Helping your students understand in a verbal world. *Teaching Exceptional Children, 33*(4), 70–74. Copyright 2001 by the Council for Exceptional Children. Reprinted with permission.

---

others are assisted to use their speech apparatus correctly, and yet others benefit from intensive programs that increase phonemic awareness. In the Specialized Instruction on this page you can learn about general interventions that teachers and other educators may use on a day-to-day basis. In the sections that follow, you can learn about two areas of particular interest: (1) the integration of speech and language services with literacy instruction and (2) augmentative and alternative communication.

Speech/Language Services and Literacy Instruction

Throughout this chapter, emphasis has been placed on how speech and language disorders can affect students' achievement and behavior. This relationship is widely recognized among school professionals, and as a result speech/language pathologists increasingly are partnering with general education teachers, special education teachers, bilingual educators, and others to ensure that all students receive the early communication assistance needed to develop crucial language and literacy skills (Boswell, 2005; Gillon, 2005).

According to the American Speech-Language-Hearing Association (Kamhi, 2003), speech/language pathologists can reinforce relationships between spoken language and preliteracy skills, provide interventions related to phonemic awareness and memory, analyze

A typical speech/language pathologist serves anywhere from 15 to 110 students; the average caseload is 49 students per week (U.S. Department of Education, 2002d).

PROFESSIONAL MONITORING TOOL

Council for Exceptional Children

Standard 7 Instructional Planning
. . . incorporate instructional and assistive technology

Courtesy of Assistive Technology Inc.

Augmentative and alternative communication (AAC) devices can provide a means for students with speech and language disorders to interact more easily with people inside and outside school.

Research Notes

Nippold, Ward-Longergan, and Fanning (2005) studied the development of persuasive writing skills in children, adolescents, and adults. The researchers used their findings to make recommendations concerning how speech/language therapists and teachers could help students develop syntactic, semantic, and pragmatic skills in this important communication skill.

PROFESSIONAL MONITORING TOOL

Council for Exceptional Children

Standard 6 Language . . . augmentative and assistive communication strategies

the language demands found in textbooks and other school materials and media, and analyze student language so that interventions can be tailored to students' needs. Speech/language pathologists also can play roles in prevention, early intervention, assessment, therapy, program development, and documentation of outcomes. Finally, they can help to advocate for literacy programs at the local and state levels.

A strong implication of this educational practice relates to collaboration (Gardner, 2006). It is essential that school professionals recognize that their efforts are far more effective if they blend their expertise (Santos, 2002). This means that general and special education teachers need to keep speech/language pathologists informed about critical curriculum topics being addressed and problems that they observe in students. Conversely, speech/language pathologists must initiate conversations with teachers to discuss student needs and plan subsequent steps for interventions. For all, clear and frequent communication is essential (Mroz, 2006).

Communication Using Technology

Many students with speech and language disorders can be helped tremendously through technology (Mechling & Cronin, 2006; Segers & Verhoeven, 2004). In addition to the examples provided in the Technology Notes on the next page, computer hardware and software, personal digital assistants (PDAs), and options now available via the Internet can help students communicate effectively and practice the skills they are learning.

Augmentative and Alternative Communication

Augmentative and alternative communication (AAC) comprises strategies that compensate for an individual's communication limitations or disabilities. AAC strategies usually are divided into two categories: (1) *unaided,* or those that do not require the use of special equipment or materials (e.g., sign language) and (2) *aided,* those that depend on some type of equipment or materials. Sign language is not considered here. Instead, the emphasis is on aided communication options. AAC can greatly benefit students with speech and language disorders (Binger & Light, 2006; Millar, Light, & Schlosser, 2006).

One example of an AAC device is a communication board. This device uses pictures, symbols, or printed words to facilitate student communication, and it can be low tech or high tech. For example, for a young student whose communication needs are fairly simple, a communication board might consist of small pictures arranged in rows and columns on a flat display. The student points to the picture that displays the desired message (e.g., "I want a drink" by pointing to a glass or "I'm hungry" by pointing to a dish). Many far more sophisticated versions of communication boards exist as well. These boards may be computerized and include a synthesized speech component. Software also exists that professionals can use to tailor the images on a communication board to a student's precise needs. Communication boards also exist for adolescents and adults that incorporate many symbols and permit communication about highly technical topics. Also available are communication boards that appear on computer monitors. When used with a touch screen, this option eliminates the need for a separate board.

Another AAC device is word prediction software. For students who have difficulty writing, this software guesses at the current word being typed and offers suggestions in a list. The student can select an option and avoid having to type the entire word, and the software ensures that words are spelled correctly. Word prediction software also serves to help composition skills. It predicts what the student's next words will be, and the student can

Many students with speech and language disorders—regardless of whether they have other disabilities as well—can learn new skills and practice emerging skills with the assistance of computer technology. This technology also can help students in their schoolwork by facilitating their reading and writing. Here are some examples of this type of software:

TypeIt4Me (version 3.0)

www.typeit4me.com

- This Macintosh computer software works with most other programs, including word-processing and database software.

- Students can create lists of words that they are likely to use, categorize them, and then click to bring up the category. By clicking on the desired word, they do not have to type it out or know exactly how to spell it.

- Students also store other information that they may need. For example, students who struggle to write can type their initials and their name will appear onscreen. They also can create abbreviations for long words to facilitate composition.

textHELP! Read & Write (version 8.0)

www.texthelp.com/page.asp?pg_id=10060

- Designed for students over the age of seven, this Windows-based software is in essence a floating toolbar that provides tools for reading and writing; it runs concurrently with other computer programs.

- The software can read back to the student text that has been composed.

- Spell-checking can occur as the student types or after he composes; spell-check includes phonetic analysis.

- Words that are easily confused are highlighted so that students can check for correct word use (e.g., *there, their; here, hear*).

- Other features include a built-in dictionary, thesaurus, and calculator and an Internet site for teachers using the software.

The Talking Series by Laureate Learning Systems

www.enablemart.com/productdetail.aspx?pid=725&dept=12&store=10

- This interactive software is designed to encourage students to develop expressive language skills and skills for using augmentative and alternative communication.

- Three programs focus on the uses of nouns and verbs.

- Activities include the computer speaking the words to students, picture matching, picture identification (finding the word that corresponds to the picture), and finding nouns that all belong to a single category.

Source: Based on Kelley-Smith, S. (2000). Can we talk? Software for language development. *TECH-NJ 2000, 11*(1), 7–10. Retrieved January 12, 2003, from www.edrs.com/members/sp.cfm?AN= ED469059.

Courtesy of Texthelp Systems Inc.

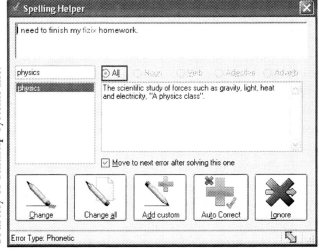

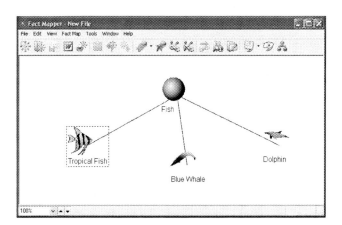

Courtesy of Assistive Technology Inc.

*T*echnology to support students with speech and language disorders is evolving rapidly and opening new avenues for communication.

 PROFESSIONAL MONITORING TOOL

Council for Exceptional Children

Standard 9 Professional and Ethical Practice
. . . methods to remain current regarding practice

either accept the prediction or substitute the intended word. One recent advance is the development of this type of software for personal digital assistants (PDAs). This innovation can help older students communicate, even without their voices, in a way that is very much accepted in today's society.

Technology for Language Practice

Technology also assists students in skill development. Perhaps you have observed students in an elementary school using a computer program to practice their knowledge of letters and sounds. Alternatively, they may have been learning how to make new words by combining various letters. Such technology is becoming commonplace and can be valuable for students who need extensive practice on basic speech and language skills. One example of such software is Fast Forword (Scientific Learning), a set of programs for students in kindergarten through twelfth grade that includes intensive skill development (from phonemic awareness to listening comprehension) using game-like exercises and immediate feedback.

Technology for students with speech and language disorders continues to advance. In some classrooms the teacher wears a microphone and the students wear or sit near receivers so that they clearly hear the teacher's voice during instruction. Technology also is emerging to help students who stutter speak more slowly to avoid hesitations and to produce natural-sounding synthetic speech for those who cannot use their own voices. Certainly, one defining feature of schools of the very near future will be the use of technology to help students communicate and learn. School professionals should stay abreast of developments in these areas, and if they are working with students using unfamiliar technology, they should seek input from specialists so that they can better interact with students and recognize if problems are occurring. At the same time, teachers should constantly monitor to ensure that technology is supporting students' communication, not interfering with it.

What Are the Perspectives of Parents and Families?

The importance of parents' participation in their young children's development is universally acknowledged, and it is the premise on which early intervention services for children with disabilities is based. When attention turns to children's speech and language development, parents' roles become, if anything, even more crucial (Guralnick, Connor, Neville, & Hammond, 2002; Mendez-Perez, 2000). Children acquire speech and language skills by observing language models, by experimenting in communication with others, and by refining their language skills based on feedback from others. How can parents and other significant caregivers provide all these experiences to young children?

Helping Parents to Develop Children's Language Skills

Have you ever observed parents with their young children? They talk to them, repeat their youngsters' words, and elaborate on their children's attempts to communicate (e.g., Child: "Me go." Parent: "Oh, do you want to go?"). Most parents intuitively interact with their young children in ways that foster speech and language development. Even so, enhancing parents' awareness and understanding of speech and language development and how to foster it can be very beneficial, especially for children with delays or disorders (Douville, 2000; Miles & Ratner, 2001).

One example of educating parents comes from a summer "sound camp" for children with speech disorders (Al Otaiba & Smartt, 2003). Parents were taught about the concept of phonemic awareness and given simple activities to help their children practice at home the skills being learned at camp. When parents were asked about their perceptions of the camp and the parent education component of it, they reported that the camp was very helpful for their children. In addition, they commented that they had a much better understanding of the concepts related to speech and language development and that they could thus better help their children at home and advocate for them at school. The parents also appreciated learning how to teach their children—for example, using small steps and occasionally repeating or reviewing skills already learned. They stressed the importance of home-based activities being family friendly, too.

> *"Most parents intuitively interact with their young children in ways that foster speech and language development."*

Another parent education program emphasized general strategies to increase parents' awareness of opportunities at home for encouraging language development (Farber & Goldstein, 1998). Parents learned how toys can stimulate children to talk and to use their imaginations. For older children, parents' discussions included the nonverbal and noninteractive characteristics of television watching and videogame playing and strategies for encouraging language use during these common child activities. Parents also discussed the importance of engaging children in games and activities that encourage language use.

Diversity and Speech and Language Interventions

Because language is a core element in every culture, speaking with parents from diverse groups about students' speech and language needs can be particularly difficult. For example, parents who do not speak English fluently may have difficulty helping their children to make sounds correctly and blend them into words. If English is not spoken in the home but school professionals are teaching it at school, students may not have enough opportunities to practice emerging skills and so may be at a disadvantage (Swanson, Hodson, & Schommer-Aikins, 2005). Based on what you have read in this chapter and your own experiences, what other issues can you identify that might occur with parents from nondominant cultures of students with speech and language disorders?

Significant differences may exist between Western cultures and other cultures. Think about augmentative and alternative communication. Most school professionals applaud the emerging technologies that facilitate student communication, give them greater independence, and assist them in their learning (Jones, Angelo, & Koskoska, 1999). School professionals not only encourage parent participation in choosing and using AAC devices, but they also rely on it. Not everyone shares this view, however. In some families, AAC might be seen as unnecessary or even detrimental because it can be intrusive in terms of family interactions (Huer, Parette, & Saenz, 2001; Huer, Saenz, & Diem, 2001). Its benefit of providing

PROFESSIONAL MONITORING TOOL

Council for Exceptional Children

Standard 2 Development and Characteristics of Learners
. . . role of families in supporting development

INTERNET RESOURCES
www.helpforkidspeech.org
The Help for Kid's Speech website is sponsored by the Scottish-Rite Foundation of Florida. Its goal is to assist parents, professionals, and others to provide better care for children with speech and language disorders. In addition to information on various disorders, the site includes tips for teachers and parents.

Laura Dwight Photography

Contemporary approaches to speech/language services emphasize the integral role of the family in setting priorities and implementing interventions.

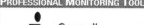

PROFESSIONAL MONITORING TOOL

Council for
Exceptional
Children

Standard 1 Foundations
. . . impact of differences in
values, languages, and customs

independence may be viewed as a reason to avoid it (Parette & Huer, 2002). For example, some Asian families may want AAC options that do not detract from the family's traditional caregiving role. These families also may presume that AAC options are the responsibility of school professionals, not families. They may even delay approving of AAC devices for their children until they observe that such technology is accepted and used by other children (Parette, 1998)

What Trends and Issues Are Affecting the Field of Speech and Language Disorders?

The complexity of the field of speech and language disorders guarantees that it is characterized by rapidly changing practice and controversy. Two important topics for professionals who work with students with speech and language disorders are (1) identifying and addressing these disabilities in a multicultural society and (2) basing student interventions on evidence-based practices.

Differences versus Disorders in a Multicultural Society

Diversity is a defining characteristic of the U.S. population. Given this, school professionals addressing students' speech and language needs must recognize how diversity affects their efforts (Kennedy, 2006; Whitney, 2005).

Language Differences

Speech and language professionals are careful to distinguish between **language differences**—variations from standard speech and language that are considered normal—and **language disorders**—impairments that interfere with language comprehension and use (American Speech-Language-Hearing Association, 2003; Bernstein & Tiegerman-Farber, 2002). One example of a language difference is an **accent,** a variation in the surface characteristics of

Many misconceptions exist regarding dialects. Here are some of the most common:

Myth: A dialect is something that someone else speaks.

Reality: Everyone who speaks a language speaks some dialect of the language; it is not possible to speak a language without speaking a dialect of the language.

Myth: Dialects always have highly noticeable features that set them apart.

Reality: Some dialects get much more attention than others; the status of speaking a dialect, however, is unrelated to public commentary about its special characteristics.

Myth: Only varieties of a language spoken by socially disfavored groups are dialects.

Reality: The notion of dialect exists apart from the social status of the language variety; there are socially favored as well as socially disfavored dialects.

Myth: Dialects result from unsuccessful attempts to speak the correct form of a language.

Reality: Dialect speakers learn their language by imitating members of their speech community who speak the same variety, not by failing to mimic speakers of the standard variety.

Myth: Dialects inherently carry negative social connotations.

Reality: Dialects are not necessarily positively or negatively valued; their social values are derived strictly from the social position of their speech community.

As you work with students, you can help all of them to understand how language differences such as dialects are part of the diversity and richness of today's society. Here are some suggestions for helping students to understand dialects:

- Use literature written in various dialects (e.g., short stories, poems, dialogue). Students can read passages out loud, compare ways people talk with ways they write, and discuss spelling variations.

- Play music with lyrics in various dialects. Have students write out lyrics and discuss the language used (e.g., its authenticity).

- Recognize and respect student dialects by allowing their use without correction during classroom discussions, when they are writing in journals, or acting out plays with dialogue.

- Have students explore the grammatical rules of a dialect. They might try to create lessons for teaching the dialect to others or try translating a poem in standard English to a dialect.

Sources: Adapted from Newton, D. W. (2004), *The reality of dialects.* Retrieved January 31, 2004, from www.westga.edu/~dnewton/engl2000/dialects.html (Originally in Wolfram & Schilling-Estes, 1998); and Language Varieties Network (2004), *Pidgins, creoles, and other stigmatized varieties.* Retrieved February 7, 2004, from www2.hawaii.edu/~gavinm/home.htm

---

language. If you have friends from different parts of the country, you may comment that one of them has a Boston accent or a Southern accent. You are referring to the way they pronounce words or make particular sounds, but you are not implying that their language is disordered. If you know individuals who learned English after learning another language, you may notice that they, too, speak English with an accent.

"In recent years professionals have worked diligently to stop the practice of trying to change students' dialects."

A somewhat different example is a **dialect** which refers to the structure of language and the rules that govern it (Shames & Anderson, 2002). One dialect that has received considerable attention is African American Vernacular English (AAVE), sometimes called *Black English* or *Ebonics.* It is spoken by many (but not all) working-class African American families, and it includes differences in some of the sounds made (*dis* for *this*) and words used (*Where is my paper at?* instead of *Where is my paper?*). The Professional Edge on this page outlines myths and realities related to dialects and provides suggestions for

dimensions of
DIVERSITY

Would you like to learn more about AAVE? This website—www.une.edu.au/langnet/aave.htm—provides information on its history and grammar as well as links to explore other dialects.

addressing dialects in the classroom. Keep in mind that dialects are differences, not disorders (Connor & Craig, 2006; Rodekohr & Haynes, 2001). In fact, in recent years professionals have worked diligently to stop the practice of trying to change students' dialects. Instead, they have focused on helping students learn to *code switch,* or to use standard English when it is important to do so and their dialect in the family, community, and other appropriate settings.

Other Cultural Influences on Communication

Accent and dialect are not the only cultural factors that may affect language. Students who are English language learners may experience difficulty in learning how to begin or finish a conversation, may have to learn to take turns during conversations, may not understand subtle humor, and may struggle to pronounce some words correctly. Likewise, they may be reluctant to initiate conversations or to contribute to them.

The examples that have been provided in this section are intended only to illustrate some of the issues related to speech and language and diversity. Comparable comments could be made for the many other cultural groups that comprise the population of this country (e.g., Laing & Kamhi, 2003; Poon-McBrayer & Garcia, 2000). All school professionals need to be aware of their students' language differences and how to appropriately work with students who do not speak standard English. Further, they need to recognize the risk of mistaking a language difference for a language disorder and seek input from speech and language professionals when they have concerns regarding a particular student's speech and language skills.

The Use of Evidence-Based Practices

Throughout education, including special education and the field of speech and language services, a significant trend is the identification of *evidence-based practices* and their use in schools (American Speech-Language-Hearing Association, 2005; Dollaghan, 2004). That is, speech/language therapists are emphasizing that the interventions used with students should only be those for which high-quality, multiple research studies have demonstrated effectiveness and systematic use by clinicians have supported their use. The trend toward the use of evidence-based practices is a direct result of the accountability movement in today's schools, prompted by the No Child Left Behind Act and its requirements as well as a trend toward improving the quality of research that is used to justify various interventions (Justice & Fey, 2004).

The implications of using evidence-based practices in speech-language services are far reaching. Here are some examples:

CHECK
Your Learning

What are *evidence-based practices*? Why have they become important to the field of speech and language therapy?

■ *Collection of data.* Speech/language therapists are expected more and more to gather systematic data that can be used to judge the effectiveness of their strategies for preventing the development of speech and language problems, their diagnostic procedures, and their methods for intervening to address student speech and language difficulties (Joint Coordinating Committee on Evidence-Based Practice, American Speech-Language-Hearing Association, 2005).

■ *Use of data for decision making.* Although decisions regarding speech and language services have always relied on data, the focus on evidence-based practices strengthens the expectation that interventions should be attempted or continued based on specific data related to the students with whom they are used and large-scale studies that document their impact. Conversely, strategies that are not supported by research or not demonstrated to be positively influencing students' skills should be discarded. An example concerns assessment tools: Hundreds of these instruments are advertised to professionals each year, and some of them lack reported research about their accuracy. Only the instruments with a strong set of data demonstrating their validity for particular groups of students and the reliability of the information they gather should be used (Research and Scientific Affairs Committee, 2004).

Professional education. Clearly, speech/language therapists need to be educated about the importance of evidence-based practices and the ways in which they should guide practices in public schools (Nail-Chiwetalu & Ratner, 2006). At the same time, teachers and other educators need to know why these practices should be central to speech/language therapists' work, how teachers can participate in further developing evidence-based practices, and what these practices imply for students and their families.

Documenting through scientific research the effectiveness of interventions used for students with speech and language disorders will take time (Coyle, Easterling, Lefton-Greif, & Mackay, 2006). However, these efforts can help ensure that the time available to improve outcomes for students will be spent as wisely as possible.

SUMMARY

Speech and language disorders have been a professional area of study since the beginning of the nineteenth century, and special classes to educate students with these disabilities were created at the beginning of the twentieth century. Since then, understanding of these students has progressed from an emphasis on the production of speech to the use of language to a comprehensive view based on the purpose of communication. Although IDEA provides a simple definition of speech and language impairments, many specific disorders are encompassed by this disability category, including receptive and expressive language disorders (i.e., those related to phonology, morphology, syntax, semantics, pragmatics) and speech disorders (i.e., those related to articulation, fluency, voice). These disorders are the second most common among students receiving special education services, occurring somewhat more often in boys than girls, and they can result from biological or environmental factors. Students with speech and language disorders vary widely in terms of their cognitive ability and academic achievement as well as in their social or emotional status and the likelihood of their displaying behavior problems. Speech/language pathologists are the specialists who evaluate students using formal and informal means to determine whether these disorders are present, but as for all students, a team determines eligibility for special education services.

Most students with speech and language disorders receive their education in typical schools and participate in general education for most of the school day. Increasingly, interventions for these students focus on blending the skills that speech/language pathologists can bring to the overall instructional program and the use of augmentative and alternative communication strategies, if needed. The parents and families of students with speech and language disorders are as diverse as the students themselves, and their preferences and concerns may in part be culturally determined. Issues facing the field include the dilemmas of differentiating between language differences and language disabilities in an increasingly diverse student population and the importance of implementing only evidence-based practices.

BACK TO THE CASES

Andrew

Andrew's parents thought he would outgrow his pronunciation difficulties. However, by kindergarten it was evident that he had not and that he required assistance. Now in second grade, Andrew works with a speech and language specialist and his classroom teacher on his sounds. One critical partner is missing: the family. (See CEC Standard 10 and INTASC Principle 10.04.) Why should his family be involved with this process? What role could they take in Andrew's therapy and educational program?

Jade

As a result of brain injury, Jade has many special needs in the speech, language, and communication areas. However, the speech/language therapist works with Jade just twice each week. If you were Jade's teacher (either special education teacher or

general education teacher), what questions would you want to ask in order to help you facilitate Jade's success as a student? (See CEC Standard 3 and INTASC Principle 3.02.) What steps would you take to ensure that Jade gains confidence so that she interacts more readily with her peers? (See CEC Standard 5 and INTASC Principles 5.03.)

Mason

Mason is ready to begin his transition planning to the postsecondary adult world. He has some ideas about what he wants to do after high school, but he and his support team (including friends, family, and teachers) must address a number of important issues. One of these issues is that Mason has little life experience beyond his circle of family and friends. Mason and his support team determine that one goal should be to get a part-time job in the computer field. You have been asked to take charge of this goal because you have considerable computer expertise. What might be your first step in helping Mason meet his goal of working in the computer industry? (See CEC Standard 7 and INTASC Principles 1.09 and 7.07.) Explain why this would be first on your list. Whom should you involve in this planning, both within and outside the school setting? Why? (See CEC Standard 6 and INTASC Principle 6.07.)

KEY TERMS AND CONCEPTS

Accent
Additions
Aphasia
Articulation
Articulation disorder
Augmentative and alternative
 communication
Central auditory processing disorder
 (CAPD)
Childhood apraxia of speech
Cleft lip and/or palate
Cluttering
Communication
Communication disorders
Dialect

Distortions
Expressive language
Fluency
Fluency disorder
Language
Language delay
Language difference
Language disorder
Morpheme
Morphology
Omissions
Phoneme
Phonemic awareness
Phonological awareness
Phonology

Pragmatics
Receptive language
Resonance
Semantics
Specific language impairment (SLI)
Speech
Speech and language disorders
Speech disorder
Speech or language impairment
Stuttering
Substitutions
Syntax
Voice
Voice disorders

REVIEW, DISCUSS, APPLY

1. Why is the definition of speech and language impairments included in IDEA generally considered inadequate for understanding the types of needs students with these disabilities may have? (Learning Objective 1)
2. The study of speech and language disorders encompasses many components. See how well you understand some of them by completing the following table. (Learning Objective 1)

	Possible Concept	Definition	Example
Disorders			
Phonology			
Morphology			
Syntax			
Semantics			
Pragmatics			
Articulation			
Voice			
Fluency			

3. How might a speech or language disorder affect a student's academic achievement? Self-concept? Behavior? (Learning Objective 2)
4. How do speech pathologists ensure that assessments of students who are not native English speakers are unbiased? What are some of the special challenges of determining whether these students are eligible to receive special education services for speech and language disorders? (Learning Objective 3)
5. Think about inclusive practices and students with speech and language disorders. Why might a general education setting be the least restrictive environment for many of these students? In what situations should some services be offered outside that setting? Why? (Learning Objective 4)
6. Why does speech/language therapy now often incorporate helping students to develop literacy skills? What implications might this have for you if you plan to be a special educator? General educator? (Learning Objective 5)
7. If you know a family with a young child, observe the parents as they interact with their infant or toddler. Based on your observations and the information you learned in this chapter, what are the most important roles that parents play in the development of children's speech and language skills? How does the family's culture affect speech and language development? (Learning Objective 6)
8. How does the concept of evidence-based practices pertain to speech and language services? Why is this concept a trend in the field of speech/language therapy? How might evidence-based practices change the approaches used by speech/language therapists? (Learning Objective 7)
9. What are *language differences*? How do they differ from *language disorders*? Why is the distinction between these concepts especially important for school professionals? (Learning Objective 7)

Go to Allyn & Bacon's MyLabSchool (www.mylabschool.com) and enter Assignment ID SIM03 into the Assignment Finder. Work through the MLS Simulation *Accountability: High-Stakes Testing for Students with Disabilities*.

Question: The teacher raises general concerns about accountability for all of her students but especially those with disabilities. How do her concerns relate to students with speech and language disabilities? You may also complete the activities included on the simulation and e-mail your work to your instructor.

5

Students with Learning Disabilities

Students with Learning Disabilities

Will Hart

learning objectives

- Define learning disabilities, explain their prevalence and causes, and outline the development of the learning disabilities field.

- Describe characteristics of individuals with learning disabilities.

- Explain both traditional and emerging approaches for identifying learning disabilities.

- Outline how students with learning disabilities receive their education.

- Describe recommended educational practices for students with learning disabilities.

- Explain the perspectives and concerns that parents and families of students with learning disabilities may have.

- Identify trends and issues influencing the field of learning disabilities.

Jermaine

Jermaine is a fourth-grade student in Mr. Hoover's class. He was identified as having a learning disability more than two years ago after he repeated second grade. Mr. Hoover has commented that Jermaine is a student of contradictions: When Jermaine is speaking in class it is obvious that he is a bright young man who has many abilities and interests. However, when he attempts to complete his assignments, it is as though his brain simply does not work properly. Jermaine reads at a second-grade level, struggling to pronounce words and often not comprehending what he has read. In math he is still learning basic facts, and he often solves word problems incorrectly because he does not know how to identify and use relevant information. Writing is also difficult for Jermaine, and Mr. Hoover usually asks him to explain what he has written because the words on the paper are jumbled and difficult to discern. To address his needs, Jermaine receives supplemental reading instruction every day, dictates test answers to a classroom assistant, is offered extra time to complete assignments that he needs to write himself, and has permission to ask classmates for assistance. Socially, Jermaine has many friends among his classmates. However, Mr. Hoover is concerned that Jermaine's challenges in learning are already having a negative impact on him; the other day he heard Jermaine telling a classmate that he hated school.

Danielle

Danielle just started middle school. She likes having several different teachers, but she is having difficulty remembering the locations of all the classrooms and the names of all the teachers. She is finding that she also has to remember to keep all her textbooks with her, take home the right materials to complete her homework, and move promptly from class to class—all tasks involving organizational skills, which are a struggle for her. Danielle is also a little worried about whether she will pass all her classes. She likes her science teacher, and completing all the practical examples and lab activities makes it easy to learn. In her other subjects, though, the amount of reading already seems endless. Danielle reads very slowly and often does not understand what she has read. She is hoping her resource teacher will have tapes of some of the books or study guides similar to those she used in fifth grade. Danielle is glad that her best friend Sophie from elementary school is in her classes; Sophie often helps Danielle indirectly by including her in conversations with other students. Danielle was identified as having a learning disability in third grade, and she has received special education services since then. In middle school two of her classes will be co-taught, and she can also work with the resource teacher during the advisory period, a time during the day when all students can receive extra assistance from their teachers.

Derek

Derek will graduate from high school this year. He was diagnosed with severe learning disabilities early in first grade and has received special education services ever since. During elementary school he attended a special education class that was located in a school across town, but in middle and high school he has attended his neighborhood school and participated in an increasing number of general education classes, receiving the support he needed in a resource room. Derek now reads at approximately a tenth-grade level, and his math skills are close to average for a senior in high school. However, he continues to experience significant problems in written language; when he was last assessed his writing skills were at an early third-grade level. Derek is an extremely likable young adult; he volunteers to help others and enjoys talking with both peers and adults. He thrives on outdoor work and can mow a yard, build a fence, or plant a garden as well as anyone. He definitely wants to get a college degree, but he has decided to start by taking two classes next fall at the community college, where he can receive support from the Office of Disability Services. He is not yet sure what he wants to do for a living, but he is thinking of working in the building industry or in landscape architecture.

Have you ever been in a class—perhaps math or a foreign language—and suddenly realized that you had absolutely no understanding of the information being presented? Even after reviewing your notes and asking questions of classmates, you simply did not grasp the concept. Perhaps the experience left you questioning your abilities and feeling incapable of learning. Have you ever become disoriented while driving in an unfamiliar area? Not only did you not know how to get to your destination, but you also were not sure which direction was north or how to get back on your way. Friends may have found your situation funny, but your sense of discomfort was tinged with panic.

Neither of these experiences by itself indicates a learning disability (LD), but it can give you a small insight into what it is like to have a learning disability and how students with learning disabilities often experience frustration and a sense of failure, particularly in school. Their special needs may affect their ability to learn to read, to compute, to speak, to write, or any combination of these. These students may experience difficulty remembering, and they may show gaps in their social skills. Students with learning disabilities often are described as "puzzle children" because they can be highly proficient in one area (e.g., math) and significantly delayed in another (e.g., reading).

Roper Starch Worldwide (www.tremainefoundation .org/ld/roper-poll.pdf) conducted a national survey to measure public awareness and understanding of learning disabilities. Included in the findings were these interesting facts: Nearly two-thirds of the public inaccurately associates learning disabilities with mental retardation, and about half attribute learning disabilities to drug or alcohol abuse by parents.

PROFESSIONAL MONITORING TOOL

Council for Exceptional Children

Standard 1 Foundations . . . historical points of view

What Are Learning Disabilities?

Compared to other disability areas, the field of learning disabilities has had a relatively brief and intense evolution (Hallahan & Mercer, 2001). The work of medical professionals, psychologists, educators, and parents all contributed to the current understanding of this disorder.

Development of the Learning Disabilities Field

The study of learning disabilities began long before the term was introduced. As early as the nineteenth century, researchers were interested in how injuries to the brain affected adults' functioning (Opp, 1994). In the twentieth century, this line of research became more focused when Goldstein (1942) studied brain-injured soldiers returning from World War I (C. R. Smith, 1998).

In the 1940s the work that had been conducted primarily with adults was applied to children. At the Wayne County Training School in Northville, Michigan—a residential facility for children with intellectual disabilities or brain injuries—psychologist Heinz Weiner and psychiatrist Alfred Strauss observed children with behavior similar to the soldiers described by Goldstein, and they concluded the children had brain injuries (Hammill, 1993). Gradually, professionals in the field began to assume brain injury or damage existed for some children even if it could not be documented. Although these children were at first called *brain injured,* the less-charged term *Strauss syndrome* was soon adopted, and it was later replaced with the term **minimal brain dysfunction.**

A Focus on Process Interventions

During the latter part of the 1940s and throughout the 1950s, emphasis shifted to designing interventions to help children's learning when they exhibited the characteristics now known to indicate learning disabilities. Professionals concluded that they should directly address the symptoms of the disorder. They developed programs to improve how their students processed stimuli—that is, the way they interpreted and acted on information in their environments—believing that academic learning would improve if students' perceptual skills could be developed. For example, Alfred Strauss and teacher Laura Lehtinen's (1947) book on working with these children recommended specific instructional approaches related to perception (e.g., avoiding the contiguous use of the easily confused letters b and d) and also removal of all distractions (e.g., teacher jewelry) from the learning environment. Kephart (1960) developed a training regimen that focused on developing children's perceptual–motor skills (e.g., balance and eye–hand coordination). Yet another pioneer in the field, Frostig, designed a program to remediate children's problems with visual perception (e.g., tracing a path with a pencil between two undulating lines) (Frostig & Horne, 1964). Notice that none of these programs taught reading or math skills; the assumption was that by focusing on distractibility and perception, the ability to learn academic skills would automatically improve.

> "During the latter part of the 1940s and throughout the 1950s, emphasis shifted to designing interventions to help children's learning when they exhibited the characteristics now known to indicate learning disabilities."

During the latter part of this period in the development of the learning disabilities field, parents and professionals were arguing that the students being studied—as diverse as they seemed—shared a disorder that had not been recognized previously, and they began to campaign for its consideration. The first public use of the phrase *learning disability* is attributed to Sam Kirk, an early leader in the field, who used the term while speaking to a parent group in 1963. By 1969 the first federal legislation acknowledging learning disabilities had been enacted. This law, the Children with Specific Learning Disabilities Act (Public Law 91-230), definitively established learning disabilities as a disability category, and it provided funding for teacher training (Lerner & Kline, 2006).

Focus on Instructional Interventions

Even as learning disabilities were being recognized formally, controversy began. In particular, during the 1960s and early 1970s the process-based interventions that had become the hallmark of the field began to be criticized. A new group of researchers failed to find that such interventions had a direct positive effect on student achievement, and they argued that direct instruction of academics, not the remediation of processing ability, was the superior way to help these students learn (Hallahan & Kauffman, 1976). When research continued to show the effectiveness of direct academic instructional approaches, interest in process methods eventually ebbed (Hammill, 1993).

From the 1980s into the beginning of the twenty-first century, there have been continued attempts to understand learning disabilities scientifically, to explore alternative instructional methods for students with learning disabilities, and to clarify the nature of learning disabilities in adults (e.g., Chiappe, 2005; Kavale & Forness, 2000a; McDermott, Goldberg, Watkins, Stanley, & Glutting, 2006; Swanson, 2000b). To meet a young adult who has a learning disability and hear his perspective on his school experiences, read the Firsthand Account.

Definitions of Learning Disabilities

Although the term **learning disabilities** was coined forty years ago and the study of learning disabilities has been pursued intensely ever since, considerable controversy still exists over what a learning disability really is. The two definitions that are noted most often and that largely shape students' programs and services are (1) the federal definition included in the Individuals with Disabilities Education Act (IDEA) and (2) the definition proposed by the National Joint Committee on Learning Disabilities (NJCLD). Each is explained in the following sections.

> "Considerable controversy still exists over what a learning disability really is."

Federal Definition

The federal definition of learning disabilities articulated in P.L. 94-142 in 1975 has changed very little since then. According to IDEA,

> Specific learning disability means a disorder in one or more of the basic **psychological processes** involved in understanding or in using language, spoken or written, that may manifest itself in imperfect ability to listen, think, speak, read, write, spell, or do mathematical calculation, including conditions such as perceptual disabilities, brain injury,

Michael's Story of Unrealistic Goals

Michael knows firsthand what it is like to be a student with a learning disability. His story explains his passion for making a difference in the lives of students with disabilities.

I was first identified as having a learning disability in third grade— but by then I had been held back twice. They told my dad that it might be best to send me to a special school because there was not much of a chance that I would learn to read. Later, he told me that he stood up and told them that I would read—within a year. For the next year I remember that every time we were in the car and stopped at a traffic light, my father would show me flash cards. I remember saying to him, "But, Dad, I don't want to look at any more flashcards." He said, "I love you," and kept on doing them. And I did learn to read.

By high school, I was very successful. I have ADHD so I have lots of energy. I was involved in everything: president of the drama club, very popular, well-liked by my teachers. I had a 3.5 GPA, a very bright future, and high hopes for myself. I was even taking honors and advanced placement classes.

So 11th grade rolled around and it was time to fill out transition paperwork. My parents had to be at the hospital because of my dad, who also has a disability, and so it was just me with the rest of the IEP team. They asked me, "What are your plans for the future?" I told them I wanted to go to college and be a special education teacher. I can still remember this . . . the psychologist was sitting to my right and he said, "We need to start thinking about more realistic goals." Now

that took me back, but here's what really kills me: I look around the table and the rest of the teachers, who knew me so well, knew how hard I worked, knew how successful I was . . . were all nodding their heads in agreement. I felt like someone had closed the door on

> *"It's important for teachers (and students) to have high expectations."*

everything I wanted to do. I got very discouraged. My grades started to drop. I was scared to death to turn in any kind of writing assignment because I thought it wasn't good enough.

After my grades started to go down, my dad, still in the hospital, had a meeting with me. I am sitting next to his bed and he asks, "What's going on? You went from an A–B student to making Ds and Fs." So I told him about the IEP meeting and how they had said I should start making more realistic goals for myself. Then my father reminded me about learning to read. What he said to me helped me decide to succeed in spite of what I was told at school.

So let's jump to college. I am currently a special education major. I have made the dean's list for the past three years. I am president of our local student chapter of the Council for Exceptional Children and vice president of the North Carolina Youth Leadership Network, an organization connecting

youth with disabilities from all over the state. I am also one of twelve members of the Youth Advisor Committee for the National Council on Disabilities, a group that advises the president on legislation pertaining to disability. All this from a person who "realistically" should not be in college.

It's important for teachers (and students) to have high expectations. My father had high expectations for me. I think one of the biggest fears of people who work with people who have disabilities is the fear that they will fail. So they lower their expectations for them to be sure they won't fail and so the programs they are in can be called successful. It is true that people with disabilities might fail, but they might not. Young people with disabilities need to know that there are successful people out there. They need to know that they are not struggling alone and that they can make it! I work with hundreds of youth with disabilities in my state and on a national level and I can tell you for every person like me there are more youth who do not make it.

Given the opportunity, youth at risk can achieve great things. I am not saying it is as easy, but we have to make this our core in the field of education. Disability is a natural part of the human experience—it empowers. If we believe that students with learning disabilities can do great things, we will see greater things than we ever believed were possible—and I'm proof of that.

minimal brain dysfunction, dyslexia, and developmental aphasia. Specific learning disability does not include a learning problem that arises primarily as the result of visual, hearing, or motor disabilities, of mental retardation, of emotional disturbance, or of

Students with Learning Disabilities

environmental, cultural, or economic disadvantage. (IDEA 20 U.S.C. §1401 [2004], 20 C.F.R. §300.8[c][10])

Because states are required to adhere to the provisions of the federal special education law, most of them use either this definition or a variation of it (Schrag, 2000). As you would expect, the definition focuses on school tasks and learner characteristics and needs, and it clearly explains that learning disabilities are distinct from other disabilities. What are other important components of the federal definition?

NJCLD Definition

The **National Joint Committee on Learning Disabilities (NJCLD)** includes representatives from thirteen professional and parent organizations concerned about individuals with learning disabilities (National Joint Committee on Learning Disabilities, 2006). This group has expressed concern about the federal definition for several reasons, most of which are related to what the definition does not address: the heterogeneity of students with learning disabilities, the impact of learning disabilities on social perception, the life-span nature of learning disabilities, and the possibility that learning disabilities can exist concomitantly with other disabilities.

Because of these perceived deficiencies in the federal definition, the NJCLD created its own definition of learning disabilities, which was revised in 1990:

> Learning disabilities is a general term that refers to a heterogeneous group of disorders manifested by significant difficulties in the acquisition and use of listening, speaking, reading, writing, reasoning, or mathematical abilities. These disorders are intrinsic to the individual, presumed to be due to central nervous system dysfunction, and may occur across the lifespan. Problems in self-regulatory behaviors, social perception, and social interaction may exist with learning disabilities but do not by themselves constitute a learning disability. Although learning disabilities may occur concomitantly with other handicapping conditions (for example, sensory impairment, mental retardation, serious emotional disturbance), or with extrinsic influences (such as cultural differences, insufficient or inappropriate instruction), they are not the result of those conditions or influences. (NJCLD, 1990)

Essential Dimensions of a Definition of Learning Disabilities

Although discussions about the definition of learning disabilities continue, most professionals seem to agree that learning disabilities include these dimensions (Kavale & Forness, 2000b):

- Learning disabilities comprise a heterogeneous group of disorders. Students with learning disabilities may have significant reading problems **(dyslexia),** difficulty in mathematics **(dyscalculia),** or a disorder related to written language **(dysgraphia).** They may have difficulty with social perceptions, motor skills, or memory. Learning disabilities can affect young children, students in school, and adults. No single profile of an individual with a learning disability can be accurate because of the interindividual differences in the disorder.

- Learning disabilities are intrinsic to the individual and have a neurobiological basis. Learning disabilities exist because of some type of dysfunction in the brain, not because of external factors such as limited experience or poor teaching.

- Learning disabilities are characterized by unexpected underachievement. That is, the disorder exists when a student's academic achievement is significantly below her intellectual potential, even after intensive, systematic interventions have been implemented to try to reduce the learning gap. This topic is addressed in more detail later in this chapter.

PROFESSIONAL MONITORING TOOL

Council for Exceptional Children

Standard 2 Development and Characteristics
. . . similarities and differences among individuals
. . . typical and atypical development
. . . educational implications

Will Hart

■ Learning disabilities are not a result of other disorders or problems, but individuals with learning disabilities may have other special needs as well. For example, being deaf cannot be considered to be the basis for having a learning disability. However, some students who are deaf also have learning disabilities.

Prevalence of Learning Disabilities

According to annual data gathered as part of IDEA during the 2002–2003 school year, approximately 2.8 million students between ages six and twenty-one had learning disabilities (U.S. Department of Education, 2004). This number represented about 4.3 percent of the entire school population.

Further exploration of prevalence data reveals several interesting facts. For example, learning disability has been the fastest-growing category of special education since the federal law was first passed in 1975. At that time students with learning disabilities comprised only 22 percent of all students receiving special education (Horn & Tynan, 2001); they now represent nearly half of all students with disabilities. Over the past ten years, the number of students identified as having learning disabilities ages twelve to seventeen has been growing. The number of students in this group ages six to eleven has dropped slightly, probably because younger students may be assigned the more general (and relatively new) designation of *developmentally delayed* (U.S. Department of Education, 2004).

> *"Learning disabilities has been the fastest-growing category of special education since the federal law was first passed in 1975."*

The matter of gender can be raised as a prevalence issue, too. Researchers generally have found that the ratio of boys to girls identified as having learning disabilities is at least 2:1 (Coutinho & Oswald, 2005; Siegel & Smythe, 2005). Many explanations have been offered for this phenomenon: Boys may be labeled as having learning disabilities more frequently because of medical factors, such as their greater vulnerability to prenatal and postnatal brain damage; maturational factors, including their documented slower rate of development; sociological factors, such as societal expectations for high achievement from males; and brain organization factors, including the greater likelihood in boys of genetically based impulsivity (C. R. Smith, 2004). In practice, girls identified as having learning disabilities as a group usually have more severe academic deficits than boys (Lerner & Kline, 2006).

Taken together, what do all these prevalence figures mean? They illustrate that learning disabilities represent a complex disorder affecting many students. They also demonstrate that the current definition of learning disabilities probably leads to inconsistency in identifying students as having this special need. In fact, dissatisfaction about who is eligible to receive services as having this disability has led to significant developments in assessment procedures. This topic is addressed in more detail later in this chapter.

Causes of Learning Disabilities

As you might suspect from the preceding discussion about the development of the learning disabilities field and the definition of the disorder, in most cases the cause of a learning disability is simply not known, and it is highly unlikely that a single primary cause will ever be identified. C. R. Smith (2004) divides the possible causes of learning disabilities into two categories: physiological causes and curricular and environmental contributors.

Physiological Causes

Several possible physiological causes of learning disabilities have been identified by education professionals and medical researchers. These include brain injury, heredity, and chemical imbalance.

First, as proposed from the earliest work in the learning disabilities field, brain injury probably causes some students' disorders. The injury may occur prenatally, as might happen when a mother consumes alcohol or drugs, contracts measles, or smokes cigarettes. An injury also might occur during the perinatal period, as when a baby is deprived of oxygen during birth. Brain injury also can occur postnatally because of a high fever, a head injury (e.g., falling from a bike or playground equipment), an illness (e.g., meningitis), or an accident (e.g., a near drowning). In the Technology Notes on the following pages, you can learn more about recent advances in understanding the brain and learning disabilities.

Considerable evidence indicates that another physiological cause of learning disabilities is heredity (Alarcon, Pennington, Filipek, & DeFries, 2000). Teachers have reported for years that many parents of children with learning disabilities comment, "He's just like his father [or mother]." Now research is supporting those claims. In fact, when one or both parents have a learning disability, their children may have as much as a 30 to 50 percent chance of also having that disorder (Castles, Datta, Gayan, & Olson, 1999). Critics of this research have noted that it does not consider possible environmental factors. That is, perhaps parents and their children share learning disabilities because of similar exposure to allergens or environmental toxins such as lead. However, studies of twins and siblings support the heritability of learning disabilities (Wadsworth, Olson, Pennington, & DeFries, 2000). The reading level of one identical twin is very likely to predict the reading level of the other, even when they are reared apart, and this holds true when one has been identified as having learning disabilities. In contrast, a nontwin sibling's reading level is much less likely to predict the reading level of the other sibling when they are reared separately. This line of research provides evidence of a genetic link.

A third physiological cause of learning disabilities sometimes mentioned is biochemical. For some children learning disabilities seem to be related to significant attention problems, which may be the result of chemical imbalances in the brain.

You should be careful in attributing learning disabilities to physiological causes. Just because a child has a head injury does not mean that a learning disability is inevitable. Likewise, just because one child has a learning disability does not mean his sibling will have the disorder. Perhaps in the future, emerging medical technology will provide scientists and researchers with new tools for studying the relationship between the brain and individuals' patterns of learning. In the meantime, professionals should consider such information intriguing but somewhat speculative.

Curriculum and Environmental Contributors

For some children learning disabilities are caused by the situations in which they live (C. R. Smith, 2004). For example, children who have poor nutrition may develop learning disabilities, as may those who live for an extended period of time in a highly adverse emotional climate. Some students have learning disabilities because of toxins in their environments, as might happen to children who develop lead poisoning because of the use of lead-based paint in older homes. Yet other children may have too little stimulation (e.g., adults who model language, access to books, experiences such as visits to the zoo) (Rashid, Morris, & Sevcik,

Advances in medical technology are making it possible for scientists to study the human brain and how it works with a precision never known before. This research is leading us to a much clearer understanding about the parts of the brain that are most critical for oral language and reading and the differences between the brains of individuals who read fluently and those with reading or learning disabilities (Shaywitz, 2003; Society for Neuroscience, 2006). Eventually, it may lead to new types of interventions for students.

Brain Structure

One area of interest to scientists is whether the brains of individuals with learning disabilities are physically different from those of others. A technique for studying the structure of the brain is the computed tomography (CT) scan, in which the brain is X-rayed and bone, brain matter, and fluids are identified (Alarcon, Pennington, Filipek, & DeFries, 2000). Using these data, a computer can then construct an image of a "slice" of the brain. CT scans have shown that the brains of individuals with LD are symmetrical in the area called the *occipital lobe* (see figure, The Organization of

The Organization of the Human Brain for Language

Word-form and sentence implementation

Frontal Lobe

Parietal Lobe

Verb mediation

Color concepts

Occipital Lobe

Verb working memory

Noun mediation

Temporal Lobe

the Human Brain for Language), whereas the brains of those without LD are asymmetrical in this area (Bigler, Lajiness-O'Neill, & Howes, 1998).

2005). When you think about all these factors, can you identify a single group of youngsters who might be most expected to have learning disabilities because of environmental causes? If your response is children who live in poverty, you are correct. These children also may be placed at greater risk of having learning disabilities because of poor medical care or low parent education level (Skiba, Poloni-Staudinger, Simmons, Feggins-Azziz, & Chung, 2005).

One other environmental cause of learning disabilities should be mentioned. Although in an ideal world this paragraph would not need to be written, some students have learning disabilities because of poor instruction (Lyon et al., 2001). When teachers use outdated instructional practices, do not consider the differences in students' maturational levels, and ignore students' learning styles, they can cause some students to display characteristics of learning disabilities. This cause of learning disabilities is one of the most controversial. IDEA specifically prohibits students who receive poor instruction from being identified as having this or any other disability on that basis. However, some professionals argue that if teaching

PROFESSIONAL MONITORING TOOL

Council for Exceptional Children

Standard 1 Foundations ... issues in definition and identification

Students with Learning Disabilities

156

Brain Function

A second area of scientific interest in brain research is how the brain functions. Several techniques are used to study brain functioning. Some studies use positron emission tomography (PET) scans or single photon emission computed tomography (SPECT) scans in which radioactive material is injected into the brain so that its activity can be measured while participants engage in a reading task. Another technique is functional magnetic resonance imaging (fMRI), which measures bloodflow during brain activity. Results of studies using these approaches indicate that oral language and reading use the same parts of the brain and that individuals with LD do not have as much brain activity in the occipital lobe during reading activities as individuals without LD (Joseph, Noble, & Eden, 2001). The figure entitled Brain Activation during Reading illustrates these brain differences.

One other technique used in the study of brain functioning is the electroencephalogram (EEG). Electrodes are attached to the head, and the amount of electrical activity in the brain can then be measured. Individuals who have LD show less of this electrical activity than individuals without LD (Fiedorowicz, 1999). The greatest differences occur when individuals are engaged in activities that require phonological awareness—that is, the ability to relate letters to specific sounds (Burns, 2002).

Cautions

Although promising, brain research also must be viewed with caution. Most of the work has been completed with adults, not children, and although it is assumed that the results are valid for both groups, this is not known for sure. In addition, although the different parts of the brain activated during oral language and reading are being mapped, it is not accurate to assume they function exclusive of each other. The relationships among the parts of the brain used for speaking and reading are not known at this time. Next, most studies have involved reading single letters or words, not paragraphs or passages. Whether brain function during the latter type of activity is different in any meaningful way from the former is not clear. Finally, information on brain structure and function is not diagnostic; that is, it does not directly tell us the nature of an individual's learning disability or the interventions that might ameliorate or compensate for it.

Source: Bigler, E. D., Lajiness-O'Neill, R., & Howes, N. (1998). Technology in the assessment of learning disability. *Journal of Learning Disabilities, 31,* 67–82.

Brain Activation during Reading

The yellow areas show where typical readers have greater brain activation during word reading, compared to those with LD.

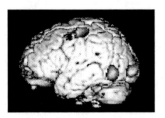 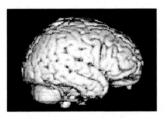

Note: Images above show left and right hemispheres of the brain.

Source: Copyright 2001 by Lynn Flowers and Frank Wood. Reprinted with permission from Lynn Flowers and Frank Wood.

---

has been so inadequate that a learning disability has been created, that student should receive the benefit of a specialized education to remediate the problem.

What Are the Characteristics of Individuals with Learning Disabilities?

Individuals with learning disabilities are an extraordinarily heterogeneous group, with different areas of strengths and special needs in the cognitive, academic, social/emotional, and behavior domains. The following sections highlight some of the most common characteristics.

PROFESSIONAL MONITORING TOOL

Council for Exceptional Children

Standard 2 Development and Characteristics
. . . similarities and differences among individuals

Cognitive Characteristics

Although students with learning disabilities typically have average or above-average intelligence, they usually display weaknesses in one or more areas of cognition, including attention, perception, memory, and thinking/processing.

Attention

Students with learning disabilities may have poor selective attention (Mayes, Calhoun, & Crowell, 2000; Zera & Lucian, 2001). One way to illustrate what this means is to think about the setting you are in as you read this paragraph. Stop to listen and look around. Is air blowing from a vent? Is there noise in the hallway or on the street? Is there a pile of other reading material right beside you? Until you were directed to notice items such as these, you likely ignored them because your attention was devoted to reading. Students with learning disabilities may have extraordinary difficulty attend-

> *"Individuals with learning disabilities are an extraordinarily heterogeneous group, with different areas of strengths and special needs."*

ing to only the important stimuli in their environments. The other reading material is as captivating as the book in front of them; the plane overhead is as noticeable as the teacher's voice.

Perception

Many students with learning disabilities exhibit perceptual problems (Lerner & Kline, 2006; Silver, 2004). *Perception* does not pertain to whether a student sees or hears but rather to how her brain interprets what is seen or heard and acts on it. For example, a student with a visual perception problem may see perfectly well the words on a page. However, when asked to read the words, the student may skip some of them. Other symptoms of visual perception difficulties include spatial orientation and judgment (e.g., bumping into things; knowing how to safely get from one point to another); the ability to distinguish right from left; labored handwriting; and overall clumsiness or awkwardness in walking, skipping, balancing, and other large-motor activities (C. R. Smith, 2004). Problems in auditory perception often include difficulties with perceiving sounds that are not attributable to a hearing loss (Kruger, Kruger, Hugo, & Campbell, 2001). For example, some students may have trouble understanding whether the word spoken was *team* or *teen, odor* or *over, pet* or *bet*. Of course, the result can be misunderstood directions, poor communication, and awkwardness in social interactions.

Memory

In addition to problems related to attention and perception, students with learning disabilities may experience problems with memory (McNamara & Wong, 2003). Everyone has two types of memory: short term and long term. **Short-term memory** is the mechanism by which a person holds information in the mind for a brief amount of time—less than a minute. Unless it is acted on in some way, it is gradually lost. One simple example is when you look up a phone number. You remember it long enough to dial it, but if you delay dialing you probably have to look up the number again unless you have consciously taken steps to remember it (e.g., by repeating it several times). **Long-term memory** is the permanent storage mechanism in the brain, and information to be remembered generally has to be transferred from short-term to long-term memory. An example might be verses from a favorite childhood song: Even if you have not recalled them for many years, you can still sing the words as soon as you hear the title "If You're Happy and You Know It" or "The Barney Song." Students with learning disabilities may have difficulty with either short-term memory or long-term memory or both.

Information Processing

Finally, students' general information-processing or thinking skills may be deficient (Geary, Hoard, & Hamson, 1999). Students with learning disabilities may have difficulty with **metacognition,** or thinking about thinking. They may lack the ability to actively consider how new

Standard 2 Development and Characteristics
. . . educational implications of exceptionalities

If you think about the characteristics of students with attention deficit–hyperactivity disorder (ADHD), you will see that some overlap can exist with learning disabilities.

information being learned relates to other information already stored or how to apply that knowledge in a novel learning situation. For example, as you read this chapter, you probably are actively relating the concepts to people you know who have learning disabilities or perhaps to knowledge you acquired in a course in psychology. You might also be using a strategy to help you remember information that may be on a test—for example, by repeating key ideas aloud. These are all metacognitive activities. Without explicit training (discussed in a later section of this chapter), some students with learning disabilities will not use such strategies to foster their learning.

Academic Characteristics

By far the most commonly noted characteristic of students with learning disabilities is their struggle with school learning. Their difficulties may occur in reading, spoken language, written language, mathematics, or any combination of these. Academic difficulties comprise the most likely reasons for classroom teachers to suspect a student has a learning disability, and such difficulties often are emphasized in the services provided by special education teachers.

Reading

Most students with learning disabilities experience significant problems in reading (Sperling, 2006; Vaughn & Edmonds, 2006). For example, many students struggle with *phonological awareness,* which is the ability to make the connection between letters and the sounds they stand for that is essential for developing reading skills. These students are not able to sound out words, and they often rely on visual cues or the context in which a word is used to determine what the word is.

Other students struggle with *oral fluency* (Therrien & Kubiana, 2006). They may read aloud in a word-by-word manner without appropriate inflection or rhythm, unable to relate the patterns of spoken language to the printed word. Students with weakness in this area often dread being asked to read aloud in class.

One other typical reading problem for students with learning disabilities is *comprehension* (Humphries, Cardy, Worling, & Peets, 2004). Unlike the student previously described who labors to say each word, some students are able to read a passage so fluently that you might assume they are highly proficient readers. However, when they are asked questions about what they have read, these students may have little or no understanding of the words. Not surprisingly, students who have difficulty with phonological awareness and oral fluency also are likely to experience weakness in reading comprehension.

You might find that some people refer to reading problems of all sorts as *dyslexia* (e.g., Bell, McCallum, & Cox, 2003). The Professional Edge clarifies the use of this term and strategies for addressing dyslexia.

Oral Language

Another academic area that can be a significant problem for students with learning disabilities is oral language. Problems usually fall into the areas of phonology, morphology, syntax, and pragmatics.

Students may have difficulties with *phonology*—that is, using the correct sounds to form words. They may struggle with *morphology,* the study of the smallest meaningful units of language (e.g., that *-ed* denotes past tense or that *pre-* means "before"). Likewise, students may have problems with *syntax,* the rules of grammar, or with *semantics,* the meanings of words or phrases. Finally, *pragmatics*—the ability to successfully participate in interactions with others—may be a weakness.

If you think about all these elements of spoken language, you can begin to see how pervasive the effects of this type of learning disability can be. For example, a student with poor oral language skills may miss subtle meanings of words during conversations or might fail to understand the punchline of a joke based on word meanings. Such a student also may have difficulty participating in conversations with classmates or adults.

dimensions of
DIVERSITY

When Hispanic American students in the primary grades were provided with supplemental reading instruction (e.g., word attack skills), their overall fluency and literacy increased. This result occurred regardless of the students' initial levels of English proficiency (Gunn, Smolkowski, Biglan, & Black, 2002).

INTERNET RESOURCES
www.dyslexia.com
At the Gift: Dyslexia you can find a discussion board and links to additional information as well as a bookstore and other aids.

PROFESSIONAL MONITORING TOOL

Council for Exceptional Children

Standard 3 Individual Learning Differences
. . . effects on an individual's life

The term *dyslexia,* which means developmental word blindness and is considered a common type of learning disability, is used a lot these days. You hear that a friend's child has dyslexia, or you see a person who is dyslexic on television, or you read that Albert Einstein and Thomas Edison had dyslexia. Dyslexia has a medical sound to it, and evidence is beginning to accumulate of an organic basis for it. Recent studies using computerized imaging show that the brain activity of students with dyslexia differs from students who are good readers (Shaywitz, 2003). For example, from an early age, and often into adulthood, dyslexics show a pattern of underactivation in a region in the back of the brain that enables first accurate and then automatic reading. This pattern of underactivity appears to be present regardless of age, sex, or culture (Shaywitz, 2003). That is why dyslexics have problems initially "cracking the code," and then problems later on developing reading fluency.

Put very simply, students with dyslexia have serious problems learning to read despite normal intelligence, normal opportunities to learn to read, and an adequate home environment. While the precise organic cause of dyslexia continues to be researched, considerable evidence suggests that reading problems associated with dyslexia are phonologically based (Denton, Foorman, & Mathes, 2003). Students with dyslexia have difficulty developing *phonemic awareness,* the understanding that spoken words are comprised of sounds. Phonemic awareness problems make it hard for them to link speech sounds to letters, ultimately leading to slow, labored reading characterized by frequent starts and stops and multiple mispronunciations. Students with dyslexia also have comprehension problems largely because the struggle for them to identify words leaves little energy for understanding what they read. They also have trouble with the basic elements of written language, such as spelling and sentence and paragraph

construction. Finally, students with dyslexia may have difficulty understanding representational systems, such as telling time, directions, and seasons (Bryan & Bryan, 1986).

Early identification for students with dyslexia is particularly urgent given recent studies showing that effective language instruction appears to generate repair in underactivated sections of the brain (Shaywitz, 2003). A large body of research (Denton, Foorman, & Mathes, 2003; McCardle & Chhabra, 2004; Oakland, Black, Stanford, Nussbaum, & Balise, 1998; Swanson, 2000c) shows that many students with severe reading disabilities benefit from a beginning reading program that includes the following elements:

1. *Direct instruction in language analysis.* For example, students need to be taught skills in sound segmentation or in orally breaking down words into their component sounds.

2. *A highly structured phonics program.* This program should teach the alphabetic code directly and systematically using a simple-to-complex sequence of skills

3. *Writing and reading instruction in combination.*

4. *Intensive instruction.* Reading instruction for at-risk students should include large amounts of practice in materials that contain words they are able to decode.

5. *Teaching for automaticity.* Students must be given enough practice so that they are able to read both accurately and fluently.

Source: Friend, M., & Bursuck, W. D. (2006). *Including students with special needs: A practical guide for classroom teachers* (4th ed., p. 244). Boston: Allyn & Bacon. Copyright © 2006 by Pearson Education. Reprinted by permission of the publisher.

Written Language

For some students, learning disabilities are manifested in written language (Brice, 2004; Graham, Harris, & Fink-Chorzempa, 2003; Wong, 2000). For example, the motor coordination required for handwriting can be overwhelming for some students. As shown in the sample in Figure 5.1, it is nearly impossible to determine what these students have written even though the words form complete sentences and are spelled correctly. For other students, the deficiency is spelling. Not only do these students labor to discern the sounds comprising words, but they also may be unable to distinguish between appropriate uses of homonyms (e.g., meet–meat; there–their) or to recognize when they have written a misspelled word (e.g., *seperate* instead of *separate; advise* instead of *advice*). Students also may have difficulty knowing when and how to punctuate the sentences they write, struggling not only with the appropriate application of periods and commas but also with the use of apostrophes (e.g., *it's—it is* instead of *its*—possessive form). Finally, they may also be uncertain about capitalizing words (e.g., *My Brother likes mexican food*).

In an era when spelling, punctuation, and many other conventions of written language can be corrected with computer software and other electronic tools, perhaps the most serious

Figure 5.1

Writing Sample from a Student with Learning Disabilities

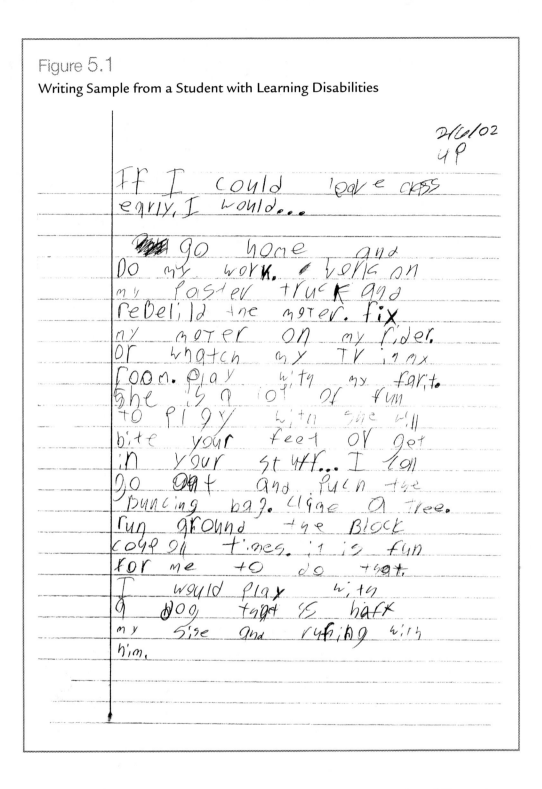

issue for students with learning disabilities in written expression is composition skill. In order to write effectively, students need to be able to organize their thoughts, present them in some type of logical order, and provide enough details to convey the intended message to readers (Williams & Ward-Lonergan, 2001). These tasks can be exceedingly difficult for students with learning disabilities like Derek, who was described at the beginning of the chapter. When telling a story, they may make assumptions about what the reader knows (e.g., not explaining who a main character is but writing as though the reader is familiar with this character) or jump from topic to topic (e.g., mixing together information about the causes, battles,

dimensions of
DIVERSITY

Wagner, Francis, and Morris
(2005) noted that recent
trends in the field of learning
disabilities, including recognition of the importance
of early intervention and
phonological awareness,
should also apply to English-
language learners but that
adequate models for assessment and intervention do
not exist at this time.

PROFESSIONAL MONITORING TOOL

Council for
Exceptional
Children

Standard 2 Development and
Characteristics
. . . similarities and differences of
individuals

and outcomes of World War II instead of presenting them as categories of information). Because of their disability, these students sometimes struggle with using adjectives to enrich their writing (e.g., *The meal was good. We had lots of stuff.* instead of *Thanksgiving dinner was delicious. We devoured turkey roasted to a golden brown, fluffy mashed potatoes, crunchy green bean casserole, and pecan pie.*). As these students move through school, they will likely find it difficult to succeed in the many school tasks that rely on clear written expression.

Mathematics

A final domain in which students with learning disabilities may experience difficulty is mathematics (Dowker, 2005; Parmar & Signer, 2005; Swanson & Jerman, 2006), a disorder sometimes referred to as *dyscalculia*. Some students are not able to learn basic math facts or fundamental computational skills. Others cannot grasp the principles of estimation, mental calculation, and probability. Yet others find mastery of fractions or decimals difficult. For some students, learning various types of measurement or concepts related to time is extraordinarily challenging. Geometry is a weakness for others. One other area that may cause difficulty is problem solving. Whether because of the reading requirement or the inability to understand the mathematical concepts that underlie the problem, students like Jermaine, who you read about in the opening to this chapter, may be unable to sort relevant from extraneous information, to recognize the correct computational procedure, or to determine whether the answer they obtain is reasonable (Fletcher, 2005; Jordan & Hanich, 2003).

Social and Emotional Characteristics

Understanding the social and emotional characteristics of students with learning disabilities is as important as understanding their cognitive and academic traits. How students perceive themselves and others and how adept they are in social situations can significantly affect their learning success (Welsh, Parke, Widaman, & O'Neil, 2001). Further, their accomplishments in life may depend on this ability to interact effectively with others. Two areas are particularly relevant: social perception and motivation.

Social Perception and Social Competence

Many students with learning disabilities may have some type of deficit in the area of social skills (Bauminger, Edelsztein, & Morash, 2005). When compared to peers without disabilities, these students tend to have lower self-esteem. They often are less accepted by their

Ellen B. Senisi

In addition to experiencing difficulties with reading, writing, math, and other academic areas, students with learning disabilities also may struggle in their social interactions with peers.

Students with Learning Disabilities

nondisabled peers than are other students, and they are more likely than typical peers to be rejected by classmates (Pavri & Luftig, 2000). Danielle, the middle school student discussed at the beginning of this chapter, experiences such difficulties.

Studies of teachers' ratings also suggest that students with learning disabilities have lower social status than other students (Al-Yagon & Mikulineer, 2004; Wiener & Tardif, 2004), a fact that may be explained in two ways. First, among nondisabled peers who value school and proficiency at school-related tasks, students with learning disabilities may be viewed as less-desired classmates because of their academic struggles. Second, the status of students with learning disabilities may be related to their *social competence*—that is, their ability to accurately receive, interpret, and respond to the subtleties of interpersonal interactions (Murray & Greenberg, 2006). Michael exemplifies problems in social competence. He was seated on the floor of the office in his middle school with several of his peers, waiting to be seen by the principal about an altercation that occurred during lunch. The boys were discussing a variety of topics including who had won the cafeteria shoving match and who had bragging rights for the lowest grades on their recently issued report cards. In the middle of this conversation, Michael chimed in, "I'm going to see my grandma next weekend." Even though the other boys' topics of conversation may not have been those preferred by an adult, Michael's comment illustrates his obvious lack of awareness of the nuances and expectations of him in this social situation. The other boys immediately began making fun of him. As you might expect, students with learning disabilities who have poor social skills often are reported to have difficulty making and keeping friends (Pavri & Monda-Amaya, 2001), and they may feel lonely and depressed, especially through adolescence and adulthood (Maag & Reid, 2006).

It is important to note, however, that some students with learning disabilities are well adjusted and well liked by their peers and teachers (Greenham, 1999). One explanation for this finding concerns the learning environment. When teachers value and respect students, focus on their abilities, and create a supportive social environment, students thrive. Conversely, when too much emphasis is placed on students' problems, they become negative about themselves and are viewed in this way by peers.

Another explanation is offered by those who hypothesize that students with learning disabilities and poor social competence form a distinct subgroup who have **nonverbal learning disabilities (NLDs)** (Court & Givon, 2003; Telzrow & Bonar, 2002). These students may read and speak fluently, but because of a dysfunction in the part of the brain that controls nonverbal reasoning, they are unable to accurately interpret nonverbal communication (e.g., facial expressions, posture, eye contact), and they fumble in social interactions. For example, a student with this disorder might not recognize that he is receiving "the look" from a teacher or parent and thus may not change the behavior at issue. Likewise, this student might keep talking during a conversation, failing to understand the signals from others that they would like to talk, too.

Understanding the social and emotional characteristics of students with learning disabilities is as important as understanding their cognitive and academic traits.

PROFESSIONAL MONITORING TOOL

Council for Exceptional Children

Standard 5 Learning Environments and Social Interactions . . . teacher attitudes and behaviors

dimensions of **DIVERSITY**

Using data from reports to Congress on IDEA, the Advocacy Institute estimates that dropout rates among students with learning disabilities vary by race/ethnicity: 18.8 percent for Asian students, 26.9 percent for white students, 32.3 percent for Hispanic students, 33.7 percent for African American students, and 44 percent for Native American students (www.advocacyinstitute .org/resources/LD_Review02 .pdf).

Motivation

Many special education and general education teachers, especially those in middle and high schools, comment that students with learning disabilities are not motivated to learn, and research suggests that this is a common characteristic (Fulk, Brigham, & Lohman, 1998; Garcia & deCaso, 2004). *Motivation* is the desire to engage in an activity. This desire can be **intrinsic** (e.g., out of curiosity, as when you complete a crossword puzzle simply to see if you can) or **extrinsic** (e.g., for payment, as when you agree to help a neighbor with chores to earn money for a planned vacation). Ideally, all students would be intrinsically motivated to learn, but many students with learning disabilities are not. This could be due to what is called their *locus of control*, which is their belief about whether their life experiences are determined by internal (e.g., personal effort and skill) or external (e.g., luck) factors. Students with learning

It is difficult to determine whether motivation is a characteristic of some students with learning disabilities because of neurological dysfunction or an effect of students' school experiences.

disabilities often attribute academic success to external factors and failure to internal factors. For example, if a student with learning disabilities does well on a test, he may comment that it is because of "good luck" or "an easy test." If the student does not pass it, he may say, "I'm dumb." You can easily see how this would eventually lead to a low level of motivation.

However, it is difficult to determine whether motivation is a characteristic of some students with learning disabilities because of neurological dysfunction or an effect of students' school experiences. For example, some students demonstrate **learned helplessness** by giving up on a task before they even try. They may do this because they have failed at so many school tasks that they would rather not begin the work than fail again, or they may have discovered that if they say they cannot do a task, the teacher or a peer will help them do it.

Behavior Characteristics

If you think about the possible results of having deficits in academic subjects, selective attention, social competence, and motivation, you probably will conclude that a significant number of students with learning disabilities (although not all) also have behavior problems. You are correct. However, it is unclear whether the behaviors are part of the learning disability or a result of the frustration that many of these students experience (Farmer, 2000). For some students, difficulties in communicating with others may lead to inappropriate behaviors (Vallance, Cummings, & Humphries, 1998). For others, the prospect of not being able to complete an academic task might cause them to act out in a sort of learner "road rage." Examples of behavior problems that have been studied for students with learning disabilities include excessive out-of-seat behavior, talk-outs, and physical and verbal aggression.

One of the difficulties in discussing the behavior characteristics of students with learning disabilities is the fact that a significant number of these students have co-morbid (i.e., occurring simultaneously) learning disabilities and **attention deficit–hyperactivity disorder (ADHD)** (McNamara, Willoughby, Chalmers, & Cura, 2005); estimates range from 15 to 70 percent or more (Forness & Kavale, 2001a; Mayes, Calhoun, & Crowell, 2000). This comorbidity factor raises the possibility that the behavior problems of some students with learning disabilities are, in fact, symptoms of a second disorder. The Positive Behavior Supports provides one example of educators' efforts to help students with learning disabilities learn appropriate classroom behavior.

How Are Learning Disabilities Identified?

During the late 1960s and early 1970s, an assessment to determine whether a learning disability existed had to include a statement from a physician because a learning disability was considered a physiologically based disorder.

In order for students to receive special education services to address their learning disabilities, they must be identified as being eligible for them. This involves assessments to determine the existence of learning disabilities. Based on the information derived from these assessments, the multidisciplinary team must decide that the disability exists and that students are eligible for services (if the disability negatively affects educational performance).

IDEA 2004 changed dramatically the basis on which students may be identified as having a learning disability. The law still permits traditional assessment procedures based on identifying discrepancies between ability and achievement. However, it also explicitly introduces and gives permission for a procedure called *response to intervention (RTI)* based on the extent to which a student's learning does not improve when specific interventions are implemented. Both the traditional and RTI procedures are explained in the following sections.

Traditional Approach to Assessment for Learning Disabilities

All students who receive special education services first go through a careful process of assessment. For students with learning disabilities being assessed in the tradi-

Teaching Students to Manage
Their Own Behavior

Many students with learning disabilities can learn to manage their own behavior. Steps to teaching them this research-based approach include the following:

1. Help the student clearly identify the problem behaviors to be changed. Try to focus on behaviors that are harming the student's classroom success. If problems are particularly serious, do not try to change too many behaviors at one time.

2. Define the behavior to be demonstrated clearly, using words the student understands.

3. Collect baseline data with the student. You and the student should monitor the desired behavior to see how often it occurs.

4. Schedule a conference with the student to discuss the behavior of concern, identify the alternative behavior, gain student commitment to try to change, and explain the student's responsibility. You should also help the student set realistic goals for increasing the positive behavior.

5. Decide with the student on how to record the behavior and how often.

6. Teach the student how to use the self-management procedures.

7. Implement the plan.

8. Monitor how well the student is doing by periodically recording the same information that the student is recording. Reward the student for being accurate in recording, even if the behavior is still not at the desired goal.

9. Follow up once goals are reached to ensure ongoing success.

Review the figure below, which is one example of a self-management recording sheet for a student. This sheet lists several behaviors, a judgment made by the teacher. How could you adapt such a sheet for use with younger students? Older students? Can you think of other situations in which this type of approach to address student behavior could be successful?

Source: McConnell, M. E. (1999). Self-monitoring, cueing, recording, and managing: Teaching students to manage their own behavior. *Teaching Exceptional Children, 32*(2), 14–21. Copyright © 1999 by the Council for Exceptional Children. Reprinted with permission.

Classroom Self-Monitoring Scale

NAME: _____   DATE: _____

CLASS: _____   TEACHER: _____

Circle one of the four choices

4 = Always   3 = Most of the time

2 = Some of the time   1 = Did not do

1. Worked without disturbing others.	4	3	2	1
2. Participated in class.	4	3	2	1
3. Listened and paid attention when the teacher was talking.	4	3	2	1
4. Asked for help when I needed it.	4	3	2	1
5. Followed teacher directions.	4	3	2	1
6. Completed class assignment.	4	3	2	1
7. Turned in completed assignment.	4	3	2	1

Student Score _____

28–24	SUPER
23–20	GOOD
19–14	FAIR
13–0	MAKE A PLAN

tional way, this process includes both formal and informal assessments. These assessments are designed to create a picture of a student's learning capacity, academic achievement in reading and mathematics, social and emotional skills, and behavior patterns.

Formal Assessments

In many school districts the formal assessments used to determine whether a student has a learning disability are either norm-referenced or criterion-referenced tests. **Norm-referenced tests** are those in which the student taking the test is being compared to a large number of students, or *norm group*. Examples of norm-referenced tests used to identify learning disabilities include intelligence tests, such as the Wechsler Intelligence Scale for Children–IV (Wechsler, 2003), and achievement tests, such as the Woodcock–Johnson Psychoeducational Battery–III (Woodcock, McGrew, & Mather, 2001). Another example is the relatively new Learning Disabilities Diagnostic Inventory (LDDI) (Hammill & Bryant, 1998), which was designed specifically to assist professionals in identifying in school-age children intrinsic processing problems related to listening, speaking, reading, writing, mathematics, and reasoning. Unlike other assessments that compare the achievement of students to all other students, the LDDI compares the learning patterns of the student only to those of students known to have learning disabilities.

    Criterion-referenced tests are another type of formal assessment that may be used during this type of evaluation for learning disabilities. These tests are designed to determine whether a student has learned a specific body of information, so they represent an absolute standard rather than the comparative standard of norm-referenced tests. One example of a criterion-referenced test nearly everyone has experienced is a driver's test. This test is designed to determine whether you have learned enough to drive an automobile safely; comparing you to others is not relevant. Examples of criterion-referenced tests to assess for learning disabilities include the Stanford Diagnostic Reading Test (Karlsen & Gardner, 1995) and the Brigance Comprehensive Inventory of Basic Skills (e.g., Brigance, 1999).

Classroom Assessments

Classroom assessment information, usually considered informal, is the second type of data gathered to determine whether a student has a learning disability. Three types of classroom assessments are most often used: curriculum-based measurement, portfolio assessment, and observation.

    Curriculum-based measurement (CBM) is designed specifically to supplement information obtained from formal assessments by sampling a student's understanding of the classroom curriculum (L. S. Fuchs & D. Fuchs, 1998). CBM may include having a student read short passages from books in the district language arts or English curriculum and answer comprehension questions. By comparing the student's reading rate (i.e., correct words read per minute) and comprehension to a sample of other students in the classroom or the district, a determination can be made about the student's learning progress.

    Teachers may complete a portfolio assessment as another type of classroom assessment. A *portfolio* is a purposeful collection of a student's work that demonstrates the quality and progress of her learning (Jochum, Curran, & Reetz, 1998). For a student being assessed for learning disabilities, a portfolio might include drafts and final versions of writing assignments, a list of books read, an audiotape of the student reading, samples of assignments and problems solved in mathematics, and some type of student self-evaluation. The intent of a portfolio is to capture a snapshot of the student's performance in the reality of the classroom.

    A third form of classroom assessment is observation. For a student to be identified as having a learning disability, federal law requires that he be observed in the general education classroom or, for young children, in a school-like environment, such as a preschool. Observation often involves getting a general sense of the student's academic and behavioral functioning in the classroom. It may also include tabulating information of interest—how often the student leaves his seat, how often the student blurts out answers instead of raising

his hand, and how the frequency of such behaviors compares to that among other students in the class.

Criteria for Eligibility

In schools using a traditional approach to identifying learning disabilities, once assessment data have been gathered, the multidisciplinary team convenes. Using all of the assessment information, the team then decides whether a student meets the eligibility criteria for having a learning disability using these questions:

1. *Does a significant gap exist between the student's ability and academic achievement?* Although a number of methods can be used for determining the presence of a learning disability and IDEA explicitly states that school districts do not have to find a severe ability–achievement discrepancy, the most common method is to compare the student's scores on an individual intelligence test with his scores on the individual norm-referenced or criterion-referenced achievement measures (Schrag, 2000) and then to consider curriculum-based measures and portfolio information. For example, if a student's measured intellectual ability (i.e., IQ) is 100 but his equivalent reading score is 80, a decision might be made that a learning disability exists. However, if the intelligence score is 90 and the reading score is 88, no significant discrepancy and hence no learning disability exists. Any other related information (e.g., information from parents or teacher records) also can be used in answering this question. Keep in mind, too, that a discrepancy may be found between ability and any area of academic achievement, including thinking skills, oral expression, listening comprehension, written expression, basic reading skills, reading comprehension, mathematics calculation, and mathematics reasoning.

2. *Is the learning problem the result of a disorder in an area of basic psychological processing involved in understanding language?* These processes are included in the definition of learning disabilities that you learned earlier and in the description of student characteristics. They include sensory–motor skills, visual or auditory processing, and cognitive skills, such as attention and memory. As the team looks at all the assessment data, it must consider whether such processing problems are present.

3. *Can other possible causes of the learning problem be eliminated?* As noted earlier, the IDEA definition of a learning disability includes the provision that the discrepancy cannot be the result of other factors including environmental factors (e.g., an unsatisfactory home or school situation), poor teaching, poverty, and poor school attendance. Similarly, learning disabilities cannot be the result of other disabilities (e.g., mental retardation, vision or hearing disability, behavior disability) or a language difference. This requirement to eliminate possible alternative explanations for a student's learning problems is called the *exclusionary clause*.

If the student's learning problems are serious enough, the other criteria are met, and the team determines the student would benefit from special education, the student is eligible to receive services as having a learning disability.

PROFESSIONAL MONITORING TOOL

Council for Exceptional Children

Standard 8 Assessment
. . . use assessment information

INTERNET RESOURCES

www.ldresources.com
The LD Resources website contains published resources and materials for individuals with learning disabilities.

A New Approach for Identifying Students Who Have Learning Disabilities

The traditional approach to identifying the presence of learning disabilities has been criticized as a "wait to fail" model because students must progress far enough in school and experience significant academic frustration to even be considered as having learning disabilities (Lyon et al., 2001). Professionals also speculate that practitioners sometimes ignore the traditional diagnostic standards for learning disabilities in order to provide services to students without having to use more potentially objectionable labels (e.g., mental retardation) and in order to provide help to those students sometimes referred to as "slow learners," who exhibit overall marginal achievement but otherwise would not be eligible for special education.

Michael Newman/PhotoEdit

PROFESSIONAL MONITORING TOOL

Council for Exceptional Children

Standard 8 Assessment ... legal provisions regarding assessment

In many ways response to intervention (RTI) is a specific application of universal design for learning and differentiated instruction. It considers learner needs, relies on changing procedures to accommodate students, and advocates basing decisions on data.

Response to intervention (RTI) represents a federally legislated option for addressing these problems (Bradley, Danielson, & Doolittle, 2005). RTI is permitted, not required, in IDEA 2004, and it is receiving widespread attention. It includes these principles:

1. It replaces the ability–achievement discrepancy criteria with a simple direct assessment of the extent of a student's underachievement. This solves the problem of identifying young children and providing early intervention because it eliminates the need to wait for a discrepancy to emerge.

2. It removes the provision that inadequate instruction, emotional disturbance, and cultural or social issues make a student ineligible for services as learning disabled. In RTI, if learning problems are extreme, the reasons for them are not as important as providing assistance to the student.

3. It requires measures of a student's achievement on well-designed early instructional interventions (especially in prekindergarten through second grade) as part of the assessment process. Doing so ensures that the quality of instruction will be high as well as provides clear documentation of efforts to address student learning problems (Lyon et al., 2001).

Three-Tiered Models in Response to Intervention

The most common procedures being used to implement the RTI approach address reading problems, and they are outlined in three-tiered models of intervention (Vaughn & Fuchs, 2003; Vaughn, Linan-Thompson, & Hickman, 2003). Here is an explanation of each tier:

■ *Tier 1.* Most students should succeed when they are taught to read using practices that have been demonstrated through research to be effective (Denton, Vaughn, & Fletcher, 2003). All students participate in tier 1, and educators are responsible for implementing proven instructional methods, including differentiation, and closely monitoring the progress of students in the core reading curriculum.

■ *Tier 2.* For approximately 20 to 30 percent of students, tier 1 instruction is not enough. That is, the gap between their skills and what would be considered average progress is significant, and it is likely, based on the data, to get worse. Based on diagnostic data gathered (Speece, 2005), students in tier 2 receive supplemental instruction that may include structured tutoring by a trained assistant or peer, additional opportunities to practice skills, and individually paced instruction. The interventions are research based, and they are in addition to the core reading instruction being delivered in the classroom.

■ *Tier 3.* If diagnostic data indicate that a student still is not making adequate progress in acquiring essential reading skills when tier 2 interventions are being implemented, even more intensive interventions are initiated. For the few students who need this intensive assistance (i.e., usually no more than 5 to 10 percent of all students), instruction usually is delivered by a reading specialist or special educator and often occurs outside the general education classroom. The instruction may include a specific reading program (e.g., Wilson Reading, Corrective Reading), but it is primarily characterized by its intensity, its repeated opportunities for practice and review, its reliance on carefully analyzed and sequenced instruction, and its use of continuous monitoring of progress. In some but not all applications, this tier is considered special education service.

Criteria for Eligibility

When RTI is the approach used to assess students for the possible presence of learning disabilities, decision making is slightly different from that in traditional approaches. The multidisciplinary team still convenes and considers the available data, but their focus is on the following:

1. Even though research-based, individually designed, systematically delivered, and increasingly intensive interventions have been implemented, is the student still exhibiting significant gaps in learning compared to what would be expected? Is it likely that, despite the interventions, the gaps will stay the same or increase instead of decrease? Because this approach to identifying learning disabilities is relatively new, in some states traditional achievement data, classroom observation data, other curriculum-based measures, and even measures of ability (all described in the preceding section) also may be considered in making a decision about eligibility. However, emphasis remains on the existence of a significant learning gap that, without additional support, will worsen over time.

2. If the team decides that the student is *nonresponsive to intervention,* he may be determined to have a learning disability.

Notice that this approach completely eliminates an ability–achievement discrepancy. It also takes out issues related to psychological processing, environmental factors, and quality of instruction. You should note, though, that RTI has raised many questions related to specific guidelines for use, including the length of time each tier should be implemented before it is determined to be inadequate, the way that RTI applies to mathematics, and the types of research-based practices teachers should be using.

Perhaps the most important question related to RTI concerns whether it is a valid approach to identifying students with learning disabilities, and controversy is growing on this topic. You can read more about this rapidly evolving debate in the last section of this chapter.

How Do Students with Learning Disabilities Receive Their Education?

Students with learning disabilities are educated in a range of settings. However, strong emphasis is placed on ensuring that these students are held to the same academic expectations as typical learners. Federal law outlines the basic requirements for how all students with disabilities receive their education. Within those guidelines, though, many options exist.

Early Childhood

Young children generally are not diagnosed as having learning disabilities for several reasons. First, the indicators of learning disabilities (e.g., problems related to reading, math, oral and written language) usually are not apparent in preschool children. Second, because the possibility of misdiagnosis is so high, professionals are reluctant to risk the negative impact on child self-perception and teacher expectations that might occur if the learning disability

In studying schools that
"beat the odds"—that is,
schools with high levels of
poverty where reading is
taught successfully—Den-
ton, Foorman, and Mathes
(2003) found that these
schools shared a sense of
urgency and commitment
to learning, had strong
instructional leadership and
accountability, relied on
strong professional development and coaching, closely
monitored student progress,
targeted instruction, and
took no excuses for lack of
success.

label is applied in error. Overall, the considerable normal differences in rates of development among young children make formal identification inappropriate; what might appear to be a learning disability could easily turn out to be a developmental difference well within the normal range (Appl, 2000).

Programs for young children with *developmental delays* (the general term you have learned, often given when young children receive special services) usually address areas indirectly related to learning disabilities. For example, such programs focus on improving children's gross-motor skills (e.g., hopping) and fine-motor skills (e.g., using scissors or crayons), their expressive language skills (e.g., naming objects, asking questions to indicate need) and receptive language skills (e.g., following simple directions), their attention (e.g., persisting in a task for several minutes), and their social skills (e.g., taking turns, playing in a group). Interventions in all of these areas help create a solid foundation for later academic tasks, and students with significant delays in these areas may or may not later be identified as having learning disabilities.

Elementary and Secondary School Services

Ninety-nine percent of school-age students with learning disabilities receive their education in a typical public school setting (U.S. Department of Education, 2004). As you can see from the information presented in Figure 5.2, approximately 48 percent of today's students with learning disabilities spend nearly their entire school day in general education settings with their peers. These statistics illustrate the strength of the trend toward inclusive practices. Only 20 years ago, just 15 percent of students with learning disabilities spent this much time in general education settings (U.S. Department of Education, 1988). However, these data vary greatly from state to state, with New Hampshire and North Dakota educating 80 percent or more of their students with learning disabilities primarily in general education and Hawaii and Massachusetts educating less than 15 percent of their students in this setting (U.S. Department of Education, 2004). What do the data for your state suggest about how students with learning disabilities receive their services? Why do you think there are such large discrepancies across states regarding placement options for students with learning disabilities?

Knowing the proportion of time students spend in general education versus special education settings does not adequately convey what an individual student's services might involve. In schools using best practices, a student in general education—whether for a large or small part of the day—would use materials adjusted for his reading level and other special needs and access a computer and other appropriate assistive technology, as illustrated in the Technology Notes on the next page. Peer supports, such as peer tutoring or a buddy system, would be in place, and a special educator might co-teach in the classroom for part of the day (Friend & Cook, 2007). In the resource setting (the usual arrangement when students leave the classroom for part of the day), the student would receive intense, individually designed, and closely monitored instruction in any academic area affected by the learning disability. A student who is away from the general education classroom for more than 60 percent of school time is in a self-contained program in which most

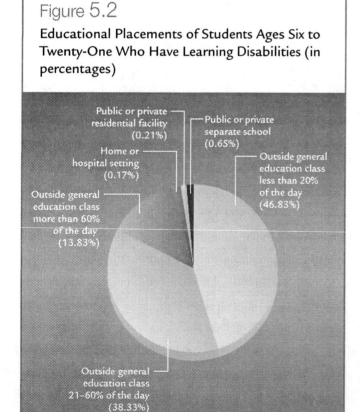

Figure 5.2

Educational Placements of Students Ages Six to Twenty-One Who Have Learning Disabilities (in percentages)

Public or private residential facility (0.21%)

Public or private separate school (0.65%)

Home or hospital setting (0.17%)

Outside general education class less than 20% of the day (46.83%)

Outside general education class more than 60% of the day (13.83%)

Outside general education class 21–60% of the day (38.33%)

Source: U.S. Department of Education. (2004). *Twenty-sixth annual report to Congress on the implementation of the Individuals with Disabilities Education Act.* Washington, DC: Author.

Current technology provides many tools to help students with learning disabilities to take in information, organize their thinking, and demonstrate their learning. Here are three excellent examples:

■ *AlphaSmart Neo* is a self-contained unit that enables students to enter and edit text and then send it to any computer for formatting or to a printer. Its rugged construction means it can survive the occasional fall from a student desk, and its simplicity eliminates the complexities and distractions of a computer. The units are operated by battery, so no wires are involved. They are compatible with both Macintosh and PC computers. Students who may be reluctant to compose by handwriting often can succeed using this widely available technology, particularly because information from one file can be pasted into another.

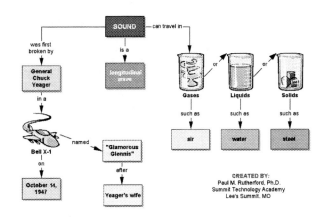

Inspiration concept map

AlphaSmart

Courtesy of AlphaSmart Inc.

■ *Inspiration Software* produces a suite of tools (Inspiration, Kidspiration, Inspiredata) that provide visual learning tools for students. For example, they can create webs or concept maps that enable them to see a visual organization of information they are learning. They also can convert information they have put into tables into clear visual representations. The software also can be an integral part of brainstorming ideas for a project or for prewriting activities. Versions of this program exist for younger or older students.

■ *Write:OutLoud* is a talking word processor software package designed for students across grade levels and reading abilities who experience difficulties writing. As the student types, it can say each letter, word, or sentence, thus providing constant feedback about what is being written. The program also has a talking spell checker. It can read information to the student that has been accessed from the Internet or another source, so it can be used to assist poor readers in preparing reports.

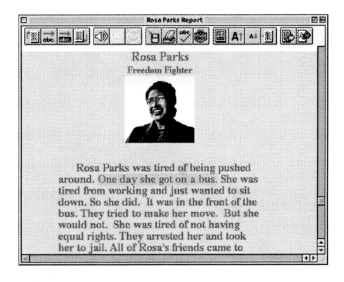

Write:OutLoud® story

Of course, any technology can only be as good as the knowledge base of the professionals teaching students how to use it. Technology specialists are sometimes used in school districts to help teachers learn how to use technology most effectively with their students with LD and other disabilities. As students with LD spend more and more time in general education settings, technology is becoming more and more integral to their education.

Source: Adapted from Quenneville, J. (2001). Tech tools for students with learning disabilities: Infusion into inclusive classrooms. *Preventing School Failure, 45*, 167–170. Reprinted with permission of the Helen Dwight Reid Educational Foundation. Published by Heldref Publications, 1319 Eighteenth St., NW, Washington, DC 20036-1802. Copyright © 2001.

or all core academic instruction is delivered by a special education teacher highly qualified in the core content areas. However, students in such settings often join general education classmates for some instruction, as well as for related arts and electives such as art, music, and technology. In middle and high school settings, students might take exploratory classes, electives, or study skills training with other students.

Inclusive Practices

As you know, decisions about where students receive their education are determined on the IDEA principle of *least restrictive environment (LRE)* and the specific needs identified in their IEPs. Within this context the issue of whether inclusive practices are the best educational approach for students with learning disabilities has been debated for many years (e.g., Carlberg & Kavale, 1980; De Simone & Parmar, 2006; McPhail & Freeman, 2005; National Joint Committee on Learning Disabilities, 2003). In the early twenty-first century it appears that fundamental questions about whether students with learning disabilities should receive at least some services with their peers are largely answered, but data suggest that over the past decade only fifteen states have clearly increased the time spent in general education for these students (McLeskey, Hoppey, Williamson, & Rentz, 2004).

Several serious issues remain to be addressed. It is important to remember the premise of this book—that inclusion is about how the adults and students in any particular school think about teaching and learning for all the students who go there. Being inclusive does not mean that students never leave the general education setting. Instead, it means that consideration is given to how a student's needs can be met within the classroom context before resorting to instruction in a separate setting. If the latter is considered in the student's best interest, it is provided for as long as it is warranted. Within that framework, professionals in the field now are thinking about the outcomes for students who receive an inclusive education versus those who receive more traditional services. The data are mixed.

> "Inclusion is about how the adults and students in any particular school think about teaching and learning for all the students who go there."

For example, Idol (2006) studied inclusive practices at eight elementary, middle, and high schools. She generally found positive results related to teacher perceptions and student outcomes. Ritter, Michel, and Irby (1999) found that parents and teachers of students with learning disabilities in an inclusive program reported higher student self-confidence, higher expectations, and improved academic progress. Rea, McLaughlin, and Walther-Thomas (2002) reported similar results for students in middle schools. They found that the students with learning disabilities in inclusive programs earned higher grades, scored at comparable or higher levels on achievement tests, and attended school more days when compared to students with learning disabilities in resource programs.

Not all the results are clearly positive, however. For example, Magiera and Zigmond (2005) explored the question of whether co-taught versus solo-taught middle school classes had differential effects on students with learning disabilities. They found no significant differences except that general education teachers interacted less often with the students with learning disabilities when the special educator was present. Vaughn and her colleagues (e.g., Klingner, Vaughn, Hughes, Schumm, & Elbaum, 1998; Vaughn, Elbaum, Schumm, & Hughes, 1998; Vaughn & Klingner, 1998) have examined the locations in which services are delivered and the academic and social outcomes of inclusion. They found that students have better social outcomes when in-class services, such as co-teaching, are available on a part-time rather than a full-time basis, and they found that both social and academic outcomes vary based on individual student characteristics. Ultimately, whether this approach is successful depends largely on the quality of the instructional practices in general education classrooms, including implementing universal design for learning (UDL) and differentiation; the availability of supports such as assistive technology; and the provision of intense, separate instruction as it is needed (Sapon-Shevin, 2003).

PROFESSIONAL MONITORING TOOL

Council for Exceptional Children

Standard 1 Foundations . . . issues, assurances, and due process rights

Research Notes

A report released by a coalition of New York City advocacy groups states that students with disabilities who are included in general education classes are three times more likely to pass standardized tests than those who are separated into special education classrooms, as long as they continue to receive the supports they need (http://specialed.about.com/library/blinclusionworks.htm).

PROFESSIONAL MONITORING TOOL

Council for Exceptional Children

Standard 4 Instructional Strategies . . . select and use instructional strategies

Inclusion Matters

Michael's Perspectives on His Education

Have you ever wondered what students with learning disabilities think of their services? Connor (2006) reported on his study of Michael, a young adult with learning disabilities who is also African American and living in poverty. Here are excerpts from Michael's story:

The kids who are placed in that special ed. classroom,
   They don't want to learn.
Most of the kids act like they don't care.
They destroy the rooms, they play around, make jokes, throw stuff. . . .
But once you're placed in an environment with regular ed. kids,
   they sit there. . . .
A totally different person, coz they don't want to embarrass themselves.
When you're placed in a room with people who they claim that is your kind,
You don't care.
"Oh, we all special ed., so we can all act the same way."
"You're here, I'm here. So something's wrong with all of us."
"He's stupid, I'm stupid, we're all in special ed."
When it starts at a young age, when it goes up, it just gets more corrupt.
"I'm special ed. I'm slow in all these classes. I don't need to do none of the work."
They don't think they're good in anything.
   It seems like teachers have pity on the special ed. kids.
   "He can't pass the test, but he's a good boy so let's just pass him"

I used to sit in the corner and like, *"This work, Oh, my God, might as well go to sleep."*
When you're in regular ed., everyone loves you and adores you.
In special ed., you're treated differently.
They have mercy on you.
When you do special ed. work, they try to help you too much.
Special class work was easy.
   Basically special ed. kids only stick with special ed. kids.
   Coz, at the lunch table if they find out that you're in special ed;
   No one's gonna hang out with you—you might as well hang out with your own kind.
   You're just lost, labeled as a reject. . . .
   In high school, no one ever really knew I was in special ed.
   Coz I'd sit there and carry myself like a regular kid.
   I'd come to all my classes. Just to make sure the hall is clear,
   I'd go into the classroom and hide in the corner, coz you don't want people to know.
   Once they find out, girls don't want to date you . . . No one wants to talk to you.
   I kept it to myself, I still do keep it to myself.

Source: Connor, D. J. (2006). Michael's story: "I get into so much trouble just by walking": Narrative knowing and life at the intersections of learning disability, race, and class. *Equity & Excellence in Education, 39,* 154–165.

The discussion of inclusive practices often overlooks the perspectives of students. In the Inclusion Matters, read the poetry of Michael, a young adult with a learning disability who received special education through junior high and high school. What does Michael's experience tell you about students' perspectives on special education and learning environment?

Transition and Adulthood

The outcomes for students with learning disabilities as they move into adulthood are as varied as the individuals who comprise this group. Some of these young adults successfully complete high school and move into postsecondary options—vocational training, college study, and employment—with confidence and success. However, the majority of young adults experience difficulties (Scanlon & Mellard, 2002). For example, Murray, Goldstein, Nourse, and Edgar (2000) followed the progress of two cohorts of high school graduates with and without learning disabilities for up to ten years. They found that the graduates with learning disabilities were significantly less likely to have participated in any form of postsecondary education, and if they did participate, they were more likely to have attended a training school or vocational program than a college or university. Others have found that adults with learning disabilities are more likely to be employed in part-time jobs, to have lower occupational status, and to earn lower wages (Collett-Klingenberg, 1998; Reder & Vogel, 1997).

PROFESSIONAL MONITORING TOOL

Council for Exceptional Children

Standard 3 Individual Learning Differences
. . . effects on life

Students with learning disabilities may attend college and receive supports there through the Americans with Disabilities Act.

Tom Stewart/Stock Market/Corbis

Research Notes

School professionals now are required to use research-based practices in their interventions with students. You can read more about this very important topic at the U.S. Department of Education website: www .ed.gov/rschstat/research/ pubs/rigorousevid/index .html.

PROFESSIONAL MONITORING TOOL

Council for Exceptional Children

Standard 4 Instructional Strategies
. . . strategies to promote transitions

Standard 5 Learning Environments and Social Interactions
. . . encourage self-advocacy and independence

Transition Planning

Why do many students with learning disabilities who are acknowledged to have at least average intelligence continue to have various difficulties as they become adults? Consider the traits and skills needed to go to college or to obtain and keep a job, including an ability to work independently and to seek assistance as needed; to be organized; to focus attention for long periods of time; to listen, speak, read, write, and compute effectively and efficiently; to problem solve; and to handle social situations with competence. These are the precise areas in which students with learning disabilities may be deficient. And because these students may demonstrate a slower rate of career maturity, poor ability to advocate for themselves, and low self-esteem, they may have unrealistic job expectations in terms of how to juxtapose their strengths and weaknesses with vocational choices (Bear, Kortering, & Braziel, 2006).

Since transition planning was added to federal special education law in 1990, increased attention has been paid to preparing students with learning disabilities for life after high school. As you know, a transition plan includes a statement of needs that begins at age sixteen and is updated annually pertaining to the student's course of study, along with a specific plan with measurable goals and an explanation to the student of his rights. However, the quality of transition plans and services is still not fully established (Carter, Lane, Pierson, & Glaeser, 2006). Hitchings and his colleagues (Hitchings, Luzzo, Ristow, Horvath, Retish, & Tanners, 2001) studied students with learning disabilities who were attending college. Of the students who had received special education services during their elementary or secondary school years, only one could recall participating in a meeting specifically to plan transition. Many of the students had difficulty explaining the nature of their disabilities and the impact their disabilities might have on career choice.

Model Transition Practices

Model practices for transition for students with learning disabilities in one high school were found to include these features (Collett-Klingenberg, 1998):

- Inclusion of career awareness and exploration activities beginning in the freshman year and continuing through high school
- Instruction related to skills needed for successful transition, including problem solving, organization, self-advocacy, and communication
- Transition-planning activities for school professionals and community members regarding the next steps that might be needed to improve activities and services

In addition, students and parents were integrally involved in transition planning, and transition-planning teams included community representatives as appropriate. Academics were given priority; however, work experiences were increasingly being incorporated into student plans, and linkages were created between students and their parents and postschool services, such as the Division for Vocational Rehabilitation.

Self-Advocacy

One other topic needs to be considered in a discussion of students with learning disabilities and transition: **self-advocacy** (Carter et al., 2006; Madaus & Shaw, 2006). First, students need to be willing to identify themselves as having a disability. Some are reluctant to do so on college applications because they fear it will affect their admission status; others have been advised by school counselors to drop their learning disability designation (Hitchings et al., 2001). In addition, students need to research and access the supports available to them from the college or university campus office designed to provide such assistance (Lock & Layton, 2001). These supports might include tutors, notetakers, and audiotaped textbooks. Finally, students need to be confident enough to articulate their needs to professors and negotiate accommodations, such as extended time for tests, so that they can compensate for their learning disabilities. Unless students learn and use strong self-advocacy skills, they are likely to drop out of college or to remain underemployed or unemployed (Field, Sarver, & Shaw, 2003; Trainor, 2005). If they have these skills, they are likely to complete college and enter the workforce much like other young adults (Madaus, Foley, McGuire, & Ruban, 2001).

PROFESSIONAL MONITORING TOOL

Council for Exceptional Children

Standard 4 Instructional Strategies
. . . teach problem-solving
Standard 5 Learning Environments and Social Interactions
. . . teach self-advocacy

What Are Recommended Educational Practices for Students with Learning Disabilities?

For more than two decades, professionals have been investigating which techniques and methods are most effective for addressing the academic, cognitive, social, and behavioral needs of students with learning disabilities. A wealth of research information now is available to guide teachers' practices (e.g., Jitendra, Edwards, Sacks, & Jacobson, 2004; Vaughn & Linan-Thompson, 2003). It indicates that two methods, used in combination, are most effective for most students, regardless of age or specific type of learning disability: direct instruction (DI) and strategy instruction (SI).

Direct Instruction

One method for effectively instructing students with learning disabilities is direct instruction. **Direct instruction (DI) is a comprehensive, teacher-led approach based on decades of research that emphasizes maximizing not only the quantity of instruction students receive but also the quality** (National Institute for Direct Instruction, 2006; Stein, Carnine, & Dixon, 1998). It includes clear demonstrations of new information in small segments, practice that is teacher guided, and immediate feedback to students on their work (Henley, Ramsey, & Algozzine, 2001). Direct instruction is based on these guiding principles:

1. Present lessons in a well-organized, sequenced manner.
2. Begin lessons with a short review of previously learned skills necessary to begin the lesson.
3. Begin lessons with a short statement of goals. Provide clear, concise explanations and illustrations of what is to be learned.
4. Present new material in small steps with practice and demonstrations at each step. Provide initial guidance through practice activities.
5. Provide students with frequent opportunities to practice and generalize skills.
6. Ask questions to check students' understanding, and obtain responses from everyone (Mather & Goldstein, 2001, p. 146).

The Specialized Instruction on the following pages illustrates the use of direct instruction in a sample lesson plan.

Strategy Instruction

One of the overall goals for all students' education is independence. Because of students' learning disabilities, achieving academic independence can be particularly difficult. Some students cannot write essays because they do not know the components of an essay and what content goes in an introduction, body, and conclusion. Others do not comprehend their textbooks because they do not have a plan for processing and remembering the information presented. Yet others struggle to take notes because they cannot decide

PROFESSIONAL MONITORING TOOL

Council for Exceptional Children

Standard 4 Instructional Strategies
. . . facilitate maintenance and generalization of skills

CHECK
Your Learning
How do the characteristics of direct instruction address the learning characteristics of students with learning disabilities?

Using Direct Instruction

Direct instruction (DI) is one of the most recommended approaches for teaching students with learning disabilities. Here is a sample lesson plan based on DI principles:

Title of Lesson: Contractions
(e.g., *he's, she's, it's, that's*)

Classroom Management: (1–2 minutes)

Grading Criteria: 15 percent reading sentences correctly, 35 percent generation of new sentences with learned contractions, 25 percent completed worksheet, and 25 percent slate writing activity.

Contingency: If the entire class's criterion level performance is at or better than 85 percent correct, students qualify for extra slate time (i.e., free choice to write or draw on their slates).

Specific Learning Outcomes: (1–2 minutes)

"Today, we are going to learn about contractions. You will learn to read a contraction alone and in a sentence. You will also learn to correctly write a contraction when given two words, and use the newly learned contraction in a sentence."

Anticipatory Set: (3 minutes)

Focus Statement. "Most often when we speak, we shorten a word or phrase by omitting one or more sounds. Listen to this sentence, 'It is raining.' Now listen again as I omit a sound, 'It's raining.' What two words did I shorten by omitting a sound?" (Students respond.) (Repeat with other examples such as "He's going to the store" and "She's at the mall.")

"When we shorten a word or phrase by omitting one or more sounds or letters, it is called a contraction."

Relevance of the Lesson. "It is important to learn how to read contractions because they are often used in storybooks, newspapers, magazines, and most material that you read. Also, you need to learn how to write contractions to use in your own writing."

Transfer of Past Learning. "We learn many new words in reading. A contraction is a special word because it is written differently than a regular word. Learning how to read and write contractions will make you a better reader and writer."

New Vocabulary Terms: (1–2 minutes)

- Contraction—shortening of a word or phrase by omitting one or more letters or sounds.

- Apostrophe—a mark that takes the place of the missing letter(s) in the contraction; it looks like a comma but is placed at the top of the line.

Teaching (10–12 minutes)

1. Review decoding words in isolation and in sentences: *he, she, it, that, is*. Have students use words in their own sentences.
   Questions
   "What is this word?"
   "Read this sentence."
   "Use this word in your own sentence."

CHECK Your Learning

How could you use principles of universal design for learning to incorporate learning strategies into instruction?

what information is essential or how to organize it. **Strategy instruction (SI)** is a highly recommended method for students with learning disabilities that addresses these types of problems. *Strategies* are techniques, principles, and rules that guide students to complete tasks independently (Friend & Bursuck, 2006). Strategies outline the steps students can take to accomplish learning tasks and provide some type of memory assistance (often an acronym) so that students can easily recall them. Teachers usually introduce strategies by helping students realize an instructional dilemma (e.g., a challenge students encounter with word problems in math) and then explaining why the strategy will help them overcome the dilemma. In the Specialized Instruction, you can see specific examples of learning strategies.

Think about strategies and students with learning disabilities. How does strategy instruction address some of the characteristics they have? In what areas do you think these students would benefit from strategy instruction? Many research-based strategies have been described in the professional literature (e.g., Deshler, Ellis, & Lenz, 1996; Deshler et al., 2001; Friend & Bursuck, 2006), and you are likely to find a strategy that can assist a student with learning disabilities regardless of her age or specific needs.

Students with Learning Disabilities

2. Define a contraction and an apostrophe.
   Questions
   "When a word or phrase is shortened by omitting one or more letters or sounds, it is called a _____."
   "What is the name of the visual mark used to take the place of the missing letters?"

3. Present examples and nonexamples of contractions and have students identify them.
   Examples:
   he's, she's, it's, that's.
   Nonexamples:
   cat, drum, bell.
   Questions
   "Is this a contraction? Why or why not?"

4. Model the sequence of steps for forming contractions.
   Example: *It is*
   a. Write the two words together without a space between them.
   b. Erase the letter *i* in *is* and put an apostrophe in its place.
   c. Read the new word by blending the sounds. Point out that the apostrophe doesn't make a sound. Have students read the word, spell it, and repeat the word again.
   d. Write sentences:
      It is hot today.
      It's hot today.
      "Do these two sentences mean the same thing? How do you know?"
      Have students read sentences with the teacher.
      Have students use the contraction in a new sentence.
   e. Repeat steps a–d with other examples (e.g., *he, she, that*) using simple sentences.

5. Do a discrimination test of irregular words and previously known words. Call on students as a group to read words by randomly pointing to each word several times.

6. Test individual students on reading contractions.

Guided and Independent Practice: (5–8 minutes)

1. Students first complete a worksheet with teacher direction and then do similar exercises independently. Students match the contraction with the two words that it is composed of.

2. The teacher provides guided and independent practice in writing the contractions on slates when the two words that make up the contraction are presented on the board.

3. Examples on board: *He is, she is; it is; that is*

4. Students will correctly write the contractions in newly generated sentences and share sentences with the class.

Closure: (3 minutes)

"Today, we learned about contractions and the apostrophe. We also learned that contractions have the same meaning as the two words that make them up. What is a contraction? What is an apostrophe? What word means the same as *it is*? What two words make up *he's*?"

Source: Jitendra, A. K., & Torgerson-Tubiello, R. (1997). Let's learn contractions! *Teaching Exceptional Children, 29*(4), 16–19. Copyright © 1997 by the Council for Exceptional Children. Reprinted with permission.

Elizabeth Crews/The Image Works

For many students with learning disabilities, intense, phonologically based interventions have been demonstrated effective for improving reading achievement.

Students with Learning Disabilities

Sample Learning Strategies

Learning strategies are effective tools for helping students with learning disabilities succeed in a wide variety of tasks. Here are two examples of learning strategies.

The AWARE Strategy for Note-Taking

The AWARE strategy is designed for high school and college students who need a systematic way to remember to take notes effectively during lectures and other instruction.

1. **A**rrange to take notes.
   Arrive early.
   Take a seat near the front or center.
   Obtain a pen and notebook.
   Note the date.

2. **W**rite quickly.
   Indent minor points.
   Record some words without vowels.

3. **A**pply cues.
   Attend to accents and organizational verbal cues.
   Record cued lecture ideas.
   Make checkmarks before cued ideas.

4. **R**eview notes as soon as possible.

5. **E**dit notes.
   Add information you forgot to record.
   Add personal details.
   Supplement notes with details from readings.

TREE for Writing

TREE is designed for elementary school students as a way to assist them in learning how to write persuasive essays.

1. **T**opic sentence.
   Tell what you believe.

2. **R**easons
   Tell three or more reasons: Why do I believe this?
   Will my readers believe this?

3. **E**nding
   Wrap it up!

4. **E**xamine
   Ask myself: Do I have all my parts?

Keep in mind that students need to be taught how to use strategies. They should see the importance of the strategy, discuss it, watch you model it, and memorize it. You should provide ongoing support until students can use a strategy independently.

Sources: Based on Hughes, C. A., & Suritsky, S. K. (1993). Notetaking skills and strategies for students with learning disabilities. *Preventing School Failure, 38*(1), 7–11. Harris, K. R., Graham, S., & Mason, L. H. (2003). Self-regulated strategy development in the classroom: Part of a balanced approach to writing instruction for students with disabilities. *Focus on Exceptional Children, 35*(7), 1–16.

What Are the Perspectives of Parents and Families?

Unlike the parents of students with significant sensory, cognitive, or physical disabilities, who may learn of their child's disabilities soon after birth, parents of children with learning disabilities often are not aware of their child's special needs until the child is enrolled in school and experiences frustration and failure in academic tasks. Parents may be surprised when they are informed about their child's disability, relieved to hear an explanation for their child's struggles to learn, or concerned about the time lost in finding effective interventions. As Mary, a college-educated professional and the mother of first-grader Guy, told school professionals as they conducted the initial eligibility and IEP meeting,

> *"Parents of children with learning disabilities often are not aware of their child's special needs until the child is enrolled in school and experiences frustration and failure in academic tasks."*

Stop. Wait. You're saying my son has a disability—a disability. You've just changed my whole world and how I think about Guy. You can't just say, "He's learning disabled. Let's write a plan for his education." I need to think about this. I need to understand better what this means. It may be routine to you, but he's my son. I can't sit here right now and make decisions. It's his life we're talking about. I wouldn't sign a contract to buy a car without a lot of thought and some careful research. How can you expect me to sign these papers about Guy's life without even knowing what I'm signing? I need to know what this means and what I'm agreeing to before I can sign anything.

Although not all parents can express their sentiments in such an articulate way, it is important to remember that the disability label often affects parents of students with learning disabilities in ways that school professionals cannot completely understand (Lardieri, Blacher, & Swanson, 2000). Many parents will have to redefine their image of their child. Especially if a child is identified during middle or high school, some parents may blame school personnel for their child's problems. Other parents may believe that they have failed their child and that they should have been able to prevent the disability. Special education teachers and other school professionals need to be aware that their attitudes toward parents, their communications with them, and their openness to parent and family perspectives can affect greatly the quality of the student's education and support received from home. In fact, one of the most common concerns expressed by parents of students with learning disabilities about school services is the frequency (i.e., too little) and focus (i.e., negative instead of positive) of communication from teachers and other professionals.

PROFESSIONAL MONITORING TOOL

Council for Exceptional Children

Standard 10 Collaboration
. . . concerns of families

Parents as Partners

Many parents of students with learning disabilities take active roles in their children's education. For example, Polloway, Bursuck, and Epstein (2001) conducted a series of studies on homework for students with learning disabilities and other disabilities. They found that school–home collaboration led to clear expectations, effective communication, and increased student success. Munk and Bursuck (2001) took a collaborative approach, involving students with learning disabilities, their parents, general education teachers, and special education teachers to create personalized grading plans. They found that the team effort resulted in a greater sense of fairness regarding grading students with learning disabilities and that students reported trying harder with this coordinated effort.

INTERNET RESOURCES
www.matrixparents.org
An excellent website for parents, the Matrix Parent Network for Parents of Children with Learning Disabilities includes a discussion board for parents to exchange ideas.

Although parent involvement is preferred, sometimes it can be a challenge. For example, Hughes, Schumm, and Vaughn (1999) examined Hispanic parents' perspectives on home reading and writing activities. They found that many parents of Hispanic children with learning disabilities provided books to their children, took them to the library, and read to them. However, some parents reported that they did not receive enough communication from school regarding how to help their children, and others indicated that their own difficulty with the English language constrained their ability to provide assistance. Torres-Burgo, Reyes-Wasson, and Brusca-Vega (1999) studied the involvement and treatment of urban Hispanic parents of children with learning disabilities in the entire special education process. They found that these parents rated their knowledge about IEPs significantly lower than non-Hispanic parents, particularly regarding the severity of their children's disabilities and the types of services received. Although all of the parents reported that special education teachers were sensitive to cultural issues, the Hispanic parents of children with learning disabilities communicated less with special education teachers than the non-Hispanic parents, and they were far less likely to report receiving advice on how to work with their children at home.

PROFESSIONAL MONITORING TOOL

Council for Exceptional Children

Standard 10 Collaboration
. . . becoming participants in the educational team
Standard 1 Foundations
. . . impact of differences between home and school

What Trends and Issues Are Affecting the Field of Learning Disabilities?

Controversy has characterized the field of learning disabilities almost since its inception, and that trend continues today. In this era in which standards are rising and accountability for education outcomes is increasing, it is not surprising that many aspects of learning disabilities are being examined under a critical lens.

Issues Related to Response to Intervention for Identifying Students as Learning Disabled

Earlier in this chapter, you learned that IDEA 2004 authorized for the first time a procedure for identifying students as having learning disabilities that is significantly different from traditional approaches—response to intervention (RTI). RTI has many benefits, including its reliance on data directly related to instruction and its potential for heading off serious learning problems through early intervention (Fletcher, Denton, & Francis, 2005; Vaughn & Fuchs, 2003). A rapidly growing body of professional literature is exploring both the applications and the viability of RTI. Not surprisingly, a number of questions are being raised regarding its use (Holdnack & Weiss, 2006; Johnson, Mellard, & Byrd, 2005; Kavale, 2005).

First, some professionals are concerned that RTI may not adequately and fairly address the diversity of students who may have learning disabilities. For example, students who are gifted and who also have learning disabilities may be able to compensate enough for their areas of deficiency that they will not be identified using an RTI model, even though a traditional approach would have highlighted a discrepancy between these students' potential and achievement (National Joint Committee on Learning Disabilities, 2005). A potential result is that RTI would underidentify students who are gifted and learning disabled. Conversely, preliminary research has raised concern regarding RTI for students who live in poverty and other high-risk situations. For these students, a real risk of overidentification may exist (Skiba et al., 2005).

A second area of concern has to do with the specific procedures that comprise response to intervention and the ways these procedures are implemented (Gerber, 2005; Mastropieri & Scruggs, 2005). Some of the questions being raised are these:

- For how long should an intervention be implemented before it is determined to be ineffective?
- How often and for how long should students receive tier 2 and tier 3 interventions (Fuchs, 2003; Speece, 2005)?
- Which research-based interventions should be used at each tier (Deshler, 2003; Semrud-Clikeman, 2005)?
- Is a three-tier model the best approach, or might four- or even more tier models, as are being designed in some states, be more effective?

A third set of concerns pertains to the resources required to effectively and fully implement RTI models. For example, implementing RTI requires that educators understand research-based interventions and strategies for data collection related to screening, diagnostics, and progress monitoring (Vellutino, Scanlon, Small, & Fanuele, 2006). The implication is that considerable professional development will be needed, and resources must be committed for that purpose. In addition, professionals need appropriate materials for assessment and instruction; again, resources must be allocated for the purchase of such items. A third example of resource needs concerns personnel; someone has to be available to gather data and interpret data and meet with others to problem solve regarding the next steps for individual students. RTI generally is labor intensive, and resources may be needed for paraprofessionals or substitute teachers to provide coverage for classroom personnel. Finally, little has been discussed regarding parents as resources, and no specific role for parents is included in most RTI models.

Response to intervention has the potential to significantly change the ways in which students who struggle to learn receive their education (Francis, Fletcher, Stuebing, Lyon, Shaywitz, & Shaywitz, 2005). However, most professionals agree that far more information is needed before RTI can be considered valid and well established (Fuchs, Mock, Morgan, & Young, 2003). Whatever your planned role as a professional educator, you should anticipate that you will be affected by RTI, and you should closely watch for developments related to its implementation.

INTERNET RESOURCES
www.jimwrightonline.com/php/rti/rti_wire.php
At the RTI Wire website, you can learn details about implementing this alternative approach to identifying learning disabilities and also access helpful tools, such as templates for gathering data.

INTERNET RESOURCES
www.interventioncentral.org
The Intervention Central website is designed to help educators find and implement research-based practices. Reading, writing, math, behavior, and motivation are among the areas addressed.

High School and College Students and Learning Disabilities

As the field of learning disabilities has matured and services have improved for older students, more and more students have successfully completed high school and continued on to college. In fact, students with learning disabilities now make up the largest single group of students with disabilities at the college level (Henderson, 2001; Scott, McGuire, & Shaw, 2003). However, a challenge accompanies what seems like a strongly positive trend: Increasingly, students are being identified for the first time as having learning disabilities during the high school years (U.S. Department of Education, 2004). Advocates applaud this as evidence of a deeper understanding among professionals about what learning disabilities are and how the increased demands in high school for student independence and responsibility expose previously unidentified learning disabilities. Critics claim that many students thus identified in high school are hoping to take advantage of the testing accommodations they may be able to obtain to improve their scores on SATs and other college entrance exams and to parlay a disability label into special treatment while in college (Siegel, 1999). The rapid increase in students identifying themselves as having learning disabilities late in their school careers has led colleges and universities to outline more carefully the documentation necessary to be eligible for services and the types of supports that can be provided (Madaus & Shaw, 2006).

> *"The rapid increase in students identifying themselves as having learning disabilities late in their school careers has led colleges and universities to outline more carefully the documentation necessary to be eligible for services and the types of supports that can be provided."*

PROFESSIONAL MONITORING TOOL

Council for Exceptional Children

Standard 1 Foundations
. . . issues in definition and identification

SUMMARY

The origin of the learning disabilities field can be traced to nineteenth-century research on the brain, but recognition of learning disabilities as a discrete category occurred in the 1960s. The definition that guides most school practices was included in the first federal special education law in 1975, and it has changed little since; an alternative definition has been proposed by the NJCLD. Nearly 50 percent of all students receiving special education services are identified as having learning disabilities, which may be caused by physiological factors or curriculum and environmental influences. Students with learning disabilities may experience problems in cognition (e.g., perception or memory), one or more academic areas, social or emotional functioning, and behavior.

Students are assessed for learning disabilities through one of two approaches. Beginning with IDEA 2004, response to intervention (RTI) may be used to determine whether a learning disability exists. In addition, traditional formal and informal assessments still may be employed. Eligibility is determined either by a failure to improve significantly or by the presence of a discrepancy between ability and achievement. Most students with learning disabilities receive their services in general education settings with some type of special education assistance. As students near school completion, attention is focused increasingly on helping them make the critical transition to adulthood. Recommended instructional practices for students with learning disabilities include direct instruction, which is a highly structured teacher-led approach for teaching students across academic areas, and strategy instruction, which includes steps to guide students so that they can achieve independence for completing common academic tasks. Parents of students with learning disabilities often are highly involved in their children's education, but sometimes barriers to participation occur. Two important issues currently facing the learning disabilities field are (1) the validity of response to intervention as a method for identifying the presence of learning disabilities and (2) whether high school and college students should be identified as having learning disabilities for the first time.

Jermaine

Jermaine is a student who has many needs, and you are a member of the IEP team that will make decisions about his placement for the next school year. Jermaine has told his general education teacher that he hates going to the special education classroom—his friends call him "retarded." Jermaine's mother, though, has indicated that she likes the individual attention Jermaine receives there and would even like additional services there. You are going to be asked to give your professional opinion about how Jermaine should receive his services next year. Prepare a statement that captures your thinking. (See CEC Standard 10 and INTASC Principles 10.01 and 10.05.)

Danielle

You will be working with Danielle during her advisory period. Prior to meeting with her for the first time, you will need to find strategies (see CEC Standard 4) and assistive technologies (see INTASC Principle 4.08) to help Danielle become more organized so that she can be independent and academically successful in middle and high school. Based on the information provided in Danielle's folder, prepare a summary of strategies and technolo-gies you think are appropriate to meet Danielle's organizational challenges. Include the rationale for your recommendations.

Derek

Derek, like many students with or without learning disabilities, is apprehensive about his choices for the future. He only has a few months remaining in high school, but there is time to enhance his possibilities of a successful transition to postsecondary education (see CEC Standard 7). You and Derek have outlined a plan for his last semester of high school. Now you must write a letter to his general education teachers and family stating what Derek needs and wants from each of them as well as your own role (see INTASC Principles 1.09 and 7.07). Be sure to include the following points:

- What might his general education teachers do to ensure that he will be able to complete college-level academic work?

- What should Derek's special education teachers do to support his transition to college?

- How should Derek's family be involved in this process?

KEY TERMS AND CONCEPTS

Attention deficit–hyperactivity disorder (ADHD)
Criterion-referenced test
Curriculum-based measurement (CBM)
Direct instruction (DI)
Dyscalculia
Dysgraphia
Dyslexia

Extrinsic motivation
Intrinsic motivation
Learned helplessness
Learning disabilities
Long-term memory
Metacognition
Minimal brain dysfunction

National Joint Committee on Learning Disabilities (NJCLD)
Nonverbal learning disability (NLD)
Norm-referenced test
Psychological processes
Self-advocacy
Short-term memory
Strategy instruction (SI)

REVIEW, DISCUSS, APPLY

1. What are the critical differences between the federal and NJCLD definitions of learning disabilities? How might school practices change if the latter definition were adopted in federal law? (Learning Objective 1)

2. Why are researchers so interested in determining the causes of learning disabilities? How might some of the areas of research explored in this chapter influence future practices for educators? (Learning Objective 1)

3. Interview the parent of a student with learning disabilities. What characteristics are mentioned by the parent? How do the child's characteristics affect school learning? Activities at home? (Learning Objective 2)

4. Response to intervention (RTI) is a radical departure from traditional approaches to identifying students as having learning disabilities. Do you think this approach will lead to more students being identified? Fewer? What might be the direct impact of RTI on you as a professional educator? (Learning Objective 3)

5. In using traditional assessment strategies to identify learning disabilities, why is it helpful to have both formal and informal assessment data? (Learning Objective 3)

6. If you are currently participating in a practicum or field experience, compare with classmates the ways in which students with learning disabilities receive their services. Are the schools inclusive? How common are resource programs? Do any students receive most of their core instruction in a special education classroom? (Learning Objective 4)

7. Do you know someone with a learning disability who is attending college? If so, what is this person's perspective on the quality of supports and services available to students with learning disabilities as they leave high school for college? (Learning Objective 4)

8. Considerable research demonstrates that strategy instruction is very effective for facilitating learning for students with learning disabilities. What characteristics do you think account for its effectiveness? What additional research-based learning strategies can you find by completing a search of the university library and the Internet? For whom might these strategies be appropriate? (Learning Objective 5)

9. What is your responsibility as a teacher in working with the parents of students with learning disabilities? How would you respond if a parent expressed concern that her child was not learning in the way expected? (Learning Objective 6)

10. Scan recent issues of newspapers and magazines. What topics related to learning disabilities appear in the popular press? Do these issues help the public's understanding of LD? Hinder it? How? (Learning Objective 7)

mylabschool
Where the classroom comes to life!

Go to Allyn & Bacon's MyLabSchool (www.mylabschool.com) and enter Assignment ID SPV7 into the Assignment Finder. Watch the video *Learning Disabilities,* in which Bridget, a teenager diagnosed with a learning disability, talks about how she deals with others' perceptions of her disability, and how it affects her.

Question: Relate Bridget's story to the material you have just read about dyslexia, social and emotional characteristics related to learning disabilities, special issues for older students diagnosed with learning disabilities, and Firsthand Account by Michael. You may also answer the questions at the end of the clip and e-mail your responses to your instructor.

Index

F

Families (of students with).
  autism spectrum disorders, 78–79, 84–85, 102–105
  Down syndrome, 23
  emotional and behavioral disorders, 46, 52, 69–70
  intellectual disabilities, 5, 8, 23, 26–30, 32
  learning disabilities, 178–179
  speech and language disorders, 133, 138–140
Fetal alcohol effect (FAE), 10
Fetal alcohol syndrome (FAS), 9–10
Fluency (as element of speech), 120
Fluency disorders, 121
Formal assessment, 54, 90, 166
Fragile X syndrome, 3, 9, 34
Functional approach (to emotional and behavior disorders), 40
Functional behavior assessment (FBA), 64–66

G

Gender
  emotional and behavior disorders and, 44, 51–52
  intellectual disabilities and, 7–8
  learning disabilities and, 154
  speech and language disorders and, 123, 133
General education
  autism spectrum disorders and, 94
  emotional and behavior disorders and, 56–58
  identification in, 53
  intellectual disabilities and, 20
  learning disabilities and, 170, 172
  speech and language disorders and, 132
Generalization (as cognitive skill), 13, 87, 90
Grandin, Temple, 81–82

H

Hall, G. Stanley, 40
Heredity (as cause of disabilities)
  autism spectrum disorders and, 83–84
  emotional and behavior disorders and, 44, 46
  learning disabilities and, 155
  speech and language disorders and, 123
High–stakes testing, 31
Hispanic students
  families/parents of, 95, 179
Home base (for students with autism spectrum disorders), 97
Home–based programs, 93, 104

I

Identification
  of autism spectrum disorders, 90–92, 102, 105
  of emotional and behavior disorders, 53–56, 70
  of intellectual disabilities, 17–19
  of learning disabilities, 164–169, 180
  speech and language disorders, 127–131
Immunizations (and autism spectrum disorders), 85
Inclusive practices
  attitudes toward, 172
  autism spectrum disorders and, 94–96
  emotional and behavior disorders and, 58–59
  intellectual disabilities, 22–24
  learning disabilities, 172–173
  research about, 172
  speech and language disorders and, 133–134
Individuals with Disabilities Education Act (IDEA)
  disability categories of, 5
Information processing (and learning disabilities), 158–159
Instructional strategies
  approaches to, 175–177
  as cause of learning disabilities, 156–157
  autism spectrum disorders and, 94–102
  deafness and hearing loss and, 47
  emotional and behavior disorders and, 59–69
  intellectual disabilities and, 19–26
  learning disabilities and, 175–178
  literacy and, 135–136
  speech and language disorders and, 131–138
Intellectual disabilities, 2–35
  age and, 7, 17, 19–20, 22–23, 29–30
  assessment and, 18
  case studies about, 3, 34, 107
  causes of, 8–11
  characteristics of students with, 11–17
  definitions of, 6–7
  families/parents and, 5, 8, 23, 26–30, 32
  gender and, 7–8
  history of field of, 4–6
  IDEA and, 5–6
  identification of, 5, 17–19
  instructional strategies for, 21, 24–26, 30–32
  litigation and, 5–6
  multidisciplinary team for, 18–19
  placement options for, 5–7, 19–24
  prevalence of, 7–8
  race/ethnicity and, 8
  research about, 4–6
  terms describing, 3, 6–7
  trends/issues in, 30–33
Intelligence tests/testing
  assessment and, 18, 166
  intellectual disabilities and, 5, 11–12, 18
Internalizing vs. externalizing behaviors, 47–49
Intrinsic vs. extrinsic motivation, 163

J

Job coach, 22

L

Language, 115–117
  assessment of, 129
  culture and, 139, 142
  definition of, 115
  development of, 116–117
  elements of, 115–117
  types of, 115, 118
Language delay, 119
Language differences, 140–142
Language disorders, 87, 117–119, 140
Language impairments, 115
Lead poisoning, 11
Learned helplessness, 164
Learning disabilities, 148–183
  age and, 154, 181
  assessment of, 164–167
  attention deficit–hyperactivity disorder and, 164
  case studies about, 149, 152, 173, 182
  causes of, 153, 155–157
  characteristics of students with, 153–154, 157–164
  comorbidity and, 154, 164
  controversy about, 179–180
  definitions of, 151–154
  families/parents of, 178–179
  gender and, 154
  history of field of, 150–151
  IDEA and, 151–153, 156
  identification of, 164–169, 178–180
  instructional strategies for, 150–151, 175–178
  legislation for, 151
  multidisciplinary team for, 167
  physiology of, 156–157
  placement options for students with, 169–175, 181
  prevalence of, 154